"Through the example of leaders from the Canadian and South African Truth and Reconciliation Commissions, Thomas Malewitz illustrates that America can learn much from neighboring countries regarding a national response to historic racial injustices. Each chapter highlights a tenet of servant leadership to encourage skills of listening and creating dialogue for future change. This book offers a novel approach to discuss, explore, and create first steps to address deep-seated injustices in America."

—**Jerry Abramson**, former director, White House Office of Intergovernmental Affairs (2014–17)

"Thomas Malewitz draws on a wide range of stories and voices to illuminate the challenging history of racial injustice in the United States and offers a compelling vision of servant-leadership that can forge new paths from past injustices toward future justice, peace, and unity. This book is rich in its analysis of history and Scripture and perceptive in its diagnosis of contemporary challenges. *Truth and Reconciliation* is an exciting new resource for anyone looking to understand our present challenges and to make progress toward a better future."

—**David Golemboski**, associate professor of government and international affairs, Augustana University

"America was built on the ideology of individualism, which is in direct contrast to the collectivist ideologies of the first inhabitants of these lands. Thomas Malewitz shines a spotlight on this dichotomy, and he provides an in-depth examination of the cultural diaspora created for native communities when they are forced to adapt to the foreign ideologies of a conqueror. Beyond this, he provides a way forward by examining servant leadership and highlighting historical examples of ways to successfully shift the mindset of object-oriented societies to a more other-centered worldview. I highly recommend this book to anyone seeking ways to promote social justice."

—**Beatriz Pacheco**, director of education, Pueblo of Sandia

Truth and Reconciliation

Truth and Reconciliation

An Exploration of Leadership and Accountability within Divided Nations and Cyclic Ideologies

Thomas E. Malewitz

◈PICKWICK *Publications* • Eugene, Oregon

TRUTH AND RECONCILIATION
An Exploration of Leadership and Accountability within Divided Nations and Cyclic Ideologies

Copyright © 2024 Thomas E. Malewitz. All rights reserved. Except for brief quotations in critical publications or reviews, no part of this book may be reproduced in any manner without prior written permission from the publisher. Write: Permissions, Wipf and Stock Publishers, 199 W. 8th Ave., Suite 3, Eugene, OR 97401.

Pickwick Publications
An Imprint of Wipf and Stock Publishers
199 W. 8th Ave., Suite 3
Eugene, OR 97401

www.wipfandstock.com

PAPERBACK ISBN: 978-1-6667-1351-0
HARDCOVER ISBN: 978-1-6667-1352-7
EBOOK ISBN: 978-1-6667-1353-4

Cataloguing-in-Publication data:

Names: Malewitz, Thomas E., author.

Title: Truth and reconciliation : an exploration of leadership and accountability within divided nations and cyclic ideologies / Thomas E. Malewitz.

Description: Eugene, OR : Pickwick Publications, 2024 | Includes bibliographical references and index.

Identifiers: ISBN 978-1-6667-1351-0 (paperback) | ISBN 978-1-6667-1352-7 (hardcover) | ISBN 978-1-6667-1353-4 (ebook)

Subjects: LCSH: Human rights. | Governmental investigations. | Reconciliation. | Truth commissions.

Classification: JC571 .M35 2024 (paperback) | JC571 .M35 (ebook)

VERSION NUMBER 02/09/24

The Scripture quotations contained herein are from the New Revised Standard Version Bible, copyright ©1989. By the Division of Christian Education of the National Council of the Churches of Christ in the U.S.A. Used by permission. All rights reserved.

To
My parents
Charles and Imogene
for their constant love and encouragement

Learn then from this story not to fear the fruits of the past, rather be circumspect in the future, that those foul passions whereby our family has suffered so grievously may not again be loosed to our undoing.

—ARTHUR CONAN DOYLE, *THE HOUND OF THE BASKERVILLES*

Contents

Acknowledgments | ix

Introduction | xi

1. The New World: America and Its Roots | 1
2. Conflict over the Sacred Land and Expansion: North America | 17
3. European Colonialization: Africa and the New Imperialism | 32
4. Manifest Destiny: America's Two-Edged Sword | 45
5. Cultural Stratification: Residential Schools | 59
6. Racial Stratification: Apartheid | 72
7. The Roots of Truth and Reconciliation: Leadership and the Dignity of the Human Person | 85
8. The Tenants of Truth and Reconciliation: South Africa | 100
9. The Tenants of Truth and Reconciliation: Canada | 114
10. Racism: A Call for Truth in America | 126
11. Genocide: A Call for Reconciliation in America | 142
12. Truth and Reconciliation: A Vision for Servant Leadership in National Dialogue | 155

Bibliography | 169

Index | 181

Acknowledgments

THIS MANUSCRIPT HAS BEEN brought together through the assistance, dedication, effort, and sacrifice of a community of extraordinary individuals. First, I would like to extend my heartfelt gratitude to Matt Wimer at Wipf & Stock for his patience throughout this progress and his continual support and grace as this topic came to fruition. I would like to extend my appreciation to Paul Pynkoski and the organizers of the Voices for Peace Conference for opening a global discussion on the Canadian Truth and Reconciliation Commission and offering a powerful inspiration of the importance of the arts in advocacy and leadership. I would like to offer my gratitude to Katherine Barry for her help and time during the final stages of the scholarship query for this manuscript. I would like to also acknowledge the encouragement and reminder to continue to write each day by my colleagues Karen Dunnigan, Kristen Harris, and Pat Todd throughout this process. Thank you to David Orberson for his consistent encouragement, friendship, and support. Likewise, to my wife, Bridget, and step-daughter, Brenna, for their time proofreading several chapters of the manuscript—I am grateful of your time and all of your suggested revisions. Finally, I am most grateful for the time, support, sacrifice, and love of my wife and step-daughters throughout this research and writing process without which this manuscript would not have been able to be completed. Thank you all very much.

Introduction

You have heard that it was said, "You shall love your neighbor and hate your enemy." But I say to you, Love your enemies and pray for those who persecute you. . . . For if you love those who love you, what reward do you have? Do not even the tax collectors do the same? And if you greet only your brothers and sisters, what more are you doing than others? (Matt 5:43–44, 46–47)

These teachings attributed to Jesus of Nazareth, during the Sermon on the Mount, create a stark contrast regarding the type of justice commonly expected or practiced in the ancient world to what was going to be expected from a disciple of this rabbi proclaiming good news. From this announcement, Jesus acknowledged and echoed the prophet Isaiah (Isa 61:1–11; Luke 4:21) that a new expectation and perspective was needed to challenge and respond to the complacent stances of injustices in the world. What was Jesus of Nazareth really calling for through this dramatic call and shift in perspective regarding acting for a more socially just society? I would argue that this perspective shifted from a lens of object-oriented, rule-based, way of life toward a more humane, person-oriented perspective; opening the door for creative and new opportunities for relationship building and service. This simple phrase "You have heard that it was said. . . . But I say to you . . ." can also serve as a catalyst and reminder for changes needed today; to create a more person-oriented dialogue in the midst of past cyclic injustices, through a lens of servant leadership in a post-pandemic reality.

A brief examination of recent global pandemics: the Bubonic plague (1346–1353), the plague of Marseille (1720–1722), the Spanish Flu

Introduction

(1918–1920), and the recent COVID-19 pandemic reveal similar trends in human behavior after a global catastrophe. Some of these behavioral trends include: a stricter stance in laws to control movement and travel which usually is followed by rebellion or riot; a separation or isolation from groups and families, where normal celebrations, rituals, or services of mourning are unable to be performed; an ideological divide and extremism often widens in belief systems that can stem from propaganda and misinformation; a shift in economics causing instability often alters classes and social statuses; and there is often a growth in stigmatization and violence. While these challenges have been present, there have also been examples of exponential creativity and growth through a renewed sense of humanism, such as during the Renaissance, the Enlightenment, and the roaring twenties during which the development of blues and jazz musical expression formed. This second trend offers hope of a future with more dialogue and recognition of human dignity after post-pandemic disequilibrium.

Times of great suffering have often led to times of profound leadership. I believe that in light of the post-pandemic reality, and growing tension in the local and global political spheres, the wisdom of servant leaders who strove for options of non-violence and peace should be reexamined in light of contemporary issues. This manuscript is offered as a brief examination and exploration to remember and reassess the wisdom of servant-leaders involved in global peace efforts, specifically the contexts surrounding the South African and Canadian Truth and Reconciliation Commissions, to gain any successful perspectives to respond to cyclic ideologies in America and hopefully create a dramatic shift from complacent stances to racial injustices and begin to engage in a dialogue based on human dignity and needed creative growth. May the phrase: "You have heard that it was said . . . but I say to you . . ." become a reminder that now is the time to examine new perspectives to address truth and reconciliation for divided nations and deep-seated cyclic ideologies.

Post–World War II Roots of Truth and Reconciliation

A powerful reminder of the limits of retributive justice can be experienced through the 1961 recordings of the trial of Adolf Eichmann, one of the highest-ranking Nazi officers tried for crimes perpetrated during the Second World War.[1] Eichmann's trial was the first experience for the

1. Prazan, *Trial of Adolf Eichmann*.

Introduction

world to hear the testimony and witness of Holocaust survivors. The archive footage offered clear signs of trauma and horror in the stories of the witnesses. The camera also caught the juxtaposed video of the unemotional response of Eichmann, who consistently maintained his innocence of the Nazi genocide, due to the fact that he was merely following orders. The American spiritual author and Cistercian priest, Thomas Merton, reflected on his recognition of the real horror of Eichmann's attitude and repose during the trial.

> The sanity of Eichmann is disturbing. We equate sanity with a sense of justice, with humaneness, with prudence, with the capacity to love and understand other people. We rely on the sane people of the world to preserve it from barbarism, madness, destruction. And now it begins to dawn on us that it is precisely the *sane* ones who are the most dangerous.[2]

Watching the film of the courtroom film from sixty years ago, as well as reading Merton's reflection of the situation initially caused me to reflect on the definitions placed on terms like civility, justice, and leadership. Jonathan Sacks, former Chief Rabbi of the United Hebrew Congregations of the Commonwealth and member of the House of Lords, offered the reminder that: "stories are where theology comes off the page and begins to transform of human possibility."[3] The interconnection of these reflections fascinated me to investigate the power of story and testimony, and caused me to wonder how leadership surrounding the incorporation of storytelling, especially in the space of a Truth and Reconciliation Commission, might become a catalyst for change in ideological perspectives.

Purpose of the Manuscript

The purpose of this manuscript is to explore and identify patterns or trends in the example of global leaders who have attempted to address deep racial divides in their own countries, and assess what might be applied in the case of America's current racial challenge. But as Sacks rightly noted, theology is an essential component of viewing human possibility within storytelling, so this manuscript will also include a theological lens when examining servant leadership in dialogue within a truth and reconciliation context. I

---

2. Merton, "Devout Meditation," 46.
3. Sacks, *To Heal a Fractured World*, 211.

Introduction

hope that these initial reflections will offer a broader and creative opportunity for seeking an option for a new approach to wrestle with America's pasts in ways that have not yet been attempted.

Many questions remain of the lasting legacy of the process of Truth and Reconciliation as well as to what extend such Commissions have in altering the long-term cultural identity of a country. There are two factors that are important to keep in mind while reading this manuscript. The first is that, in some sense, the romanticism surrounding the global response to the Truth and Reconciliation Commission of South Africa's and end of the apartheid past has come to a close. With the death of the revered bishop and theologian Desmond Tutu, on December 26, 2021, one of the foundational and consistent voices of hope and change in the South African Truth and Reconciliation process (1996–2003) was laid to rest, though there is still much to continue to learn from his compassion, leadership, and wisdom.[4] Secondly, there seems to be an expansive awareness and creative explosion surrounding recognition of the dignity of First Nations identity in these initial years following the Canadian Truth and Reconciliation Commission (2008–2015). The arts, literature, and music genres are having a renaissance in Canadian educational and arts engagement. Is this rising enthusiasm similar to the first years of hope experienced in South Africa in the 2000s? Or is this a sign that the hope instilled through Truth and Reconciliation Commissions can endure past the legacy of the first-generation advocates and bridge non-violent unity for future generations in North America?

For the Reader

To help establish the connectivity of the exemplar countries and the chosen themes of contextual history, servant leadership, and the tenets of Truth and Reconciliation between South Africa, Canada, I have attempted to include a structure for the manuscript that weaves together both theory and practical application for the reader.

First, as indicated through the table of contents, the chapters of the manuscript are grouped together in four historical contextual sections. Chapters 1, 2, and 3 explore initial foundations and consequences of

---

4. Battle, *Desmond Tutu*; Battle, *Reconciliation*; Dalai Lama XIV and Tutu, *Book of Joy*; Tutu, *God Has a Dream*; Tutu, *No Future without Forgiveness*; Tutu and Tutu, *Book of Forgiving*.

Introduction

colonialization; chapters 4, 5, and 6 explore the significant effects that led to deep racial divide and injustices, chapters 7, 8, and 9 explore the tenets and momentum of change and Truth and Reconciliation; and finally, chapters 10, 11, and 12 explore stories from America's recent past, and attempts to apply some of the wisdom and lessons learned to address racial leadership issues.

Along with this historical lens, each chapter will focus on one of the essential components of servant leadership as posited in Robert Greenleaf's *Servant Leadership*.[5] Examples of the theme will be demonstrated using quotations and stories throughout the chapter to help illustrate the consistency of the example of servant leadership in contrast to past historical actions. The following list outlines the tenets of servant leadership examined in each chapter. Chapter 1: A servant leader is service-oriented; chapter 2: A servant leader possesses awareness and preparation; chapter 3: A servant leader is community-oriented; chapter 4: A servant leader is goal-oriented; chapter 5: A servant leader listens for understanding; chapter 6: A servant leader recognizes the importance to withdraw and reorient; chapter 7: A servant leader is present to the now; chapter 8: A servant leader is methodical: focusing on one action at a time; chapter 9: A servant leader purposefully uses language and imagination; chapter 10: A servant leader possesses foresight; chapter 11: A servant leader needs to witness acceptance and empathy; and chapter 12: A servant leader focuses on healing and serving.

Finally, each chapter will also incorporate the following parallel structure to create a sense of consistency for the reader:

1. An introductory quotation with a brief contextual explanation of the chapter

---

5. Greenleaf, *Servant Leadership*, 21–53. As a note to the reader: Servant Leadership, as a leadership model, is not accepted as readily throughout the globe as compared to inside of the United States due to its heavy reliance on Western constructs and values. The tenets of Servant Leadership do bear parallel resemblance to the Global Leadership and Organizational Behavior Effectiveness (GLOBE) Research Program's study of Humane-Oriented Leadership, which is accepted more in international leadership theory and practice. Although I have included the leadership experiences of global leaders from the First Nations and South Africa, I have chosen to use Servant Leadership in lieu of Humane-Oriented leadership in this context because of the direct connection of its tenets to Judeo-Christian practice and theological underpinning with Servant Leadership, which will be explored throughout this manuscript. For more information regarding the similarities between Servant Leadership and Humane-Oriented Leadership see House et al., *Strategic Leadership across Cultures*; and Winston and Ryan, "Servant Leadership."

Introduction

2. "Servant Leadership" offers a section of text that examines and explores an example from Scripture that can offer an illustration and witness of the specific tenet of the servant leadership focus

3. "The Challenge" is a section of text dedicated to the acknowledgement of past historical issues of injustice, in the effort of transparency for dialogue

4. "A Call for Change" offers a direct historical response to issues of injustice presented in the previous section from the lens of servant leadership

5. "At the Crossroads" involves an example of decision making regarding the issues of historical injustice and the creation of a process forward, some examples throughout the chapters demonstrate positive movements for change, while others demonstrated a resistance to change

6. "Learning from Global Witnesses of Leadership" offers a global example of servant leadership related to the chapter topic that may not be directly related to the historical context but exemplifies the aspect of servant leadership for a further examination of responses to contexts of injustice

7. "Lessons in Servant Leadership" offers three concise summary characteristics exemplified through the examples of servant leadership presented throughout the chapter

8. "For Further Reflection" uses the previous three "Lessons in Servant Leadership" summaries for direct activities, from the arts, literature, or historical story that engage the topic for further investigation and dialogue

Invitation to Explore a New Way

American Leadership theorists, James Kouzes and Barry Posner, challenge that stronger leadership stems from moving from a state of compliancy to a stance of disequilibrium. "To become a better leader, you have to step out of your comfort zone. You have to challenge the conventionally ways of doing things and search for opportunities to innovate."[6] Their reminder regarding the need to expand beyond one's perspective of comfort also echoes through the work of global leaders who challenge scholarship in the field of

---

6. Kouzes and Posner, *Learning Leadership*, 100.

Introduction

leadership theory to explore beyond traditional examples and learn from nontraditional and unconventional examples of leadership as well.[7]

As I examine leadership through the lens of Truth and Reconciliation I hope that the reader finds some semblance of hope that even though in the darkest points of Apartheid in South Africa or the horrific traumas explained in the residential schools of Canada that there is a glimmer of light that can offer initial steps towards a future of authentic dialogue and conciliation in the pangs of America's past and future identity. I posit that the future of America rests not only with the acknowledgement and response of the issue of the consequences of slavery and its generational trauma in the identity of American citizens, but it also rests on the acknowledgement and response to the genocide of the indigenous whose First Nations were displaced, systematically murdered, continuously lied to and broken trust with, and forced to live on reservations.

You have heard it said . . . that history does not change, or maybe that history just repeats itself, or that the past is just the past . . . but I challenge you, the reader, let us open a door to new and creative possibilities of hope to stop the cyclic national violence and racial divide, and seek new avenues of forward movement toward reconciliation.

---

7. Guramatunhucooper, "Theory Leadership from Africa"; Sacks, *Lessons in Leadership*; and Smith, *Leadership Lessons*.

1

The New World

America and Its Roots

Humankind has a long past, and it is all present, for, like all beings in history, we are where we are, inevitably, because of where we came from. Even though free choice is partly responsible for our present situation, free choice itself cannot be exercised groundlessly. Any choice is made at a given time in a given situation and thus depends on the options that the time and situation provide, that is, the options of the past has brought into being.[1]

THE TWENTY-FIRST CENTURY HAS seen a resurgence in iconoclastic responses to people, stories, and symbols from the past that elicit a visceral response in the mind of contemporary cultural attitudes, beliefs, and ideologies. The colloquial phrase associated with this movement of iconoclasm is referred to as cancel culture,[2] and this movement can be seen illustrated from the actions of group extremes from both sides of the political spectrum, conservative and liberal. From the call for the removal of books, names, and statues from the American historical record to destroying the lives of individuals through public opinion and social media, this process

---

1. Ong, *Fighting for Life*, 9.

2. The cancel culture movement refers to an extreme form of boycotting or removal of a person or symbol based on ideological differences. For additional scholarship on the cancel culture movement and its effects on communication and societies See Clark, "Drag Them"; and Norris, "Cancel Culture."

is changing the landscape that will define the country's narrative for future generations and create a different, and likely more, perpetually critical lens into the history of America's past. This book was not written to explore a moral response to this iconoclastic movement or the removal of historical symbols that these books, names, and statues represent, but rather offer a reminder that the permanent removal of historical records may limit our ability to one day wrestle with the historical accounts and stories of the past in a process to seek an opportunity of reconciliation for the future.

Many of the examples or stories in this manuscript may create a visceral response in the reader, as they should. Discussion surrounding the consistent lack of the recognition of human dignity based on an individual's race throughout history is something that should not be ignored. Listening to the stories of the past can remind us of the consequences of such actions and hopefully inspire future generations to not engage in such forms of division and injustices. The examples that have been incorporated into this text, such as: the genocide of residential schools, the terroristic bombing of the 16th Street Church in Birmingham, and the horrific and traumatic experience of Amy Biehl's murder in South Africa are only a few of the countless examples that could be included for examination on this topic. Throughout the research of this manuscript, though, I have chosen to include examples that would highlight how servant leadership might offer a path for a future of reconciliation through a history of such atrocities, and throughout which a leadership of magnanimity could offer an avenue for change in the face of such horror and violence. Although these examples might recall some of the most challenging aspects of history, they were included as a reminder not to dwell in a perspective of anger that seeks retribution for past evils but to learn from the wisdom present in such volatile times. As indicated in the opening quotation by cultural historian and Jesuit, Walter Ong, it is essential to recognize that the actions of individuals in the nation's past has laid a foundation of the moment we current experience; for all of its strengths and weakness, justice and injustices. We must now find a determination toward a more unitive direction for the future.

This manuscript hopes to follow in that same vein. It was written as an opportunity to explore just a few historical stories of the past to help elicit conversation for forward movement, by learning from the examples of the wisdom of servant-leaders who have attempted to lead the way of addressing injustice and seeking a process forward in their cultures and during their times. As will be demonstrated through the recounts of tumultuous violence and the traumatic experiences throughout the historical governmental structures surrounding the Truth and Reconciliation Commission of South Africa as well as the anguish of testimonies offered during the Truth and Reconciliation Commission of Canada surrounding the abuses of the forced residential schooling of First Nations youth, this process is not easy, quick, or absolute—it cannot be. Examining the past involves an examination of generations of trauma and involves the acknowledgement of consistent loss of trust in authorities that should have protected human rights instead of exploit them. I posit, though, that there are trends in the leadership present during these two specific examples that offer insights that might assist America in starting to address the continuing issues of injustice plaguing the promises of a government that purports to be a nation of life, liberty, and pursuit of happiness.

In the most challenging and divided political circles, there are moments when political differences can be placed aside for the betterment of the whole. Rabbi Jonathan Sacks recounted an experience that illustrated this to him through how the leading members of Britain's divisive political parties were able to evolve in a moment from being rivals to having an open friendship. In 1995, during a flight to attend the funeral of the fifth prime minister of Israel, Yitzhak Rabin, who had been assassinated by an extremist for his dedication and efforts as an advocate for peace between Israel and Palestine, the British politicians were able to put political differences aside and express a civility that recalled their duty as public, social servants through the experience of that sacred moment.

> It was a conviction that they shared about politics: that it exists to reconcile the conflicting desires and aspirations of people within a polity, and to do so without violence, through reasoned and respectful debate, listening to, while not agreeing with, opposing views, and trying as far as possible to serve the common good.[3]

This desire to strive for the common good, as Sacks stated, recognized that beneficial leadership is grounded in an underlying dimension of service for others.

---

3. Sacks, *Morality*, 214.

Truth and Reconciliation

America and the Need to Wrestle with Open and Honest Dialogue

America is a nation acknowledged to be founded from a desire for religious liberty. It also has deep fundamental roots in the humanist movement of the Enlightenment, as well as Scriptural traditions and legacy, and a search for the common good. But the country is on a trajectory that seems to have forgotten its own history and stories, and continues to be haunted by its past; a past that is often overshadowed by its material development instead of an honest account of the price that was paid to achieve such development. It is a country that has a dichotomous and contradictory history of: freedom and slavery, liberty and subservience, life and death. Hopefully, the American experiment remains far from its conclusion, but it continues to show many pains of growth through the lack of offering fulfillment to its promise of being a land of liberty. As I wrote this book another struggle surrounding the recognition of dignity and identity is taking place in Memphis, Tennessee, as the city is engulfed in a critical response after the excessive beating and death of an African American male at the hands excessive police violence. Such responses of anger and violence have become far too common place, and the pressurized emotion of generational trauma is boiling over, where violence seems to be the only proportional response for many to the countless and unresolved injustices stemming from officer-involved deaths.

Although 2020 is primarily remembered for the COVID-19 pandemic, and the governmental isolating precautions from the disease, it also saw a summer of revolt and protesting, and/or riots, as a response to the injustices surrounding the officer-involved deaths, especially in Kentucky and Minnesota. The centuries of frustration and silence has evolved into an active vocal response, where mottos like "say her name," have become an oral reminder of the human loss, especially of black women throughout the past decades.[4] The frequency of protests and the lack of acknowledgement of human dignity based on race in America is only increasing as the frequency of large scale urban violent physical altercations manifest every ten years, or sooner. A quick examination of the last four decades reveals that the 1980s Miami saw the first race riots since the 1960s Civil Rights Movement. The 1990s is remembered for the L. A. riots, the 2000s in Cincinnati, 2010s in Ferguson, Missouri, and the 2020s in Minneapolis and Louisville,

---

4. Crenshaw et al., "Say Her Name."

The New World

and they still occur today in Memphis. There is a clear sense of unrest and unresolve in America that affects the present. The question must be posed: what type of leadership is needed to assist in finding a more non-violent resolution for the racial issues that plague the American ethos?

Since the global witness of the unconventional process of South Africa's Truth and Reconciliation commission, 1996–2003, the concept of Truth and Reconciliation and its form of restorative justice has become a byword in the contemporary rhetoric as a response to injustice and the search for civility between cyclic and divisive ideologies throughout the world. In recent years there has been a growing call to action in the media for a Truth and Reconciliation commission to respond to the racial divide present in the ethos of American society, especially in the wake of the protest and unrest during the summer 2020.[5]

In January 2021, Democratic New York Representative Alexandria Ocasio-Cortez indicated that an investigative commission was in the process of being discussed as a possibility to respond to racial issues in America. "There's absolutely a commission that's being discussed, but it seems to be more investigating in style rather than truth and reconciliation."[6] The following year, President Biden's administration announced that a Disinformation Governance Board was created within the Department of Homeland Security to help secure and offer guidance between accurate information and disinformation. This Board only lasted three weeks and was subsequently terminated in April 2022. Although not directly parallel to a commission inspired by the tenets of Truth and Reconciliation these recent examples illustrate that there is movement in the American government to respond to the need for investigation for truth and to resolve racial tensions through a perspective that involves some form of truth telling efforts.

Additionally, there have been movements outside of the realm of the federal government to start the process of self-reflection and examination through Truth and Reconciliation efforts in America at local levels.[7] So, the questions are raised what would a national Truth and Reconciliation Commission look like in the United States? Are pundits on either side of the political aisle seeking authentic dialogue and reconciliation for past

---

5. Martin, "Healing U. S. Divides."
6. Swoyer, "Alexandria Ocasio-Cortez," para. 1.
7. Grassroots Law Project and their initiative with their partnership with district attorneys in the cities of Boston, Philadelphia, and San Francisco. Also see Greensboro Truth and Reconciliation Commission (2004–2006) in chapter 12.

wrongs? Is a Truth and Reconciliation Commission possible in the current American political climate?

With the recent demonstrations, and the force for change so poignant and prominent in current American politics and policy, it is essential to examine and assess the historical context that have defined contemporary culture in America as well as explore the trends in the leadership of Truth and Reconciliation commissions that addressed similar racial issues at a national level to see what insights that they might offer through their own benefits or pitfalls, if such a commission is viable and/or warranted in America. Although Truth and Reconciliation Commissions have been researched and analyzed from various perspectives to find fruitfulness in the process, it is extremely important to examine the role of the perspectives of leadership demonstrated through the authorities who called, and led, Truth and Reconciliation Commissions. In what ways do the leadership skills demonstrated offer the ability to examine and discuss a marred historical past in a lens aimed at a future wholeness and dialogue of growth toward possible reconciliation? For the listening and storytelling process required to offer open dialogue it must first be essential to examine a leadership model that could offer such a mindset to focus on the needs of being service-oriented rather than object-orientated.

Servant Leadership: Being Service-Oriented Minded

Servant leadership and its tenets will be the model and lens through which we will examine the leadership examples presented throughout this manuscript. The foundational tenet of servant leadership rests on being orientated toward service. This chapter will use the tenet of service-oriented leadership to explore the first roots of the American consciousness and reflect upon how its foundations have been formed through the sacred, and where individuals have overlooked the sacred. The need to examine the past to recognize the sacred present will lay a foundation for a more service-oriented future for dialogue and awareness for reconciliation.

Jacob/Israel: A Leader Whose Service-Oriented Conversion Offers a Witness of Reconciliation

An example of struggle and growth from an object-orientation to a perspective of service-orientation in Scripture can be illustrated throughout the story of Jacob, later known as Israel. Jacob's youth offers an example of an object-orientation, someone who was willing to barter, trade, and trick others for personal gain. Jacob convinced his older brother Esau, through a situation of disadvantage and hunger, to trade his birthright for a bowl of stew (Gen 25:29–34). Jacob also, through disguise and guile, tricked his blind father to bestow the father's blessing upon him instead of his older brother (Gen 27:5–29). Out of the need of his own self-preservation, from the danger of death at the hands of his brother, Jacob fled his homeland to the land of his ancestors.

After working with distant relatives, becoming a victim of trickery himself, and ultimately raising a family for over a decade Jacob felt a call to return to his homeland. While still in the distance during his journey back to the land of his youth, Jacob received news that his brother Esau heard about his return and was going to meet him with an army of 400 men. Before engaging his brother, though, Jacob encounters a mysterious individual and so ardently desires a blessing of protection from the "angel" that Jacob wrestles the individual in desperation, trying to not allow the individual to leave without bestowing a blessing. As morning dawned, and the struggle came to an end, Jacob indeed received a blessing but not in the way he anticipated. The mysterious individual blessed Jacob by changing his name to Israel (Gen 32:22–32). The significance of this change also manifested a change of character and change of heart. Jacob no longer had the intention to trick his brother for self-preservation but shows honor to his brother.

The story of Jacob offers an example of servant leadership that evolves from a position of an individual-oriented perspective of claiming and conquest of something that does not belong to him to a conversion of heart and new identity. After the conversion, Jacob lives in the reality of a service-oriented relationship, seeking reconciliation with his estranged brother through a reparation from the blessings that he worked for throughout his absent years. The Scriptural text offers a happy ending of reconciliation as Esau accepts his brother's return and does not seek vengeance for past wrongs. Can the story of Jacob offer insight into the roots of America, as a parable, of claiming discovery and conquest to a future of reconciliation?

The Challenge

Much of the history, or stories, surrounding the origins and development of America as the New World begin with the year 1492. Throughout Europe this was a time of discontent, disequilibrium, and instability. In the wake of the technological revolution of the printing press European society was trying to redefine and come to a new understanding of its identity and place in the world, much like today due to the technological changes brought about by the development of the internet. Turmoil was brewing theologically with the pre-reformers which led to challenges of traditional perspectives. Humanity was poised for a time of monumental change. But, again, the focus of this change was object-oriented—the expansion of empires, the need for additional sources of revenue for brewing wars, and a desire for financial and political independence and sustainability. The search was on for new leadership perspectives in the evolving European empires.

The imperial drive was in full force. Linda Tuhiwai Smith, professor of indigenous education and de-colonialization, clearly defined the extent of this culture of imperialism:

> Imperialism tends to be used in at least four different ways when describing the form of European imperialism which "started" in the fifteenth century: (1) imperialism as economic expansion; (2) imperialism as the subjugation of "others"; (3) imperialism as an idea or spirit with many forms of realization; and (4) imperialism as a discursive field of knowledge. . . . Imperialism in this sense could be tied to a chronology of events related to "discovery," conquest exploitation, distribution and appropriation.[8]

In the height of the pre-Reformation theological struggles, Spain and the Church were on a mission of reclaiming power through expansion and exploitation of discovery. The following offers a brief account of major events that defined the year 1492, and the mindset of the authorities who led the expansion to the New World. Smith's points regarding imperialism ring clear in the events stated below of that time period.

The calendar year 1492 began with a religious victory for the Christian monarchs, Ferdinand II and Isabella I, over Muhammed XII and Islamic control of Spain through the conclusion of the Granada War, which lasted from 1482 to 1491. Although the decade long war ended the previous year the control of the city was finally surrendered to Ferdinand II in the

---

8. Smith, *Decolonizing Methodologies*, 23–24.

beginning of the month of January 1492. Later that same month, Christopher Columbus convinced the Spanish monarchy to fund his voyage to find a new route to the East Indies. By March, Ferdinand II and Isabella I sign the Alhambra Decree, or Edict of Expulsion, a law that forced the expulsion of all practicing Jews, unless they formally converted to Christianity, from Spain and its territories by July 1492.[9] A new pope also was elected to lead the Church in August 1492, Rodrigo de Borja, the infamous Pope Alexander VI, one of the most controversial papal successors in Christian history. In September, Columbus set sail from European seas, and lands in the "New World" the following month, October 1492.

After Columbus's return in 1493, Pope Alexander VI officially defined, divided and declared that the lands discovered by Columbus were to be considered under the jurisdiction of Spain through the Papal Bull "Inter Caeter":

> With this proviso however that none of the islands and mainlands, found and to be found, discovered and to be discovered, beyond that said line towards the west and south, be in the actual possession of any Christian king or prince up to the birthday of our Lord Jesus Christ just past from which the present year one thousand four hundred and ninety-three begins. And we [Alexander VI] make, appoint, and depute [Ferdinand II and Isabella I] and your said heirs and successors lords of them with full and free power, authority, and jurisdiction of every kind.[10]

This brief reflection on the European perspective of conquest and dominance of that time period illustrates the context of an imperial culture focused on an object-oriented society. A society structured upon the growth of material possessions, economic value, and personal legacy.

A Call for Change

With global expansion and the declaration accepting and blessing the lands claimed by the Spanish empire in the name of the Church, and as the head of the Church, Pope Alexander VI, through "Inter Caeter," effectively stated that indigenous, or non-Christians, were deemed to be treated as subjects under Christian control and were not recognized with the same dignity as Christians. The power of this decree shaped the future of exploration

---

9. The law was not officially revoked by the Spanish government until December 16, 1968. See Eder, "1492 Ban on Jews," 1.

10. Alexander VI, "Inter Caeter," para. 6.

for centuries, as the written word of the Papacy was used to legitimize the actions of generations of explorers and settlers. Only the same level of authority could reverse such a decision and direction.

The Papacy continued to be challenged from without and within as Pre-Reformation theological issues continued to escalate throughout Europe, through moderate and extreme positions against Church teachings. As the Reformation took hold in Europe through the preaching and writings of Martin Luther, John Calvin, and Ulrich Zwingli, it took over forty years before a response was once again pointedly addressed by the papacy in regard to the dignity of indigenous individuals in the New World. Pope Paul III (1468–1549), who presided and actively oversaw a responsive Church to the Reformation, was the first Pope to also actively respond to the generations of the malformed and malicious conscience of the explorers and settlers through his papal bull, "Sublimis Deus:"

> [T]he said Indians and all other people who may later be discovered by Christians, are by no means to be deprived of their liberty or the possession of their property, even though they be outside the faith of Jesus Christ; and that they may and should, freely and legitimately, enjoy their liberty and the possession of their property; nor should they be in any way enslaved.[11]

Pope Paul III's bull responded and revoked the previous papal used to justify the approval and enslavement of indigenous across the empire, but the new bull became a source of struggle of power with the Spanish Crown who vehemently opposed its decree. As Black Catholic historian, theologian and Benedictine priest, Cyprian Davis commented: "In 1537 Pope Paul III issued the bull 'Sublimis Deus,' which detailed the rights of the Indians and the injustice of their enslavement. Yet, in many respects the papal bull remained a dead letter."[12]

Although dismissed in history due to political pressure, "Sublimis Deus" along with the work of the converted Dominican friar and indigenous advocate, Bartolomé de las Cases, movements of change began to slowly address the injustices common place during early perspectives of American history.

---

11. Paul III, "Sublimis Deus," para. 4.
12. Davis, *History of Black Catholics*, 21.

The New World

At the Crossroads

The life of Bartolomé de las Cases (1484–1566) offered a tangible example of a servant leader whose story parallels that of the story of Jacob and the history of the development of the roots of America. Bartolomé lived during the height of the imperialism during the Spanish conquest and served as *encomendero*, the land grantee, throughout the conquest of Cuba. In 1514, though, he had a conversion of heart and attitude from conquest to compassion, where he renounced his own indigenous slaves returning them to the governor of the region and started in earnest to advocate on behalf of better treatment and recognition of dignity of the indigenous.

Through authorship and physical pleading with the monarch of Spain, Bartolomé de las Cases was involved with the development of the administrative position of the Spanish colonies known as the "Protector of the Indians." For over fifty years Bartolomé de las Cases traveled between the colonies and Spain advocating, legally defending, and preaching against the inhumane treatment of the indigenous population. His account, *A Short Account of the Destruction of the Indies*, written in 1542 and published ten years later, became the first recognized evidential record of the atrocities perpetrated by the colonists toward the indigenous population.[13]

A contemporary witness of the legacy of advocacy of awareness initiated by Bartolomé de las Cases five hundred years earlier, Cistercian priest and monk Thomas Merton continued in a similar tradition and challenged the deeply rooted prejudice within America history in the mid-twentieth century. Without reservation Merton called out America's institutional treatment of its diverse races:

> The ultimate violence which the American white man, like the European white man, has exerted in all unconscious "good faith" upon the colored races of the earth (and above all on the Negro) has been to impose on them *invented identities*, to place them in positions of subservience and helplessness in which they themselves came to believe only in the identities which had thus been conferred upon them.[14]

Merton's reflection regarding inventing identities by society challenged and created a pause for reflection about the accuracy of the historical stories being told. Historically, as the Spaniards invented villainous identities and

---

13. Bartolomé de las Casas, *Short Account*.
14. Merton, *Ishi Means Man*, 9.

applied them to the indigenous population, as recorded by Bartolomé de las Cases, an aggressive behavior of response was then justified in the minds of the colonists, especially as the object-oriented value system believed it needed defense and protection of its material gains from outsiders. How can a service-oriented view develop in the midst of culture of invented and harmful negative identities?

Collaboration toward Community

For insights into perspectives of collaboration it is important to examine servant-oriented examples. Reflecting on the historical expulsion of Jews from Spain in the fifteenth century Harold Kushner, the American rabbi and Jewish scholar, reflected on how the forced conversion, exile, and suffering experienced at the time was not merely mourning a loss of land or possessions, but also evolved into a challenge of humanity to re-engage the world that had been shattered into pieces. Instead of seeking reacquisition or retribution of the land through violence, Kushner reflected that the Jewish mindset of that time of suffering was that "[i]t became humanity's task to repair the world by finding those fragments, recognizing the hidden holiness of ordinary deeds and moments, and painstakingly putting the broken world back together again."[15]

Professor and Jewish scholar Alan A. Block also explored how the traditional Jewish practice of *teshuvah* could offer insight into the foundations of a service-oriented leadership ethic and perspective of education: "[i]n teshuvah, we turn toward the world to begin the healing that our ethical absence from it has made necessary."[16] This perspective offers insight into a spiritual dimension for a call to better the world which lacks order because of ethical absences. Such a view of social change challenges the status quo and complacency of perspectives dominate in an object-oriented society.

In 1967, Martin Luther King Jr. also challenged that the very orientation of government and policy needs a dramatic and dynamic shift from a primary lens of materialism to a lens of human dignity:

> We must rapidly begin the shift from a thing-oriented society to a person-oriented society. When machines and computers, profit motives and property rights, are considered more important than

---

15. Kushner, *Lord is My Shepherd*, 140.
16. Block, *Classroom*, 1.

people, the giant triplets of racism, extreme materialism, and militarism are incapable of being conquered.[17]

Thomas Merton, like King, saw the call to address the need for a perspective shift in the American culture. "[Merton] recognized the oppressive effects of European colonization as it happened to indigenous peoples, African-Americans, to black and brown and southern hemisphere person the world over."[18] Similar to King's perspective of curing the disease of racism, Merton called for the acknowledgement that racism, prejudice, and stigmatization will only begin to change in culture when individuals begin to change their hearts.

The 1960s brought a painful awareness of the lack of progress of unity between the races through the Civil Rights Movement. This societal movement also brought a renewed interest into indigenous scholarship that had previously not been seen or experienced.[19] There was a recognized interwoven experience of the Black Americans and First Nations as subjects of a similar distorted mindset, that through immoral and inhuman leadership both racial groups continue to be separated, isolated, and treated without compassion through the law grounded in an antiquated lens that disregarded their life and dignity.

Learning from Global Witnesses of Leadership

Sometimes it can be easier to see and recognize issues from an outside lens or perspective. It is worth noting that there is evidence that global politicians have recognized the struggle within America's cultural divide and racial issues. In June 1990, just months after his release from prison earlier that year in February, Nelson Mandela set out on a world tour to lobby for the end of apartheid and support of the African National Congress (ANC) through the call of continued sanctions and levering pressure on the South African government to end the legal system of racial segregation that still persisted. Mandela was received as a celebrity by many Americans looking for further change in their own country. Mandela's travel throughout America was carefully watched by federal agencies, as he had previously been acknowledged as a political terrorist in his homeland as

---

17. King, "Beyond Vietnam," para. 47.
18. Savastano, "Introduction," xv.
19. See Deloria, "Indians."

Truth and Reconciliation

his past actions and history continued to be placed upon him, establishing hesitancy in the minds of many political leaders of an authentic change in his character through his call for change and non-violence.

In his autobiography, *The Long Walk to Freedom*, Mandela recounts two fascinating and telling comments that occurred throughout the North American trek of this Freedom Tour. These insights indicate, that even to Mandela, that there is a connection that exists bonding a universal experience between South Africans, Americans, and Canadians. I recount Mandela's comments below as a reminder that individuals outside of America and Canada recognize common injustices and trauma that have affected the dignity and recognition of its citizens. While recalling his time in New York, Mandela wrote that even though he was in prison in South Africa he became very familiar with the discrimination, economic inequality, and racism that black Americans faced:

> I spoke to a great crowd at Yankee stadium, telling them that an unbreakable umbilical cord connected black South Africans and black Americans, for we were children of Africa. There was a kinship between the two.... In prison, I followed the struggle of black Americans.[20]

During the same global tour, his plane had to stop to refuel in Goose Bay, in the province of Labrador, Canada. Mandela recounted that he left his plane and spoke to a group of young people standing at the airfield fence, who were there hoping to see him. He wrote about the encounter on multiple occasions and was continually captivated and fascinated with their education and interest in global affairs.[21]

> [I]n talking with these bright young people, I learned that they had watched my release on television and were familiar with events in South Africa. . . . The Innuit are an aboriginal people historically mistreated by a white settler population; there were parallels between the plights of black South Africans and the Innuit People. What struck me so forcefully was how small the planet had become during my decades in prison; it was amazing to me that a teenaged Innuit living at the roof of the world could watch the release of a political prisoner on the southern tip of Africa.[22]

---

20. Mandela, *Long Walk*, 583.
21. Mandela, *Conversations with Myself*; Mandela, *Long Walk*.
22. Mandela, *Long Walk*, 584.

Though both of these recollections were brief, Mandela points to a reality that is not often recognized: there are parallels in the struggle of racism that similarly affect individuals in South Africa, America, and Canada. Racism is a global problem that continues to affect populations across the world. It is rather telling that as each of these countries, South Africa and Canada have made attempts to address their racial challenges and past injustices; America watches its global neighbors and their leaders creating a way to discuss and have dialogue about their sins, while there has still been little movement to address the problems still plaguing America.

Lessons in Servant Leadership

- **Being Service-Oriented:** Servant leaders demonstrate a dedication to be service-oriented and to help others rather than being object-oriented, focusing on individual success or personal praise. Advocacy through a service-oriented mindset seeks the good of the other by first acknowledging the dignity or sacredness of the other. Service-orientation aims to promote and support the dignity of others.

- **Cultivate an Atmosphere and Culture for the Conversion of Heart:** Servant leaders cultivate an atmosphere and environment for the opportunity of a conversion of heart through charity and compassion. Such change of perspective needs the opportunity of cultivated growth and willingness of growth, in their own perspectives and others. Through the examples like Bartolomé de las Cases and Nelson Mandela, an individual's past does not completely define or dictate all future behavior or perspectives. The potential for conversion of heart is foundational to allow those being served to rise with their potential instead of being relegated to a perpetual stereotype.

- **Honestly Assess and Reflect on Past Events to Develop Trust through Transparency:** Servant leadership demands an honest assessment of the confluence of actions and events that have, through the past, defined the present. Reflection on the contextual present can allow leaders to develop trust and transparency for future leadership by analyzing and understanding how events affected relationship between leaders and followers.

For Further Reflection

- **Being Service-Oriented:** What further ways might the insights of Nelson Mandela, regarding the parallels of the histories and racial issues in Canada and South Africa as well as their subsequent Truth and Reconciliation Commissions, offer as an opportunity to explore further global perspectives as a response to the continual racial unrest in America? After reading Thomas Merton's challenge of fruitful advocacy in "Letters to a White Liberal" (1963), reflect on what ways servant leadership and a more service-orient minded response in the nation as well as media to injustice might offer the first steps in a process toward dialogue and reconciliation in America?

- **Cultivate an Atmosphere and Culture for the Conversion of Heart:** The arts can play an essential role for offering creative opportunities of storytelling and viewing historical events from multiple perspectives. Listen to the following songs. Use their lyrics to compare and contrast the perspectives of the artists' messages: Buffy Sainte-Marie's "My country 'Tis of Thy People You're Dying" (1966), Paul Simon's "American Tune" (1973), or Nathan Rogers's "Mary's Child" (2004) as well as his follow-up ballad "The Jewel of Paris" (2009). How does the narrative of the story of America differ in the lyrics of these songs? In what ways are the musicians telling the same story? How might the lyrics of these, and similar stories, offer a springboard for dialogue regarding American and its roots, and create and cultivate an atmosphere for conversion of heart?

- **Honestly Assess and Reflect on Past Events to Develop Trust through Transparency:** In his account, *A Short Account of the Destruction of the Indies*, Bartolomé de las Cases recorded atrocities that occurred to the Indigenous peoples by the explorers during the 1500s. After reading his account, honestly reflect how such events of the past continue to be present in the deep consciousness and pathos of the structure of American culture. In what ways did those actions create a trajectory for leadership decisions throughout the history of the country? Ultimately, how might the transparency of this, and similar, accounts offer a new perspective for advocacy and servant leadership in the future?

2

Conflict over the Sacred Land and Expansion

North America

The problem with bridging gaps in worldviews is further compounded by the fact that the world has physically been altered by the advent of technology. Since mythology emerges from the Earth itself, the mythology too has changed. Once the mythology changes, so too does the way in which we relate to the world.[1]

THE CELEBRATED FIRST NATIONS author and eminent storyteller, Thomas King, rightly stated: "[h]istory is the stories we tell about the past."[2] It is easy to assume that the annuals of history taught and passed down through social studies courses are strictly objective in nature. Thomas King reminds us, though, that the presentation of facts in such courses, that leave the reader with an interpretation of objectivity and neutrality about events, people, and places of the past, are actually infused with a subjective perspective that is carried through the voice of the interpretations of the historian or storyteller. Not only do the way that generations recount stories of history create a predisposition to the presentation of events, people, and places as well as prejudices based on the lack of particular voices present in such histories, but our own cultural mindset and contemporary mores

---

1. Duran and Duran, *Native American Postcolonial Psychology*, 64.
2. King, *Inconvenient Indian*, 2–3.

indirectly create and influence biased interpretations and meanings on the historical accounts we hear and tell.

The exploration and expansion during the imperial conquest of North America did not merely illustrate an inherent lack of dignity for the indigenous people who were already present, but also a lack of dignity was expressed for the sacred land that was being claimed in name, as an imperial possession. Unacknowledged by the fifteenth century European explorers, and settlers who came afterward, the land itself holds a sacredness beyond being just one in a number of personal possessions. In the tradition of the indigenous peoples, the land continues to be viewed as a sacred gift to be cultivated, nurtured, and treasured, while in contrast the Europeans saw the land as an object or resource to be mined and used for material and personal gain. The prophet Joel offered a poignant insight and reflection of the nature of communities of this object-oriented perspective: "Before them the land is like the garden of Eden, but after them a desolate wilderness, and nothing escapes them" (Joel 2:3).

What was the cause of the development and migration to the New World? Historians could attribute it to the error in calculation and navigation by Columbus, who was trying to find his way to India. Historians could also attribute that the migration to the New World was a search for freedom and escape from religious intolerance. It could also be claimed that the move to the New World was warranted as an opportunity to create a new heaven on earth; a land that could be based entirely on Scriptural values, in direct contrast to the theological wars raging throughout the European continent at the time. Indigenous historian and scholar Roxanne Dunbar-Ortiz recalls how this perspective influenced the British colonial mindset:

> Great Britain, emerging as an overseas colonial power a century after Spain did, absorbed aspects of the Spanish racial caste system into its colonialist rationalizations, particularly regarding African slavery, but it did so within the context of Protestantism, which imagined a chosen people founding and raising a New Jerusalem.[3]

Early American preachers, like Cotton Mather, also believed that the New World could be the location to usher in an apocalyptic revolution of starting humanity from scratch, or a redux of Eden. As mentioned previously, these are some of the stories that have been told to justify individual actions

---

3. Dunbar-Ortiz, *Indigenous Peoples' History*, 38.

of that past time. None of these stories justify the egregious actions of the explorers or settlers at all.

By looking at such historical accounts from another perspective, though, one that recognizes the sacred present in reality, a different picture emerges. What if the land was already what was hoped for by the explorers and settlers, but they could not recognize its sacredness because of their myopic object-oriented perspectives? What could we learn of the sacredness of the land by those already present before the contact of any Europeans arrived? How would their insights help heal the brokenness brought to the land through its conquest and devastation? How could being service-oriented instead of object-oriented offer a more conciliatory relationship with the sacred presence that had been neglected by the early explorers and settlers?

In his 2015 encyclical on the care of the earth, "Laudato sí," Pope Francis offered a clear and stark reminder that the indigenous peoples had a beautiful relationship and tradition of recognizing sacredness of the land well before first contact with European explorers:

> [I]t is essential to show special care for indigenous communities and their cultural traditions.... For them, land is not a commodity but rather a gift from God and from their ancestors who rest there, a sacred space with which they need to interact if they are to maintain their identity and values. When they remain on their land, they themselves care for it best. Nevertheless, in various parts of the world, pressure is being put on them to abandon their homelands to make room for agricultural or mining projects which are undertaken without regard for the degradation of nature and culture.[4]

This serves as an important reminder as we examine the past, live in the present, and look to the future that it is necessary to have awareness of the sacredness that is present in the land and the need to prepare to engage in better relationship with the environment.

Servant-Leadership Lens: Recognizing the Sacred through Awareness and Preparation

Along with a service-oriented perspective, awareness and preparation serve as additional tenets that define the servant leadership model. To change perspective from an object-oriented society to a service-oriented society it is essential to develop the awareness and recognition of the value of the

4. Francis, "Laudato sí," para. 146.

sacred already present in our environment, as well as learning from that awareness to prepare for an authentic encounter with the sacred that will lead to advocacy and missionary service for others.

The Scriptures are full of call narratives where individuals perceive a calling through the awareness of, and encounter with, the sacred. The story surrounding the calling of the famous Israelite leader and prophet Moses offers a clear example of this tenet of servant leadership, awareness and preparation.

Moses: A Foundational Servant Leader Whose Awareness and Preparation Led to Freedom and Liberty

It cannot be ignored or neglected that the roots of a leader as servant is a much older concept than the leadership theory of the twentieth century, or even the age of the Enlightenment, but exemplars offer testimony and witness of this stye of leadership from antiquity. I would like to examine the characteristics of the Israelite prophet and leader Moses as one such example. In the Jewish theological perspective, rabbi Jonathan Sacks clearly reminds the reader that "[t]he highest accolade given to Moses is that he was "the servant of the Lord" (Deut 34:5). Moses is given this title eighteen times in the Tanakh as a whole."[5]

The origin story of Moses's earliest adult life is marked with controversy, as he is portrayed as a murderer and coward while serving in Egypt. He ultimately had to flee for his life into the wilderness from Pharaoh (Exod 2:11–15). After settling into the life of a shepherd, under the guidance of Jethro, his father-in-law, a priest and a figure of parental wisdom, Moses encountered a miraculous sight in the wilderness, that of a burning bush. As he approached the wondrous sight Moses became aware of a voice calling his name, and which declared as he approached: "Come no closer! Remove the sandals from your feet, for the place on which you are standing is holy ground" (Exod 3:5). This intriguing and revealing command of Moses is not a statement from an object-oriented perspective, addressing the lack of cleanliness of his feet or his sandals, but rather an introduction into a service-oriented lens based on a tangible connection with the sacred presence that surrounded Moses.

This service-oriented view demanded that the barriers of the physical, Moses's sandals on his feet, be removed so that Moses could be fully aware

---

5. Sacks, *Lessons in Leadership*, 207.

Conflict over the Sacred Land and Expansion

of the direct contact of the sacred ground and to connect with the sacred present of that encounter through the land. It is through this initial awareness that Moses began his preparation for a new relationship established upon a new calling and future missionary service.

Theological questions could swirl about this moment: Did the ground just become sacred in that moment? Or, was the ground always sacred but was Moses unable to recognize the grace that was already present around him because of his past sin or limited perspective and awareness? Without the time to theologically explore these rhetorical questions I would like to propose, though, that this story offers a direct reminder to the reader that there is much more that is sacred that surrounds us than we often recognize. Although this moment in the life of Moses was an encounter of such awareness that leads to discovery about truth present in the world, it was not something that Moses could claim as his own or become a conqueror over. The encounter was a calling to a relationship, where he needed to let go of his previous perspective of life for a new one.

Likewise, it is not through the act of claiming, discovery, or founding that gives sacredness to the land that the first Europeans encountered as the New World, but rather the land was, and still is, sacred in itself; something that the First Nations peoples were aware of, already recognized, and deeply revered. Much like the Moses running from his past when in Egypt, the initial settlers of the New World desired to escape from their past authoritarian governments' control to find a new life. Instead of creating a new future, though, they forged and anchored their perspective in a myopic cultural perspective without preparation to engage a new and collaborative future. There was no attempt to have awareness to remove the sandals and to touch the ground to authentically encounter the sacred in the mind of the explorers and settlers, rather they claimed the encounter of the new lands as a possession to add to the long collection of material things that defined the struggle for power in the war-torn European continent. The First Nations people were well aware of the lack of recognition of the sacred in the encounter between explores, or the settlers, and the land since the first European arrivals. This awareness is recalled plainly through the following indigenous wisdom offered by Potawatomi member Robin Wall Kimmerer, professor of environmental biology and scholar of indigenous connectivity with the land and environment:

> [S]ince Columbus, some of the wisest of Native elders still puzzle over the people who came to our shores. They look at the toll on

the land and say, "The problem with these new people is that they don't have both feet on the shore. One is still on the boat. They don't seem to know whether they're staying or not." This same observation is heard from contemporary scholars who see in the social pathologies and relentlessly materialist culture.... America has been called the home of second chances. For the sake of the peoples and the land, the urgent work of the Second Man may be to set aside the ways of the colonist and become Indigenous to place. But can Americans, as a nation of immigrants, learn to live here as if we were staying? With both feet on the shore?[6]

The Challenge

The great change in the character of Moses came through his awareness, openness, and willingness to engage the divine encounter. One of the great travesties recounted through the stories told of the foundation of the land called America is that the sacred land was never encountered, but only conquered. There was no openness to the divine encounter, no recognition of the sacredness of the divine presence surrounding the land or the peoples of the land, but only the perspective of dominance, material value, and ownership of those resources. With the power that is present in the mindset of a conqueror there also comes a dominant position of power in belief to define, label, name, and create enduring reference based on a victor's possessive perspective over objects that have been conquered. This dominance in definition allowed the explorers to restructure defintions by distinguishing, labeling, and separating based on categories that existed as perceived or different from European standards and the interpretation of indigenous life. Thomas Merton again indicated that this deeply rooted classification and separation still continued in the twentieth century by indicating that American racism at its core was from when:

> [People] instinctively censor their own ideas of themselves and others: the traits they *like* [sic], they tend to see in themselves and in their friends. The traits they don't like they see in strangers, aliens, and those who are different from themselves. Then they feel they can punish these other people for being different, bad,

---

6. Kimmerer, *Braiding Sweetgrass*, 207.

Conflict over the Sacred Land and Expansion

or wrong, etc. Instead of having to admit evil in themselves, and having to live with it, they project it on others.[7]

The object-oriented society of the Europeans created legal definitions and boundaries for a society in a new environment based on dividing and defining the value or worth of materials versus persons. Those who communicated, lived, and worshipped the same way as the main-land Europeans were labeled as civilized, while those from indigenous communities who were present in relationship with the land and revered the sacred presence of the environment, were deemed uncivilized. In his text *The Clash of Civilizations*, Samuel Huntington, American historian and political analyst, exposed the cyclic nature of such perspectives of cultural dominance:

> Civilized society differed from primitive society because it was settled, urban, and literate. To be civilized was good, to be uncivilized was bad. The concept of civilization provided a standard by which to judge societies. . . . Europeans devoted much intellectual, diplomatic, and political energy to elaborating the criteria by which non-European societies might be judged sufficiently "civilized" to be accepted as members of the European-dominated international system.[8]

This division in lifestyle created a seismic cultural shift in the expectations of society and recognition of human dignity between civilized and primitive communities. Unfortunately, from its first, the development, expansion, and importance of America has placed an object-oriented value above a person-oriented value. Likewise, the ancient civilized Egyptian empire deemed civilized in comparison to the uncivilized Moses, believed he could not pose any type of importance or threat to their regal system. The traditions and grand Egyptian dominance and legacy could not learn or be affected by one outsider, an insignificant primitive shepherd who was a cultivator and steward of the land.

Walter Echo-Hawk, Pawnee Native American law professor and author, indicated that the land ethic of the Europeans has continued to be a miscarriage of authentic relationship with the sacredness of the land. The act of assimilation and suppression does not offer the opportunity to listen and become in tune with the sacred presence and natural rhythms of the land. Although the Europeans may have claimed their territory, they are

---

7. Merton, "Letter to Betsi Baeten," 358.
8. Huntington, *Clash of Civilizations*, 40–41.

still at a loss of how to engage the land and be authentically fruitful, but continue to remain strangers in a land that is still foreign to them:

> Thus, European settlers immigrated to distant lands to Christianize natives, subjugate them, and steal their resources. A land ethic based on those notions cannot easily be developed for colonized land, because, in nearly every colony, the colonists did not adapt to the land as the indigenous peoples had done. . . . In that sense, settlers were, from a cultural standpoint, very much strangers or aliens to the land they colonized, although the immigrants obtained stewardship of the land.[9]

The concept of being a steward of a land that one is a stranger in, and remains a stranger with, offers a powerful metaphor of a leadership perspective that blindly creates policy based on no tangible connectivity with concrete data or followers, to analyze or make informed decision from. As illustrated in the servant leadership model, there is a closeness of relationship that is inherent in learning and recognizing the needs of those to be served. Without an intimate knowledge of the effect actions have within the relationship, with the land or others, there is little opportunity to gather data needed to make conscientious decisions through a servant-minded lens. As rightly lamented and remembered, the leadership demonstrated by the explores and settlers illustrated an object-oriented conquest and possessive transaction without regard to future consequences upon the land or consequences for future generations. As Richard Twiss, Sicangu Lakota Oyate educator and author, astutely stated:

> More than four hundred years of missions cannot be undone. The effects will linger for decades to come. We cannot go back to a point in time before the avalanche of American assimilation buried our people under the social, political, economic, and spiritual fallout of the cultural bomb of colonialism.[10]

It was not only the Europeans explorers and the settlers who created a divide and rift between the relationship between the land, the First Nations, and life in the new world, but some of the first leaders of the United States government continued with similar and damaging perspectives of the use of land and human beings in the name of progress and expansion of the fledgling nation. The expansion of acquired land for America exponentially

---

9. Echo-Hawk, *In the Light*, 141.
10. Twiss, *Rescuing the Gospel*, 216.

grew. The Treaty of Paris (1783), which marked the conclusion of the Revolutionary war, drew new physical boundaries for Europeans between America and British North America, later known as Canada to the north and the Mississippi River to the west, that had not previously existed. No consideration was paid, nor negotiation was conducted with the First Nations regarding the redistribution of land. It was only the European powers that bartered, controlled, and negotiated for the control of the territories in the new world among themselves. Scholars, Roxanne Dunbar-Ortiz and Dina Gilio-Whitaker, further explained the implications affecting First Nations in the second exponential expansion of land throughout the Louisiana Purchase in 1803:

> [T]he Jefferson administration, without consulting any affected Indigenous nation, purchased French-claimed Louisiana Territory (formerly Spanish) from Napoleon Bonaparte. This territory comprised 828,000 square miles, and its addition doubled the size of the United States. The territory encompassed all or part of multiple Indigenous nations, including the Sioux, Cheyenne, Arapaho, Crow, Pawnee, Osage, and Comanche nations, among other people of the bison. It also included the area that would soon be designated Indian Territory (Oklahoma), the future site of the forced relocation of Indigenous people from east of the Mississippi.[11]

The expansion of the land in the name of the expansion of American came at the displacement and expense of the land of the First Nation peoples who already resided in the regions. The lack of awareness and preparation of such expansion and its consequences came at a cost; although not recognized at the time, this consequence continues to define the ethos of American object-oriented focus and relations between cultures and races that comprise the United States of America.

A Call for Change

What was the great discovery of the new world? For an object-oriented society discovery was only assessed by profitability and accumulating more materials for greater wealth and value, usually well beyond the excesses of what was needed. This perspective of excessive accumulation was reviled in some native cultures as such actions were deemed as a disease or disorder. For pre-contact indigenous cultures the importance of the community was

---

11. Dunbar-Ortiz and Gilio-Whitaker, *"All of the Real Indians,"* 70.

of paramount importance instead of the material growth of one individual within the community. In the documentary *I AM*, which explores connectedness between humanity and the world, former psychotherapist and author Thom Hartmann referenced Peter Farb's book *Man's Rise to Civilization* as he explained perspectives of first contact cultures and their view on excessive material gain. A common belief within first contact cultures was that "[t]he idea of accumulation of private property beyond your needs was considered a mental illness."[12] America, as a country, still continues to wrestle with trying to find balance with national and global resources, and how the consequences of that desire affects hope for its future and global presence. There have been examples of leaders within American government, though, who have demonstrated a recognition of the sacredness of the land and a servant awareness and preparation for the future regarding its preservation.

One example of an American President who possessed a keen awareness of the sacredness present in the land, and prepared for the future through an example of service for future generations, was Theodore Roosevelt. Discussing Theodore Roosevelt as an individual who demonstrated aspects of a servant-leader is extremely complicated as his historical accounts include much more controversial actions than what is appropriate for the present point. Through Roosevelt's extensive travel throughout the continent, he encountered and experienced the sacredness of the land through its beauty and recognized that its value ought to be protected and preserved. His awareness of wanting to protect the land for future generations was a progressive concept for his time. He anticipated that the industrial development that occurred in the United States would easily continue to affect and damage the natural beauty of the continent, as the land would only be revered and valued as a commodity, as precedent had been to that time. Although Roosevelt had awareness of a sacred aspect of the land so that it needed to be preserved, he neglected to recognize the same sacred presence in the populations he encountered during his travels. He lacked the service-oriented lens of recognizing the dignity of the people he encountered and in many cases treated them with extreme violence, especially indigenous peoples from the West and South.

It is important though to explore Theodore Roosevelt's awareness and preparedness for the recognition of the establishment of the National Parks reservations. As the Presidential historian Doris Kearns Goodwin

---

12. Shadyac, *I Am*, 59:30–59:40.

indicated, Roosevelt believed that the establishment of the National Parks for future generations of America was one of his finest decisions.[13] Throughout the Industrial Revolution evidence was clear that the value of the land was going to be continually sacrificed for the sake of industrial development and progress. In the wake of the destruction and devastation left behind, Roosevelt made the decision to ensure protection for certain regions of the land. Historical author and environmentalist Wallace Stegner stated: "National parks are the best idea we ever had. Absolutely American, absolutely democratic, they reflect us at our best rather than our worst."[14]

Stegner's comment offers a powerful reminder that the decisions of an individual, like Theodore Roosevelt, can at one time make a decision that has great bearing on the future in one regard, while another decision can have the worst consequences in a different situation, exemplifying the best and worst of what the consciousness of America citizens can offer. Here it is important to recall that an iconoclastic movement to remove historical account from memory because of the worst that individual had offered will also affect the history surrounding the positive aspects that the individual had offered as well. Roosevelt's vision for a preservation of the land, from a recognition of its sacred presence or just because of the beauty present across the nation, offers a tangible example of how a leader offers service for future generations through the awareness and preparation to establish a new vision of a relationship with the land through a service-oriented lens instead of an object-oriented lens of abusing and merely using the land for material gain.

At the Crossroads

Randy Woodley, Keetowah Cherokee theologian and leader in indigenous studies, offers a powerful reminder of the difference between how the sacred land is approached in the American consciousness versus the peace-seeking relationship of indigenous tradition:

> Place is concrete—time is abstract. Within the American myth of *pseudo-place*, most American identity is formed. Because of the inherent dualism in the American myth, the land can have been stolen through egregious means and the national myth can call

---

13. Goodwin, *Leadership in Turbulent Times*, 355.
14. See National Park Service, "Learn & Explore."

Truth and Reconciliation

the nation free.... The dualistic American myth of *pseudo-place* is inextricably woven in the fabric of history and passed down from generation to generation. Piling injustice and lies one upon the other ensures that there will be no chance in the land for God's intended way for us all to live in shalom.[15]

As Deborah McGregor, Anishinaabe Professor of Environmental Studies and indigenous scholar also indicated, an authentic awareness of the insights and traditions of the sacred land and our relationship with it depends on the essential awareness to prepare to conduct research from a perspective that is more in harmony with the sacred space:

> To truly "decolonize" research, *Indigenous research*—research that is formulated from an Indigenous perspective (i.e., is based on Indigenous world view and Indigenous knowledge, and responds to Indigenous needs and inquiries) must begin to play a central role in a broad spectrum of research undertakings. Whereas the vast majority of research is currently defined through a Western science-based/biased lens.... Indigenous theories and knowledge and world views must increasingly become a *starting point* for new research efforts.[16]

A starting point for a new direction of dialogue and research can begin with examining the stories told about the land, especially the origins of the land and its sacred nature. Storytelling has the opportunity to creatively explore and offer an avenue for a new awareness of the beliefs and symbols of differences and similarities held in origin stories. Establishing this foundation can prepare for further thorough dialogues and discussions, starting from common ground—metaphorically and physically. Jody Wilson-Raybould, We Wai Kai Canadian lawyer and former member of Parliament, recalls that the power of storytelling in indigenous culture is that it offers an avenue to engage truth. Regarding the importance of storytelling, especially recounting origin stories, in the process of seeking reconciliation she claimed: "[c]reation stories articulate how and why humans were created, and how we ended up where we are. With that, they help explain a way of comprehending our reality and how we should act in the world."[17] By reexamining the foundational stories of creation one may view our environment from a new perspective, offering an opportunity to

---

15. Woodley, *Shalom*, 135.
16. McGregor, "From 'Decolonized' to Reconciliation," 819.
17. Wilson-Raybould, *True Reconciliation*, 33.

reassess the value of our relationship with our surroundings as well. Such storytelling moments can create a movement that place historical accounts with new understandings to create a reverberating change for the future course of morality, policy, and expectation.

Learning from Global Witnesses of Leadership

An example of an individual who traversed the experiences of black, indigenous, and white in early America was Christian missionary and educator Betsey Stockton. Stockton was born in slavery in Princeton, New Jersey. When she became freed, she was educated through family connections by tutorials at Princeton Theological Seminary. Stockton spent her life in service as a Christian educator and missionary, serving and opening schools in Hawaii, educating black children in Philadelphia, and educating indigenous children in Canada between the early to mid 1800s. Her work stands as a testimonial and witness of servant leadership through her awareness and preparation to adapt and use the experiences she received throughout her early life in pedagogical methods as a tool to offer liberty for those living in poverty and on the fringe of society.

Although she was involved with starting schools for the children of non-royal descent in Hawaii, as well as successfully creating growth in achievement and numbers for schools of black children in Philadelphia, she nonetheless continued to move to locations where she felt her preparation was needed most. In 1829, she became aware and prepared for the need of her skills in Grape Island, Canada. She used her teaching expertise and linguist knowledge to serve the Ojibwa in the missionary school.

As Constance Escher, historical researcher and scholar on Stockton, indicated indigenous members in 1800s Canada desired education, as it meant an avenue of survival and possible security of land in the European system of law.

> Native leaders who asked for help to acquire languages did so to hold onto ancestral lands and to convert these to farms. Schools in bilingualism were requested by the Ojibwa as a tool to minimize cheating by the Anglo fur traders.[18]

Offering the opportunity for an education, Stockton offered indigenous peoples their own avenue to prepare and continue to be aware of

---

18. Escher, *She Calls Herself*, 135.

the systems in place in the European governmental structure to keep and cultivate their sacred connection with their community and the land.

Lessons in Servant Leadership

- **Grow in Awareness and Openness to a New Lens and Perspective:** Servant leaders must be willing to have an awareness and openness to growth in perspective and developing a new lens into the lived experiences of others. Possessing awareness of the needs and perspectives of others offers the opportunity to collect and assess new data for future decision making for a service-oriented mindset.

- **Possess an Active Preparedness for Dialogue:** Servant leaders should possess an active preparedness and anticipation for continual movement in dialogue. This may require consistent engagement with, and learning about, the contexts that affect the community. Being prepared leads to evolving strengths in further servant-leadership traits, such as foresight and remaining goal-oriented.

- **Serve in Recognition for the Dignity of All:** Servant leaders serve, through word and action, for the recognition of a deep and continuous desire for unity of all human beings. Humanity at its core is already one. It is not only important for service-oriented leaders to believe that, but to also inspire others to believe and live for the unity of others, no matter of ethnic, racial, or sexual differences

For Further Reflection

- **Awareness and Openness to a New Lens and Perspective:** Read *The Education of Betsey Stockton* by Gregory Nobles or *She Calls Herself Betsey Stockton* by Constance Escher and reflect on how Stockton was consistently aware of how the experiences of her life allowed her to serve others through administration, education, and her missionary work. Reflect on your own life experiences, what strengths have you gained that could be used in new capacities for the betterment of others? How might you be open to becoming a servant leader through your unique gifts and talents in your community, or globally?

- **Possess an Active Preparedness for Next Steps in Dialogue:** Begin an active preparedness to touch sacred ground, even though it can be an unnerving process, by removing the barriers that block direct connection with the sacred presence in the land, and with others. It is essential for an authentic servant-minded perspective and fruitful dialogue for change. Read Henry David Thoreau's *Walden* (1854) or Wendell Berry's *The Peace of Wild Things: And Other Poems* (2018). Compare and contrast the emotion and language used by the authors to describe the beauty and grandeur of nature. What barriers currently limit your ability to appreciate and understand the dignity and sacredness of your community and environment?

- **Serve in Recognition for the Dignity of All:** As mentioned previously, arts and music can serve in an instrumental role of serving and sharing the message to recognize the sacred dignity of the earth. Listen and reflect on the following songs: Spirit of the West's "Homelands" (1986), Bruce Cockburn's "Stolen Land" (1987), Michael Jackson's "Earth Song" (1995), and/or Chenoa Egawa & Alex Turtle's "Song for the Sacred Elements" (2013). How was the sacredness of creation and the land presented through the rhythms and instrumentation of the songs? What feelings did you experience through the song? How did the musicians illuminate beauty and reverence for the land as well as challenge complacency through these songs? How can music offer an avenue to become more servant-oriented and environmentally connected and conscious?

3

European Colonialization
Africa and the New Imperialism

At any point in history, colonialism has at it roots an interventionism enabled by paternalism. It involves someone intervening in the lives and the decisions of others and claiming that it is for the good and well-being of the people being colonized. In this way, colonizers take the moral high ground even as they take control of the lives of others.[1]

OBIANUJU EKEOCHA, NIGERIAN AUTHOR, biochemist, and scholar offers a haunting and scathing reminder that colonial actions of the past can easily occur in the future, under new forms and under different names. The colonization of the European explorers and settlers offer another example of this type of moral justified intervention in the lives of the indigenous peoples of South Africa by claiming land, objectifying human beings, and eroding the earth to mine for natural minerals and resources to increase their personal gain and wealth. It would be ignorant to state that the direct effects of colonialization have stopped and have been removed during the twentieth-century movements of independence of the governmental leadership emancipating from European control. The deep effects of colonialization extend well beyond the historical imperial control of the governmental structure and the land. There remains psychological effects of

---

1. Ekeocha, *Target Africa*, 138–39.

the caste system that was developed and maintained for centuries, as well as international structures that perpetuate an indirect influence of global decisions through dominance over the region based on superior moral justifications.

As Michael Battle, American theologian and scholar of the life and writing of Desmond Tutu, illustrated: "[m]any Afrikaners think of themselves as descendants of those seventeenth-century Calvinist rebels who fled religious persecution in Europe. For them, God created the Afrikaner people with a unique language, philosophy of life, history, and tradition."[2] This divinely-ordained perspective directly led to the physical separation of race and class between this group of privilege from the indigenous population of South Africa, as well as to the creation of laws that legitimatized the continual dehumanization of black South Africans for centuries.

The history of colonialism in South Africa bears a similar and tragic resemblance to the conquest of North America. Similar to the discovery and settler expansion of the lands of North America, South Africa's narrative history bears a parallel resemblance through the European development of the land, but with a new form and a different label. The historical and looming Columbus—like figure of South Africa's past could be applied to Dutch explorer, Jan van Riebeeck (1619–1677). van Riebeeck was an administrator for the Dutch East India Company who was instructed with securing the trade routes between Europe and Asia. He encountered the region of Cape Town in April 1652, and claimed the region and later fortified it as a location that could be used to control the trade route between the Netherlands and the East Indies. Unlike Columbus, though, van Riebeeck had not always received historical remembrance as a national hero until the mid-twentieth century, when his legacy was infused as part of the construction of national settler ideology. The national settler ideology was a perspective fostered by the white Afrikaners who claimed lineage of the Dutch founders of Cape Town, and was brought to prominence in the 1950s with the coinciding of the 300th anniversary and celebrations of van Riebeeck's arrival in Cape Town.[3] Through this celebration, van Riebeeck was re-imaged as a Founding Father of South Africa by the Afrikaner controlled government and remained a symbol of a new revered hierarchy throughout the remaining years of the Apartheid government.

---

2. Battle, *Reconciliation*, 17.
3. See Rassool and Witz, "1952 Jan van Riebeeck."

Truth and Reconciliation

Although travel and trade were present around the Cape before van Riebeeck's settlement in Cape Town, his presence established the first colonial development for the Netherlands in South Africa. The population in the colony grew quickly and needed to expand agriculture to develop a sustainable food source. With the local lands not always suitable for good farming, the Dutch colonists continued to expand further inland and began to interfere with the indigenous Khoikhoi farmers which escalated to war in the mid-1600s. As the colony expanded the lands surrounding the Cape for the Netherlands, the European wars of the late 1600s between British, French, and the Netherlands also expanded beyond the geographical mainland and brought the colonies into the war stemming from Europe. Although the Netherlands originally staked a claim on the land of South Africa, possession switched from the Dutch to British empire until it remained in the control of the British in the early 1800s.

As was the case with the explorers of North America, European colonialization continued to spread across the globe as financial burdens rose and resources for imperial authorities ran low through expansion of the empire and war efforts to retain those lands of the empire. Author and historical theologian Valentine Ugochukwu Iheanacho offered a powerful reminder that colonialism, and its direct religious connection through missionaries, planted deep roots into the African consciousness because of the lens that defined the settlers' beliefs, cultural place, and time regarding the search for power, pleasure, honor, and wealth:

> It is in this horizon, in the shadow of missions and colonialism, that the history of Christianity on the continent may be described as one of the many vicissitudes of Africa. . . . As people are normally children of their time, the missionaries and their mother churches in Europe bore the imprints of their time with regard to colonialism.[4]

As precious natural minerals and resources were found by the settlers in the lands of South Africa, the rush for acquisition and possession occurred. This rush to claim lands and its resources directly paralleled the experience of the Gold Rush of California, whose byproduct led to the displacement, mass removal, and the mass murder of the indigenous of the region.[5] The rush that affected South Africa similarly occurred over the desire for the possession of the gold and diamond mines as well as the desire to become

---

4. Iheanacho, *Historical Trajectories*, 12.
5. See Shaler, "Indigenous Peoples."

economically prosperous and comfortable in the luxurious climate of the South African Cape. British historian, and scholar of pre-colonial Africa, J. D. Fage indicated that:

> The presence of diamonds was recognized in 1867, and diggers were soon rushing into an area around the confluence of the Vaal and Orange rivers which were found to be exceptionally rich in diamond-bearing soils. . . . The discovery of the diamond fields and their acquisition by Britain for the Cape Colony meant that the latter achieved the means for an economic take-off.[6]

This desire for living a comfortable life of economic stability and luxury became a temptation of the European inhabitants of South Africa. This object-oriented perspective and focus on material possessions instead of the dignity of the human beings already present on the land was in direct opposition against the traditional perspectives of African pre-contact societies, and was rather a myopic perspective of individual prosperity and entitlement that set the stage for further historical separation between the races as well as its legal foundations.

Servant-Leadership Lens: Being Community-Oriented

In the last chapter, we examined that the Torah contained a phrase that repeatedly entitled Moses as a servant leader. Another phrase frequently used throughout the Torah parallels another aspect of Greenleaf's servant leadership theory, which focuses on reminding the Jewish faithful to remain community-oriented. This prominent and repeated phrase throughout the Hebrew Scriptures is: "remember you were slaves in Egypt . . ." (Deut 5:15; 8:14; 15:15; 16:12; 24:18). This phrase is used as a preface, and as a consistent reminder, that the Israelite people were called to act with a sense of charity and justice toward outcasts, foreigners, and the less fortunate in a reciprocal way to what the Israelites had received from YHWH throughout the process of their escape from slavery and ultimately finding liberty in their promised land.

---

6. Fage, *History of Africa*, 382.

Amos: A Foundational Servant Leader Calling for Community Inclusion of the Outcast

After the death of King Solomon, the once united Kingdom of Israel separated into two distinct governed regions. The Israelites of the Northern Kingdom quickly fell away from following the Torah and forgot their call of remaining vigilant to the needs in the community. They instead strived to live a life of luxury, prosperity, and entitlement after settling in the land. The nobility in Samaria also neglected the poor and outcast in favor of their own comfort.

In response to the actions of the separation of the least in the community, the prophet Amos was called to challenge the complacent behavior of the wealthy nobles in Samaria, the capital of the Northern Kingdom of Israel, who had turned a blind eye to those living in poverty within their midst (Amos 4:1). Amos was a shepherd from the lands surrounding Bethlehem, a small region from the Southern Kingdom of Judah. During his mission Amos left his homeland and traveled to the separated Northern Kingdom and served as an advocate for individuals of a similar social class as himself. A very challenging position to be in, Amos trusted that his calling to demand a more community-oriented view of all Israelites, fueled by his desire for a needed change of hearts and minds, would lead a more community-oriented perspective. This call for change was dynamic, pointed, and focused on the awareness of a coming judgment. For Amos, justice needed to flow as a river to clean away the land of the malaise that poisoned the people (Amos 5:24).

Amos remained community-oriented throughout his approach to fulfill his ministry as a servant leader by brashly illustrating the disparity of the lifestyle of those who had the luxury of comfortable and complacent living versus those who did not (Amos 6:1). Through his challenging words and mission, his prophetic message focused on a call for reorientation toward unity, within the community. During the time of governmental restructuring, and the division from one kingdom to two kingdoms, much of the focus of the life of the Israelite nobility separated from a local awareness of the needs of the poor, losing sight of much of the service-oriented expectation that Moses attempted to instill during the tribal years of wandering in the desert and collective survival.

Amos's mission seemed to have not been accepted or received well, or heeded, as further prophets like Hosea were also called to continue the plea for the Israelites to come back their roots and change the focus of their hearts from material idolatry. Nonetheless, Amos's judgment of the complacency in the midst of poverty stands as a witness of the need to focus on the whole community instead of the satisfaction of individual achievement alone.

Much like the inhabitants of Samaria during the time of Amos, the wealth and luxury of the European colonists of South Africa came at the expense and neglect of the indigenous South Africans. This colonization was not just based on the mere removal of natural resources to enrich an empire, but it also included the permanent acquisition and development of the land, resources, and ultimately a complete displacement and division of the population of the area. As the Ghanaian historian and politician Adu Boahen recounted:

> European settlers in southern Africa, unlike their counterparts in the rest of Africa, were from the beginning interested in establishing permanent homes in their new environment, with its appealing temperate climate, fertile agricultural land, cheap African labour and abundance of materials.[7]

This stratification of the population and lack of regard for the sacredness of the environment offer a parallel example of the experiences of Amos. The white European settlers lived a life of ease and comfort while those in poverty had to work in exhausting and brutal conditions of the mines. Amos's call of judgment continues to ring true—that as we neglect the least among us and remain individually focused instead of community orientated, there is truly no way to find the type of authentic unity that can bring together and sustain a just way of living.

The Challenge

Boahen explained that the historical injustices in South Africa effecting indigenous black Africans was not just rooted in the individual garnering of wealth by the Europeans, but just over a generation these actions of racial separation became legalized through laws that were enacted to ensure that the races would remain economically and physically isolated from each other permanently, leading the whites to their life of luxury and the black Africans to objectivation and poverty.

> By the late 1890s . . . the hut tax, forced labour, severe suppression of traditional beliefs and customs and, especially, land alienation

---

7. Boahen, *Africa under Colonial Domination*, 94.

were introduced. This foreign interference intensified in proportion to the settlers' increasing need for cheap indigenous labour to work on farms and in the mines, and for the hut tax to meet at least part of the administrative expenses. Africans were compelled to vacate their homelands to make room for white settlers and to serve as army "volunteers."[8]

As the strength of the oppressive white government grew, the determination for liberty also manifested within the black African population. There was a desire to fight back for their previous tribal independence and for the sovereignty of the lands. To try and respond to this rising determination and opposition to the forced legal separation more measures were taken by the white government to divide and conquer the black resistance. Africa historian and scholar, David Chanaiwa stated that:

> When it became clear that repressive laws and police violence alone were failing to break up African determination, the Nationalist government . . . recommended the notorious bantustan policy. . . . [This] policy was a basically a "divide and rule" technique designed to balkanize African nationalism and to buy time while consolidating white supremacy. The idea was to revive and revitalize ethnic rivalries of the Mfecane era by reversing the unifying factors of Pan-Africanism, education, intermarriages, urbanization and nationalism.[9]

Laws were continued to be drawn up and enacted to limit the rights of the blacks of South Africa. The 1913 Natives' Land Act established geographical boundaries defining where black Africans could live, which amounted to only ten percent of the actual physical region available. Ten years later, in 1923, The Natives Act established designated townships which were set up as black only communities of residence that limited the physical view of poverty to outside of the urban experience. The townships were locations where black Africans were allowed to rent homes but were limited from purchasing them; again, another symbolic gesture that seemed to offer affordable living, but really was an illusion of independence and autonomy. The law also limited the presence and time that blacks could spent in urban areas and lead to removal and deportation of unemployed blacks to outside the cities. The 1927 Black Administration Act followed, and allowed the white government leadership to displace entire community

---

8. Boahen, *Africa under Colonial Domination*, 103.
9. Chanaiwa, "Southern Africa," 258–59.

of blacks to a totally different region of the country without less than an hour notice before the forced displacements.

In the wake of World War II, the movement of white nationalist supremacy rose in South Africa, as the Afrikaner leadership aligned with the rise and vision of Adolf Hitler. The British population in South Africa still outnumbered the Afrikaans, so ultimately South Africa aligned with Britain throughout the war. As white South Africans went to war, there was an increased need for black South Africans to fill in the jobs, and continue the industrial work for the war effort. But after the war concluded, the black South Africans were quickly removed from the jobs, the response of which developed into a strike that resulted in the death of hundreds of black workers. This reignited the rise of black militancy, and only fed Afrikaner leadership to argue that the nature of black South Africans was violent, uncivilized, and uncontrollable. The increased violence from oppressed black South Africans led to an anxious and fearful white Afrikaner leadership to ratify the full and official acceptance of the systematic doctrine of Apartheid segregation in 1948.

A Call for Change

In the ensuing laws of oppression, groups and movements were developed to offer voice against the rising tide of a single focused political white nationalist ideology. The first politically organized response of black Africans to the laws of separation by the Afrikaans was the development of the South African Native National Congress, which was founded in 1912. Later renamed and re-envisioned, the movement became known as the South African National Congress (ANC). The ANC was a responsive voice to the growing hostility toward, and lack of access of, the black population of South Africa. The ANC was organized as a movement focused on the rights of the black African community inclusion through petitioning the government for restored access to dignity and land. As petitioning consistently failed, though, the movement starting demonstrating through actions of nonviolent resistance. By the 1950s, the ANC evolved into a campaign of defiance which started to include violent responses to the government overreach and unjust laws in response to the ossification of the system of Apartheid throughout the country.

Probably the most famous member of the ANC and black resistance was Nelson Mandela, who grew up throughout the rise of the Apartheid system in the 1940s. From his youth with the ANC, Mandela committed himself to opposing the white nationalistic rule of the Afrikaans. Leadership scholar Julian Barling recounted:

> Mandela had the unusual opportunity of observing both Black and White roles models, including situations in which Black teachers defied White authority. . . . Mandela's early life was replete with situations in which he saw others challenge authority and did so himself, and he both witnessed and practiced leadership.[10]

After the official governmental adoption of Apartheid, Mandela became even more active and oppositional to the laws enforced on the black African population. He participated in the Defiance Campaign of 1950s and was repeatedly arrested for his leadership of the movement of black African resistance. Although he originally began as a nonviolent resistor, after a decade of experiencing a lack of change but continual tightening of authority from the Afrikaans government, Mandela started to argue that nonviolence was virtually unnoticed and elicited no response, so he turned to actions of violence to evoke needed change. He joined the South African Communist Party (SACP) in the 1960s, and began to believe that violence was the only answer to combat the unjust treatment of black Africans under the Apartheid system. Through the inspiration of the SACP, Mandela co-founded the militant group, *uMkhonto we Sizwe* (the Spear of the Nation), and led actions of terror against the oppressive Afrikaans leadership and rule of law that they created. He was ultimately arrested and put on trial to be executed in prison in 1962, for being an aggressive agitator, treasonous conspirator, and violent terrorist revolutionary. Through the support of international leverage from the United Nations, Mandela and other black South African leaders condemned to death for treason were spared state sanctioned executions and were committed to sentences of life in prison.

At the Crossroads

There is much that needs to be re-examined in the history of pre-contact South Africa community relationships that has been obscured in light of the recent and traumatic historical narrative established by the European influence upon the indigenous South African peoples. African history and international studies professors Adeyinka Ajayi and Lateef Buhari offer that

---

10. Barling, *Science of Leadership*, 125–26.

the nature of pre-contact African communities was primarily predicated on dialogue and agreement:

> The methods of performing conflict resolution in the traditional African societies are as follows: mediation, adjudication, reconciliation, arbitration and negotiation. It also includes employing extra-judicial devices and usage of legal maxims to persuade or convince the disputants about the implication or otherwise of their behavior. These methods have been effective in traditional African Society.[11]

These narrative-based practices lay a foundation for authentic dialogue in the midst of conflict resolution: mediation, adjudication, reconciliation, arbitration and negotiation. Such actions ungird the restorative justice processes and practices incorporated in the South African Truth and Reconciliation Commission to address an avenue for forward movement of unity for the country from its Apartheid past, which will be discussed in further detail in chapter eight. It is important to recognize that these aspects of community restoration were already part of the legacy of the pre-contact South African consciousness and were not a novel approach to addressing conflict in the traditional African societies.

Not only did these dialogue techniques offer a narrative for restorative justice but it was believed that this style of conflict resolution offered healing for the brokenness present in the community due to the conflict, as Ajayi and Buhari also stated:

> Conflict resolution performs a healing function in African societies. It provides opportunity for the examinations of alternative positive decisions to resolve differences. Failure to resolve conflict over access to commonly valued scarce resources, and over divergent perceptions of socio-political situations, has the high potential of degenerating into genocide or fratricide.[12]

For traditional African communities, it was essential to find resolution to differences for the survival of both groups, or individuals, in disagreement. Without the goal of seeking unity between the parties, the conclusion would result in violence, and likely death. It is also important to note that the goal of the good of the whole community continued to be present in the mindset of black South Africans during the Apartheid government. As indicated

---

11. Ajayi and Buhari, "Methods of Conflict Resolution," 149.
12. Ajayi and Buhari, "Methods of Conflict Resolution," 152.

through the vision of a united South Africa under Nelson Mandela, Desmond Tutu, and other resistors to the apartheid system there continued to be desired work toward conflict resolution in a post-apartheid government through the use of the traditional African conflict resolution practices.

Learning from Global Witnesses of Leadership

Although Nelson Mandela and Desmond Tutu have become two of the most globally recognized and remembered leaders during the change from the Apartheid regime to a democratic South Africa, other leaders also demonstrated a community-oriented witness and goal of united racial community through service. Another example of this type of servant leader is Rev. Peter Storey.

Storey is a white South African who served as a South African Methodist minister, former president of the Methodist Church of Southern Africa, and former president of the South African Council of Churches. His faith informed the goal that drove his advocacy to end the system of apartheid in South Africa. Storey led grassroots efforts that evolved into international outcries for assistance to raise global awareness and witness to the injustices being perpetrated by the South African government. Like the prophet Amos, Storey's actions and words became a herald of needed change for a call for a renewed perspective of being community-oriented.

One example of this call for justice was illustrated in 1984 when Storey quickly moved into an action of solidarity with other clergy to protect black South Africans against the plans of the Afrikaans government of another mass relocation effort. Storey recounted this collaborative experience in his memoirs, *Protest at Midnight*:

> My co-leader was Roman Catholic Archbishop George Daniel, and our delegation was a mix of seven clergy with on-the-ground experience in the barren resettlement areas where victims of the policy were dumped. We were armed with a powerful exposé of the government's "Relocation" policy. . . . Already three-and-a-half-million black people had been robbed of their citizenship, uprooted—some more than once—and sent to so-called bantustans. The regime was planning the same fate for at least two million more black people, and the only thing that could stop them was massive international pressure led by the UN.[13]

---

13. Storey, *Protest at Midnight*, 148.

Storey left his country as an advocate for a call on behalf of the voiceless to end the injustices of the system of apartheid, and led into the first democratic elections of South Africa. He later continued to seek nonviolent resolutions to the decades of violence by spearheading the movement for a gun-free South Africa.

Committed to peace and justice, Storey remained steadfast to his community-oriented mission through service which resulted in many white members of his congregation leaving and rejecting his prophetic message for change. As also demonstrated through the life of the prophet Amos, fulfilling the call for the change of heart is a task of great suffering.

Lessons in Servant Leadership

- **Being Community-Oriented:** Servant leaders have goals that are community-oriented. The outcome through their service is not for their benefit alone, or may not be for their benefit at all. The focus of being community-oriented is to offer a betterment for unity and stronger communal relationship for all.

- **Herald for the Poor and Outcast:** Servant leaders are willing to advocate and become a herald for the poor and outcast. Through their positions of influence, servant leaders offer their skills to give voice to the voiceless and to create lasting opportunities for those who have historically been rejected to actually contribute to future influential decision-making processes.

- **A Witness of Light in the Midst of Darkness:** Servant leaders offer hope through the illumination of their actions and words. Their witness stands as a testimony against the injustices that exist in their midst, as a beacon of hope. Servant leaders need to be a visible embodiment and example for those being neglected and shine through the darkness of injustice.

For Further Reflection

- **Being Community-Oriented:** The prophet Amos and Rev. Peter Storey can be viewed as example of servant leaders who served as heralds against the injustices that segregated the peoples of their time, based on the inequalities of luxury and wealth. Who might be a similar contemporary example of a herald against injustice based on economic disparities? Through what ways is that individual advocating for the less fortunate and calling for societal change? How are you contributing to the voice of change in situations of socio-economic injustice in your community?

- **Herald for the Poor and Outcast:** Read the United Nations adoption of the Nelson Mandela Rules, the standard minimum rules for the treatment of prisoners, adopted in 2015. The United Nations adaption of the Mandela Laws is a constant reminder of the importance of treating all human life with dignity. How can the goal of treating incarcerated citizens of society with dignity offer insight into the vision of a country or nation as a whole? Examine the incarceration rates for your local community, what does the data show you about how justice is interpreted in that area? How does your society offer opportunities for individuals to be reintegrated into society after being incarcerated?

- **A Witness of Light in the Midst of Darkness:** Listen and reflect on the following songs: Sam Cooke's "A Change is Gonna Come" (1964), Ladysmith Black Mambazo/Paul Simon's "Homeless" (1986), and/or Dave Matthews Band's "Don't Drink the Water" (1998). How do the lyrics challenge the listener to think about the perspective of community, or lack of community, through the topic and feeling of the song? What feelings did you experience through the song? How can music offer an avenue to become more community-oriented and conscious of the challenges of those who might be separated from community because of homelessness, illness, or economic struggles?

4

Manifest Destiny

America's Two-Edged Sword

I did not know then much was ended. When I look back now from the high hill of my old age, I can still see the butchered women and children lying heaped and scattered all along the crooked gulch as plain as when I saw them with eyes still young. And I can see that something else died there in the bloody mud, and was buried in the blizzard. A people's dream died there. It was a beautiful dream . . . the nation's hoop is broken and scattered. There is no center any longer, and the sacred tree is dead.[1]

THESE WORDS OF BLACK Elk, which were later used as the concluding epitaph of Dee Brown's chronicle of Indigenous American history *Bury My Heart at Wounded Knee*, convey the devastation and utter emptiness left as a consequence of the movement West, and the rally cry of Manifest Destiny. The suffering and yearning of Black Elk's comments offer a hollow memory in contrast to the traditional historical accounts of the glory of expansion and frontier life. In the 1960s, the image of a dream was once again, and famously, evoked by Martin Luther King Jr. as a cadence in his speech on the march on Washington, DC, at the country's capital. These powerful images of a dream lost, or a dream unfulfilled, offer a clear statement that the hopes within the human race have not been respected in the

---

1. Brown, *Bury My Heart*, 446.

same fashion. Manifest Destiny, which led to the expansion of the country also bears a lingering and unfulfilled dream or promise for both black and indigenous peoples, remains a two-edged sword in the historical identity of the country.

The development and expansion of America, as a country and an idea, evolved exponentially after the first arrival of the initial explorers and settlers. The Founding Fathers of the country had been influenced by the cultural rise of the movement of the Enlightenment within European philosophy. Philosophers such as John Locke and Thomas Paine influenced the mindset of the thinkers of the time through the claims that a representative government is more ethical and offered more freedom than a system based on a monarchy, even if benevolent. As the ideas of autonomy and liberty solidified into the ethos of the American consciousness it became a movement and criteria for the definition of a civilized governance and lifestyle.

After the War of 1812, much more focus was paid toward expansion of territory through treaties or war with the indigenous communities that resided on the land. As settlers migrated West they were often escorted and protected by the U. S. Cavalry.[2] When treaties with indigenous leaders were signed, they were often broken or substituted for a second, third, or fourth revision of the treaty which continued to displace the indigenous peoples from their land and further from any potential prosperity and liberty. It can be said that this was a time of being goal driven, but that goal created consequences causing extreme detriment to black and indigenous peoples. This movement eventually evolved into a divinely destined rally cry and was spread across the continent as a missionary venture. The belief, or motto, of Manifest Destiny emerged from the brief that a divine mission was instilled in the nation to evangelize and expand this new ethical government founded on democracy, the voice of the people, and capitalism, an individualistic perspective based on promises of potential prosperity and wealth.

The hope of prosperity had its limits, though, depending on the populations that its promise was intended for. As Joel Edward Goza, professor of ethics and author on community advocacy, recounts "[f]rom slavery to Jim Crow to the colorblind age, racism always required mythologies to provide illusion of harmony and progress in the midst of crisis."[3] The expansion of the West, during the era of Manifest Destiny, came at a time of crisis in the identity of America and was marketed under the guise of a divine calling.

2. See Pevar, *Rights of Indians*, 43–54.
3. Goza, *America's Unholy Ghosts*, 17.

This ideology created a powerful and profound mythology and illusion that continues to endure in historical narratives. The enduring consequences of the era have brought much more of a divide in population than the prosperity it initially promised. Theodora Kroeber, early to mid-twentieth-century anthropologist and author, offered a description of the goal driven context and outcome of the ethos of frontier life, as she stated:

> [I]t is perhaps well to remind ourselves that the best and gentlest of them [people of the frontier] did not question their right to appropriate land belonging to someone else, if Indian—the legal phrase was "justifiable conquest." However broad and real governmental and popular approval was, this invasion was like the classic barbarian invasions—a forced intrusion upon a settled population, and its replacement by the intruders.[4]

To be service- and goal-oriented, instead of goal driven, indicates that an individual is not obsessed about personal gain, expansion, or conquest but rather dedicated to their goal or outcome of service toward others. An authentic perspective of service resides in a heart that recognizes the sacred that exists in and through our environment. This chapter seeks to explain the difference of being goal driven and goal-oriented through a lens of service, in light of such historical narratives.

Servant-Leadership Lens: Being Goal-Oriented

Scripture is full of examples of goal-oriented individuals who followed in a faithful response to a specific call or action. The example used for this chapter, the prophet Jeremiah, offers a testimony of an individual steadfast in direction for his goal, and though enduring consistent suffering still maintains focus on remaining oriented toward that goal. The resilience and determination demonstrated throughout his story offers an important aspect of being goal-oriented in service to others, even in the midst of rejection, instead of goal driven to the extent of displacing others to achieve the desired outcome.

---

4. Kroeber, *Ishi in Two Worlds*, 47–48.

Jeremiah: A Servant-Leader Calling for a Change of Heart

The prophet Jeremiah was called to become a servant-leader at a young age (Jer 1:6–7). From that early time in his life, he was called to prepare the remaining Jewish population in Judah for a drastic change of life, and lifestyle. Although they were prosperous at the moment, there was a judgment coming for them in the near future that would change that way of life. Jeremiah's prophetic mission, like Amos before him, arose during a time of faithlessness and turmoil in the Jewish community. Jeremiah's prophetic goal was to serve as a messenger to the people of Jerusalem that the great power of Babylon was going to defeat the holy city; this was not welcomed news to that population. Jeremiah was commissioned for a ministry of grief, as the king and people consistently rejected him and his message, but nonetheless he remained goal-oriented. As Jeremiah was reminded throughout his ministry: "For surely I know the plans I have for you, says the Lord, plans for your welfare and not for harm, to give you a future with hope" (Jer 29:11).

The future of hope ultimately promised in the prophecy of Jeremiah was not to come quickly or without burdens. The Jewish people were challenged through Jeremiah to leave their past worship of material idolatry behind and focus on a new goal—the goal of a new law written on their hearts (Jer 31:33). This new law would create a new purpose and future for the community. Coming at a defining moment of change, Jeremiah indicated that no matter what choice the Jewish people decided the outcome would be the same; namely the city will ultimately fall and the nation of Babylon will defeat them. The goal of Jeremiah, though, was not a simple or superficial one. It was not to alter the course of the fall of the city or to find a secret way to be victorious over Babylon in war, but he was called to try to change the hardened hearts of the inhabitants of the capital city of Judah, Jerusalem. He needed to convince the Jewish people that even in the midst of a defeat at the hand of the enemy, those who remained faithful would still be protected through the struggle, suffering, and purification that was to be endured. The options offered through the prophecy of Jeremiah were that the Jewish followers could fight against Babylon and get defeated, dispersed, and killed; or they could allow the Babylonians to take the city without a great loss of life (Jer 21:3–10). Either way, Jeremiah indicated that the city would fall and the future seemed bleak for the inhabits whose faith relied on their materialistic wealth alone.

Jeremiah remained steadfast in his determination to pursue the goal of proclaiming the divinely inspired word to the inhabitants of Jerusalem that encouraged a conversion of heart to preserve the population instead of a war, which would lead to the destruction of human life. His warnings fell on deaf ears, particularly as the king of Jerusalem was swayed by the positive, but empty messages of potential prosperity and victory over the Babylonians from the messages of false prophets (Jer 23:16–19). For remaining oriented toward his goal, though, Jeremiah was labeled a traitor, thrown into an empty cistern to die from the elements by the king of Jerusalem—though he was later retrieved, and then he ultimately was taken against his will to Egypt by Jews who hoped to escape the Babylonian destruction (Jer 43:5–7). From this hard life of grief, the title "the weeping prophet" is often associated with Jeremiah. The Psalmist invokes a similar emotion of suffering and loss, which parallels the emotional heartache of Jeremiah's prophetic message, when in the midst of the taunts of the Babylonians asking for the Jewish exiles to play their beautiful and sacred songs of Zion for their entertainment, the Exiles remember that the city of their joy lay in ruins (Ps 137).

As servant leadership scholars Milton Sousa and Dirk van Dierendonck stated: "the humble service side of servant leaders (as perceived by followers) can work as a catalyst of their action side by improving the relationship of trust with followers."[5] The trust of the humble message of Jeremiah was unfortunately only appreciated by a few, a remnant, until after his forced exile in Egypt as his prophecies came to fruition. Jeremiah's words still continue to stand as a testimony and witness of the ardent focus of fulfilling a service-oriented goal; a goal that may not be attained in one's own lifetime but nonetheless one motivated for the future betterment for others. In the growing global tension Jeremiah offers a message of courage: "Do not be fainthearted or fearful at the rumors heard in the land—one year one rumor comes, the next year another, rumors of violence in the land and of ruler against ruler" (Jer 51:46).

The Challenge

The historical record of America includes countless stories of violence and war within its borders. Pulitzer Prize winning author and journalist, Isabel Wilkerson offers a disclaimer that it is often easy to disregard or overlook

5. Sousa and van Dierendonck, "Servant Leadership," 17.

Truth and Reconciliation

the egregious aspects of violence that has defined history that Americans, as individuals and as a country, have been culpable of. It is essential to remember that "[h]uman history is rife with examples of inconceivable violence, and as Americans, we like to think of our country as being far beyond the guillotines of medieval Europe or the reign of the Huns"[6] but that is not the case. Throughout the 1800s black and indigenous peoples had to remain constantly vigilant of the rumors of violence in the land as well as the terrors at the hands of many of the rulers within the federal government.

By 1851, many treaties initiated by the federal government with leaders of the First Nations were being forged. Red Cloud, leader of the Oglala Lakota, refused to sign a treaty with the government because as he prophesized and warned: "The White man lies and steals. . . . My lodges were many, but now they are few. The White man wants all."[7] The powers and principalities that came to conqueror the First Nations brought with it a darkness that distorted and enveloped the relationship between the two groups thereafter,[8] as promises were substituted for lies and honesty for manipulation. As Bob Drury and Tom Clavin, American historians and journalists recounted:

> Red Cloud's warnings would prove prescient: the mid-1860s were a psychological turning point in white-Indian relations in the nation's midsection. Earlier European colonialism had involved not only the destruction of Native peoples, but also a paternalistic veneration. . . . Now, however [that] was a receding memory, a newly muscular America was replacing it with a post-Civil War vision of Manifest Destiny . . . attitudes were reconfigured with cruel clarity, particularly among westerners. Even whites who had once considered Indians the equivalent of wayward children . . . were beginning to view them as a subhuman race to be exterminated or swept onto reservations by the tide of progress.[9]

As the expansion of American claimed territory grew, so did the goal of increased control and power that was driven by the object-oriented perspective of individual and/or national prosperity. Although the United Stated federal government promised treaties, and words of peace were

---

6. Wilkerson, *Caste*, 152.
7. Drury and Clavin, *Heart of Everything*, 4.
8. It is important to note that in Oglala Sioux rituals the symbolic meaning of darkness refers to an ignorance that clouds or distorts the soul. See Brown, *Sacred Pipe*, 36.
9. Drury and Clavin, *Heart of Everything*, 4.

Manifest Destiny

offered and given to indigenous peoples, the treaties and promises were often broken by laws enacted for the sake of land expansion and power. Thomas King recounted an example attributed to war general and later American President Andrew Jackson:

> In 1830, when . . . fulfilling an election promise to his western, and southern supporters, [Jackson] pushed the Removal Act through Congress, he did so to get rid of thousands of Indians—particularly the Cherokees, Choctaws, Chickasaws, Creeks, and Seminoles—who were not dying and not particularly interested in going anywhere."[10]

Wilkerson also included another, and more grotesque, example of the actions of Jackson at this time, as well as a demonstration of how easily power can allow darkness to blind an entire society to the horrific acts perpetrated against members of its least protected communities throughout history:

> Andrew Jackson, the U. S. President who oversaw the forced removal of indigenous people from their ancestral homelands during that Trail of Tears, used bridle reins of indigenous flesh when he went horseback riding. And . . . into the twentieth century, African-Americans were burned alive at the stake, as seventeen-year-old Jesse Washington was in Waco, Texas, in 1916 before a crowd of thousands."[11]

As expansion occurred, the goals continued to change and this drove the frontier settlers to displace the indigenous of the region. The 1870s gold rush brought to light some of the worst of human behavior, through greed and the desire of quick material gain. This exponentially quick influx into California created a disequilibrium in the culture too quickly to control. As the population migrated before any governmental control was established in the region, much of the law was left unto the frontiersmen themselves. Without accountability or responsibility being goal-driven can devolve into a relative and individualistic moral code, instead of a view of communal recognition of the dignity of others. Kroeber offered a powerful insight into the drive of hedonism and materialism of time:

> The Anglo-Saxons . . . reversed the ratio of whites to Indians, coming in inundating numbers—there were as many as a hundred thousand of them in a single year. They lacked any formal

---

10. King, *Inconvenient Indian*, 34.
11. Wilkerson, *Caste*, 152–53.

Truth and Reconciliation

church control and, during all the fateful years for Indian survival, were without adequate state or military restraints, so that both the excesses and cruelties and crimes, and the efforts to bring them under some sort of surveillance and control, were pretty much up to frontiersmen themselves.[12]

With this mass migration, driven by an object-oriented perspective, a genocide occurred to large groups of the first inhabitants of the region, and led to a diaspora of the remaining indigenous peoples of the land.[13] The darkness consumed the perspective of the white expansionists, as evidenced through the American novelist and historian Dee Brown, as recounted in the interchange between General Philip Sheridan and Tosawi, during the surrender of Comanche. As Tosawi, a Comanche chief, introduced himself to Sheridan he included along with his name that he was a good Indian. The general's reply to Tosawi's statement was the infamous retort: "[t]he only good Indians I ever saw were dead."[14]

A Call for Change

To change the hardened hearts and write a new law of compassion within the whole community, individuals rose to change the status quo. Chief Joseph (1840–1904), leader of the Nez Perce tribe from the region of the Pacific Northwest, stands as an example of a voice in the wilderness calling for a new, community-oriented goal. Standing his ground in the face of being forcibly removed to a reservation and away from his homeland, as well as being involved in some of the worst encounters with American troops in the West, Chief Joseph tried to seek refuge in Canada. He and his tribe were ultimately cornered by United States troops and defeated. Too weary to continue to fight any longer, and assessing the magnitude of the carnage resulting from his peoples' death, Chief Joseph and the remaining members of his tribe surrendered and were sent to a reservation in Washington. Even after suffering the loss of his land and forced removal of his people to another land, Chief Joseph continued in earnest toward his goal through advocacy for his people and restoring relationship with the land, similar to the suffering of the prophet Jeremiah.

---

12. Kroeber, *Ishi in Two Worlds*, 43–45.
13. See Shaler, "Indigenous Peoples."
14. Brown, *Bury My Heart*, 170.

Chief Joseph's resistance and advocacy for peace was delivered through prophetic words to the national capital of America. He called judgment upon the nation for the injustices and ill treatment of the indigenous peoples, and that of the sacred land. In 1879, he gave a scathing report in Washington, DC, which included the following challenge:

> If the white man wants to live in peace with the Indian he can live in peace. There need be no trouble. Treat all men alike. Give them the same laws. Give them all an even chance to live and grow. All men were made by the same Great Spirit Chief. They are all brothers. The earth is the mother of all people, and all people should have equal rights upon it.[15]

In this statement Chief Joseph offers a clear distinction between an object-driven goal and a community or servant-oriented goal. His clear statement for equality in treatment, law, and relationship, especially with the land, lays the foundational difference of the desired goal and outcome.

What is the image of a future of hope look like? One of peace or one of war? The goals and priorities of pre-contact associations between indigenous tribes could be characterized as an authentic relationship grounded upon peace and wisdom within the sacred land. Joseph Epes Brown, American intellectual and Native American scholar, offers an essential insight into the symbolic ritual meaning and power of light and darkness, from Oglala Sioux tradition: "we see the light which destroys darkness, just as wisdom drives away ignorance."[16] Chief Joseph's call for peace attempted to offer light to the darkened landscape and relationship, which had been the precedent for centuries and had infected ignorance throughout the land and the people of the land.

At the Crossroads

Frederick Douglass (1817/1818–1895) became a similar prophetic voice of the injustices perpetrated against blacks in America. Douglass was an escaped American slave, abolitionist, and political firebrand who rose in a time of crisis spanning before and after the Civil War. His advocacy laid the foundations for future generations of Americans as movements of race and gender equality intensified well into the early twentieth century.

15. Chief Joseph, "Indian's View," 431.
16. Brown, *Sacred Pipe*, 40.

Pulitzer Prize winning author David Blight reminded that Douglass purposefully assumed the mantle of a prophetic voice for change in the perspectives of Americans.

> Douglass's wartime apocalypticism breathed with Old Testament fire and justification. . . . Douglass's subject was less the shaping of policy than it was to persuade a people to rise, make holy war, and answer God's call to repent and sacrifice. "The land is now to weep and howl amid ten thousand desolations," he cried early in the war.[17]

Like the prophet Jeremiah, Douglass remained goal-oriented as he challenged societal complicacy, injustice, and nationalistic isolationism. He was not just focused on racial injustices but he also advocated for the rights of women, and became a catalyst for the movement toward women's suffrage. Douglass was also not a stranger to being rejected for his authentic and challenging oratory. When asked to speak for the Rochester Ladies' Anti-Slavery Society on the fourth of July 1852, he did not refrain from placing the racial disparity existing in America front and center without apology, through the prophetic reminder:

> The rich inheritance of justice, liberty, prosperity and independence, bequeathed by your fathers, is shared by you, not by me. The sunlight that brought life and healing to you, has brought stripes and death to me. This Fourth July is yours, not mine. You may rejoice, I must mourn. To drag a man in fetters into the grand illuminated temple of liberty, and call upon him to join you in joyous anthems, were inhuman mockery and sacrilegious irony. Do you mean, citizens, to mock me, by asking me to speak today?[18]

Psychologist and author, Chanequa Walker-Barnes stated that the values solidified through the American 1800s, although focused on individual freedom and human growth, also created the byproduct of limiting opportunities for Americans, based on specific criteria. The interconnectivity that exists at the very the structure of how the culture of the society is defined and sustained has formed the avenues needed for success, as well as the limitations of that access to certain essential opportunities, such as educational opportunities. To aim for a goal of inclusion and unity there needs to

---

17. Blight, *Frederick Douglass*, 434.
18. Douglass, "What, to the Slave," para. 37.

be structural changes that allow opportunities of liberty and freedom to be available to peoples of all races.

> America prides itself on its individualism, particularly the notion that "we are what we make ourselves." American nationalist rhetoric heavily emphasizes the virtues of liberty and freedom of conscience. This emphasis obscures what scholars of race and gender studies take for granted: individual identity—especially as it relates to race and gender—is not formed in a vacuum, but is heavily dependent upon cultural constructions of what it means to be human, to be male or female, and to be Black, White, Latina.[19]

The late 1800s of America saw a time that begin a shift with the rise of servant leaders who began to establish small but lasting changes to some of the systemic limitations woven into the fabric and structure of the society. Education became the new battleground for access and the defining lines of American society. There were opportunities developing that had not existed in the same way previously, such as the focus of the dedicated building of schools for the education of black and indigenous children, by heiress Katherine Drexel. The push for vocational education and the focus of development of African-American owned businesses, development, and innovation was promoted through the work of Booker T. Washington. W. E. B. Dubois was also instrumental in bridging the 1800s into 1900s through his advocacy for the equality of educational access in higher education and integration of communities through location and mind by. The tide was beginning to change to offer access that previous generations did not allow or recognize.

Learning from Global Witnesses of Leadership

The darkness of ignorance in America began to be combated through examples of dedicated innovators and servant leaders who brought a brighter light to the landscape of America. One such individual, who broke barriers and stereotypes in American society, was Augustus Tolton. Rev. Augustus Tolton was the first publicly acknowledged black Catholic priest in America. Although there had been priests in America that passed, or did not openly discuss their race, Tolton became the first to boldly proclaim his race.[20]

---

19. Walker-Barnes, *Too Heavy a Yoke*, 80–81.
20. See Davis, *History of Black Catholics*, 146–51.

Tolton was born into a family of slaves. His mother was a slave originally from Kentucky who was sold to a family in Missouri. Tolton's father served and died in the Civil War, fighting for the Union. As a single widow, Augustus's mother run away from the life of slavery with her children and made the arduous journey to Illinois, a free state. There young Augustus and his brother began Catholic school, but were quickly kicked out because of racial tension that arose.[21] An Irish priest, from the neighboring parish invited the children to attend his school and Augustus's vocation began. Overtime Augustus felt a call to the vocation of Catholic priesthood, but no Seminary in the America would accept him.[22] His only alternative was to attend Seminary formation in Rome.

Tolton travelled to Rome and discerned his formation studying to become a missionary to Africa. In 1886, just before leaving his post-ordination destination for Africa there was change to Tolton's location of service by the administrator of the missionary seminary. Giovanni Cardinal Simeoni, the prefect of the Holy See's Congregation for the Propagation of the Faith, recalled the order to send Tolton to Africa and decided to send him to become a missionary to America. It is recorded that Simeoni declared: "America has been called the most enlightened nation; we will see if it deserves that honor.... If America has never seen a Black priest, it has to see one now."[23]

Tolton's experience returning as a priest to America was initially one of welcome, but after a local change of pastor at a neighboring German parish, in Quincy, Illinois, Tolton began to struggle from the racist treatment from his neighboring brother priest, Fr. Michael Weis. In a letter to his friend and mentor Simeoni, Tolton stated:

> There is a certain German priest here who is jealous and contemptuous. He offends me often and hurts me deeply. He abuses me in many ways and asks that I leave and has told the bishop to send me away. I would gladly go elsewhere just to be rid of him. The bishop too has given me this advice.[24]

This harassment and torment did not deter Tolton from his oriented goal of ministry to the people, though without the Bishop's support to resolve the tenuous situation Tolton ultimately moved away from his hometown

---

21. Davis, *History of Black Catholics*, 152–62.
22. See Ochs, *Desegregating the Altar*, 54.
23. Heinlein, *Black Catholics*, 54.
24. Duriga, *Augustus Tolton*, 49. See also Ochs, *Desegregating the Altar*, 78.

Manifest Destiny

Quincy, Illinois to Chicago for the remainder of his ministry. Writing to Cardinal Simeoni, Tolton explained: "This German priest is very bitter: he is full of hatred against me. To keep the peace, the bishop has asked me to look for another diocese."[25] Tolton continued to minster in Chicago and become an instrumental voice for the American Black Catholic Congress, along with black activists and advocates like Daniel Rudd as well as through the support of Rev. John R. Slattery, the first General Superior of the Josephites. Simeoni's challenge of America to the presence and representation of Black Catholics could no longer be dismissed or ignored.

Centuries after the challenge of America by Simeoni, Thea Bowman, Black religious sister and educator, rightly continued to challenge racial representation of the United States Catholic Bishops in America into the late twentieth-century:

> [W]ithin the Church, how can we work together so that all of us have equal access to input, equal access to opportunity, equal access to participation? Go into a room and look around and see who's missing, and send some of your folks out to call them in so that the Church can be what she claims to be, truly Catholic.[26]

Lessons in Servant Leadership

- **Being Goal-Oriented Instead of Goal Driven:** Servant leaders keep their vision on the orientation of their goal for the community. That goal may not be achieved in the way that initially is expected, so there will likely need to be some adaptability and flexibility of perspective of the goal, instead of an unchangeable, obsessive goal driven focus for one outcome achievement at all costs.

- **Challenge of Inhumane Stereotypes:** Servant leaders need to be transparent, poignant, and purposeful with their actions and words to clearly indicate the reality of a given situation. Although this clarity of the reality may not be accepted or popular, servant leaders challenge the foundations of inhuman stereotypes to acknowledge and help recognize the human dignity of the other.

- **Thinking of Outcomes as a Communal Experience:** Servant leaders are focused on the outcomes for the betterment of the community.

25. Duriga, *Augustus Tolton*, 50.
26. Bowman, *In My Own Words*, 42.

How does this effect the whole? How will it effect the next generations? The sense of the betterment of community remains a foundation of the planning and strategy of a servant leader.

For Further Reflection

- **Being Goal-Oriented Instead of Goal Driven:** Research the history of the Ghost Dance and the prophecy of First Nations leader, Wovoka. Explore the recordings of the Ghost Dance chants by anthropologist James Moody, through the Library of Congress. What was the purpose and symbolic meaning of the Ghost Dance ritual? Why was it believed to be such a danger to American expansion and the goal of Manifest Destiny? Compare and contrast the goal orientation of the Ghost Dance within the tribes of the First Nations with the goal driven mentality and desired outcome of the American federal government. Explain the differences present in the approach of each group.

- **Challenge of Inhumane Behavior:** Read Frederick Douglass's keynote speech from July 4, 1852. Douglass begins by praising the work of the vision of the nation and the Founding Fathers. How do his words constantly indicate the difference between the rights and luxuries of white Americans versus black Americans? How does Douglass challenge the perspective of the crowd? Throughout the speech in what ways did Douglass incorporate Scripture to illustrate his role as a prophet proclaiming the injustices in America? Do you think that Douglass's prophetic message was successful? Why or why not? Explain.

- **Thinking of Outcomes as a Communal Experience:** Read the lyrics and compare and contrast the perspectives offered in the following songs: They Might Be Giants's "James K. Polk" (1996), Guster's "Manifest Destiny" (2006), Old Crow Medicine Show's "I Hear Them All" (2006), and Rhiannon Giddens's "At the Purchaser's Option" (2017). Do the lyrics of these songs present a goal-oriented or goal driven perspective? How might the lyrics of these, and similar, songs offer a springboard for a dialogue regarding the effects of Manifest Destiny and its consequences on American society?

5

Cultural Stratification

Residential Schools

> Residential schools are not "ancient history." It may seem as though they belong to a dim past, due to the horrific conditions the 150,000 children (of whom 6,000 died or disappeared) were subjected to, but the last one closed in 1996. That's not ancient history.[1]

THIS HEART WRENCHING QUOTATION offers an all too horrific reminder that the supposed ills of the past are still very much present, and continue to define and effect the present and future. The rally call of Manifest Destiny, as well as migration to conquer and civilize the West and First Nations, evolved from a physical displacement of the indigenous peoples from the sacred land to a displacement of the indigenous peoples from their culture, heart and mind through the kidnapping and government sanctioned indoctrination of their children. As previously mentioned, educational institutions became the focus for cultural conditioning and through legislation from the federal governmental boarding schools were opened and sustained to civilize the children of First Nations. Mi'kmaq-Acadian Director of Indigenous Studies and theologian, Terry LeBlanc discussed the consequences of authorities that do not listen for understanding, but rather impose their beliefs upon other communities:

---

1. Joseph and Joseph, *Indigenous Relations*, 66.

> Harmful theologies have resulted when church leadership has focused on its theological and doctrinal work first through the lens of the fall separating the material world from its spiritual nature—the essence of God's impartation in all of creation. Theologies that label people "godless heathens" suited only to servitude or that argue to "kill the Indian, save the child" proceed from this place of thought.[2]

Residential schools, or Indian industrial schools as they were commonly referred to America, were developed in the mid-nineteenth century as a method of assimilating indigenous children into a civilized culture.[3] Some of the initial ground work for residential schooling was based on Christian missionaries of the 1600s who used education as the avenue to convert and evangelize the indigenous population. These initial schools were abandoned during the political instabilities due to the war between England and France, throughout the struggle of claiming of, and the desire to conquer, the land. As the war decreased, especially the conclusion of the War of 1812, the interest rose again of residential schools; a new conquest, not of the land, but of the mind. The oldest consecutive running residential school in Canada was the Mohawk institute which opened in 1834 and continued until the 1970s.[4]

Throughout the history of residential schools, in Canada, the most schools operating at one time was 80 schools, in 1931. The 1930s also saw the highest percentage of children that attended residential schools which included roughly thirty percent of the entire population of school-aged children of indigenous lineage throughout the country. During this new conquest, there was no opportunity to learn or listen to grow in understanding about one's own culture or identity, but any aspects of that part of the indigenous child's life was attempted to be erased away for a new and more civilized way of living.[5] Offering insight into the spiritual harm of identity and alienation, Thomas Merton, advocate and spiritual author, stated:

> Alienation begins when culture divides me against myself, puts a mask on me, gives me a role I may or may not want to play. Alienation is complete when I become completely identified with

---

2. LeBlanc, "Spirit And Spirituality," 74.
3. See Regan, *Unsettling the Settler Within*.
4. See National Centre for Truth and Reconciliation, *Knock on the Door*.
5. See Regan, *Unsettling the Settler Within*.

my mask, totally satisfied with my role, and convince myself that any other identity or role is inconceivable.[6]

Servant-Leadership Lens: Listening for Understanding

Servant leadership scholars James Sipe and Don Frick indicated how important the art of listening is as a key tenet of servant leadership. "The best way to connect in empathy is to *listen*, to listen with full presence and attention. Robert Greenleaf said listening is the primary skill of a Servant-Leader."[7] Listening can be one of the most challenging aspects to habitually exercise, especially in an atmosphere full of confusion and distraction. Nonetheless, listening for understanding establishes the bedrock for authentic relationship and trust.

The transition of the people of Israel between a settler, tribal governances and the development of the kingship came with much confusion, distraction, and tension. Throughout the attacks and periodic times of becoming a vassal state to neighboring nations, the fledging Israelite nation relied on the role of Judges to serve as great military leaders and warriors to bring the people back into independence. The cycle of attack, and vassal dependence, and the need for a Judge continued in the history of Israel until the calling of Samuel, an individual who served as the final Judge as well as the first prophet for the Kingdom of Israel.

The story of the calling of Samuel offers an illustration of the essential aspect of listening for understanding within servant leadership. Samuel lived during a tumultuous time period of the history of Israel, although the priests in Israel continued to offer sacrifice and follow the law established by Moses in actions, their hearts were not present in those actions. As Scripture indicated even the high priest Eli and his family closed their ears and hearts to the understanding of the Lord (1 Sam 2:12–17). The calling, and life, of Samuel demonstrates the importance of listening for understanding in the life of a servant leader.

---

6. Merton, *Literary Essays*, 381.
7. Sipe and Frick, *Seven Pillars*, 57.

Samuel: A Servant-Leader Listening to the Cry of the Isolated and Lost

Young Samuel grew up in Shiloh, the city where the priests of Israel fulfilled their duties under the guidance of the high priest Eli. Samuel was dedicated to God and left at Shiloh to be raised by Eli (1 Sam 2:11). The calling of Samuel occurred through an example of listening for understanding when he heard a voice calling his name. Hearing a voice calling in the night, Samuel believed initially believed that it was the priest Eli who was calling him. Samuel ran to Eli, but Eli had not called young Samuel. Twice more Samuel heard the voice calling his name and still believed it was Eli. Only after the third time did Eli recognize that the voice that was calling Samuel was the Lord. After this third encounter Eli prepared young Samuel, if you hear the voice listen for understanding by being present and attentive to the calling. Samuel did hear the voice calling again, and responded as Eli had prepared him: "Speak, for your servant is listening" (1 Sam 3:10). Listening with attention, Samuel learned about his role in the future leadership of Israel and the changes that were about to occur to realign Israel to a more faithful way of life in line with the Law given through Moses.

Through attentive listening and understanding of what was to be expected of him in his faithful relationship with God, Samuel is remembered as a great warrior that led the defeat of the Philistines, but more importantly a prophet who ushered a prophetic voice of renewal for the actions and hearts of the Israelites. Throughout his ministry Samuel was revered for his leadership by the Israelites (1 Sam 7:15).

Service-oriented leadership is predicated on listening to the other and being attuned to the words and their meaning, which can be an extremely difficult discipline when we are overexposed to noise and live in a lifestyle of consistent distraction from such intent focus. Samuel needed to first recognize where the voice originated, then he needed to acknowledge that he was present in the sacred moment to listen with focus. It must be acknowledged that listening is much more of a complex operation than merely hearing a sound, or sequential grouping of sounds. Authentic listening involves dedication to correct interpretation and understanding of the message received.

In his Rule for communal living, Benedict of Nursia (480–547) challenged his followers to "[l]isten . . . and incline the ear of your heart."[8]

---

8. Dysinger, *Rule of St. Benedict*, 3.

Following in the example of Samuel, this crucial aspect of servant leadership recognizes that listening is not a function of the ear alone, but also with the heart which holds a special component within the action of reception and dialogue to the communication of the other. Without the attention of the heart words may be heard but not affect change or feeling in the individual. Words can be challenging as well as become a catalyst for growth, but without a heart of understanding needed for growth to better learn about the circumstances a relationship can be stunted or not occur at all.

The Challenge

In the late 1800s the American and Canadian government, through the cooperation of President Ulysses S. Grant and Prime Minister John A. Macdonald, commissioned a report on the development and structure of the industrial-boarding school system. Nicholas Davin, journalist and Canadian politician, was sent to investigate the American Indian industrial schools and serve as the author of the report. His *Report on Industrial Schools for Indians and Half-Breeds* was conducted and presented in 1879. Davin's report supported and encouraged the structure of the boarding school method over the tradition of day schools.[9] The Davin Report laid the blueprint for the further atrocities in regard to the structure of the residential school system: "All the representatives of the five civilized nations declared their belief that the chief thing to attend to in dealing with the less civilized or wholly barbarous tribes was to separate the children from the parents."[10] Not only did the Davin Report encourage separation of the indigenous child away from their parents, but it also encouraged not allowing parents access to their children so that any contact would limit and not remove the civilized teachings that the children received.

Jesse Wente, Anishinaabe and First Nations journalist of the arts, argued that instead of trying to civilize or support First Nations children Davin's report and recommendation created a vacuum that aborted any potential of human growth.

> The system was built to support our deaths, not our lives. That's why inequality reigns to this day. That's why there were more

---

9. Day schools were educational institutions where First Nations children went to school during the day but were able to return to their families, and primarily raised in their homes. For further information see Fast and Collin-Vézina, "Historical Trauma," 127.

10. See National Centre for Truth and Reconciliation, "Davin Report," 14.

Indigenous children in state care in 2019 than at the height of the residential schools system. . . . Individual Canadians care about our lives, but the state simply does not. The cost is too high, both financially and existentially.[11]

As the Canadian government allied with Christian educational institutions, education became the battleground for the cultural wars between the Anglo and the First Nations. The residential educational system established boarding schools that were founded on an atmosphere and environment devoid of care, predicated on fear of judgment and retribution, and isolating for the argument of better social conditioning.[12] The action of the schools desired to remove all direct connectivity of the children with their First Nation culture and heritage. A stark dichotomy created a division between the lens of good and bad between Anglo Canada and First Nations. There was no interest in understanding cultural differences or listening to the needs of the other. The residential schools system was designed as a monologue of the Anglo culture, life, and identity, and the goal of assimilation. As Pamela Rose Toulouse, Anishinaabe and indigenous curriculum specialist, reminded the toll that the support of legislation, such as the Indian Act, which funded the residential schools program, had and continues to have on the indigenous population:

> The negative effects of the Indian Act continue to be loss of language, culture, health, and life, along with lower educational attainment. For example, Indigenous peoples have the highest rates of diabetes, lower graduation rates and participation in STEM fields, and the highest rates of suicide and incarnation. The positive outcomes include the strengths of Indigenous peoples, whose resiliency resulted in newfound hope.[13]

A Call for Change

As laws of the Canadian government were ratified and enacted to define, divide, and label indigenous peoples there was little interest in listening to understanding the needs or recognizing the dignity of the indigenous population. As long as laws were in place that served the best interest of

---

11. Wente, *Unreconciled*, 191.
12. Truth and Reconciliation Commission of Canada, *Knock on the Door*, 9–16.
13. Toulouse, *Truth and Reconciliation*, 22.

Cultural Stratification

Anglo Canadian then the indigenous population would continue to suffer, from generation to generation, through maltreatment in loss of land, mind, and memory of identity and space. In their co-authored book focusing on Indigenous relations and paths for engaging in efforts for reconciliation Bob and Cynthia Joseph, leaders at the Indigenous Corporate Training Inc., describe the effects of lasting legislation on Indigenous communities throughout the history of Canada.

> Prior to 1960, Aboriginal Peoples were denied the right to vote. Well, they could vote if they gave up their Indian status and treaty rights, but then they were denied certain rights that came with living under the *Indian Act*. . . . As long as there is the *Indian Act* and the *Constitution Act*, there will never be "equality," as is often called for in rhetorical conversation. When Indigenous Peoples hear the terms "equal" or "equality," they hear that they would have to give up their constitutionally protected rights in order to be afforded that equality. They hear, "We can be equal only if we give up our human rights to be who we are as a people."[14]

When the definition of the very words that should offer a sense of commonality are distorted based on a history of mistrust a new beginning, or starting place, needs to occur. Listening to the stories of the other to understand the meaning of the emotion, language, and significance shared within the relationship can offer the first step in beginning to understand the experience and needs of the other.

As the federal view of residential schools program started to wane in the 1950s, not because of the atrocities occurring to the children, but because of the lack of success and financial burden of residency of the children, residential schools started to close in favor of placing First Nations children into the public school system. This change in perspective regarding education did not change the governmental lens of still wanting to assimilate Indigenous children, though. Instead of having First Nation children live at a boarding school environment, the children were still taken from their homes but were now beginning to be placed in the state-run foster care system. This removal of children as well as the loss of cultural identity became known as the Sixties Scoop. The Sixties Scoop extended from the mid-1950s to the 1980s, and involved the foster relocation of roughly 20,000 indigenous children. Similar to the residential school tenets, Indigenous children placed in foster homes were often denied any knowledge of

---

14. Joseph and Joseph, *Indigenous Relations*, 120.

their heritage or information about their lineage. The effects of the Sixties Scoop are still being witnessed in the lives of countless individuals who are just now realizing their indigenous heritage late into their lives, and trying to resolve a lifetime of confusion regarding their own identity, often struggling with profound and traumatic experiences from such realizations.[15] Roughly one third of all children in the Canadian welfare program are indigenous children, and around seventy percent of those children were placed with non-indigenous families.[16] Raven Sinclair, professor and Cree/Assinniboine/Saulteaux survivor of the Sixties Scoop, examined data involving the removal of indigenous children and challenged that other perpetuating injustices may be present as well:

> The Indigenous child removal system has an unprecedented scope. If we reflect upon the cultural, language, and family disruption that over 180,000 years of foster care, exacerbated by five generations of residential school trauma, potentially inflicts upon Indigenous children, families, and communities, we should be very alarmed. When these statistics are juxtaposed with the reality that Indigenous people comprise between 4 and 17% of provincial populations and yet up to 85% of all the children in care, our concern should increase exponentially.... It may well be true that generations of residential school trauma created the conditions for increased child apprehensions, but it is also likely that systemic and institutionalized structures have emerged that are enabling and encouraging overrepresentation. Critics are arguing that provinces are fostering Indigenous overrepresentation because the financial benefits contribute to income security for those involved in the child welfare system.[17]

At the Crossroads

Before the European explorers and influence of the settlers, there were measures in place within indigenous communities to keep guidance and order within the tribal governances. As contact occurred, many of these traditional methods of governance were forced aside and replaced by the newer and Enlightened European governing customs and beliefs that respected

---

15. See Csontos, "Truth and Decolonization"; Wilson, *Beautiful Scars*.
16. See Sinclair, "Identity Lost and Found."
17. Sinclair, "Indigenous Child Removal System," 14.

a more democratic process of elected officials.[18] Leadership professor and social justice advocate, Kem Gambrell stated that in contrast to the European structure of government, the Indigenous Collectivist Mindset created values that sustained the community and its future.

> Having a strong sense of traditions is not just something that [Indigenous Collectivist Mindset (ICM)] possess or does, but involves deeper cultural norms that have been passed down for generations. . . . For ICM individuals, [compassion, humility, respect, and generosity] are vital to how collective understanding and its related behaviors are passed from one generation to the next. Through these teachings, not only does one learn how to operate in the world as part of community, but a strong sense of belonging is also developed.[19]

The loss of traditional community building and community values severed the lineage of the generational education from parents to children. This abrupt and mandated separation of children from parents created generational trauma that continues to be present in the lives of indigenous communities. With the attempted destruction of the Indigenous Collectivist Mindset the residential schools and Sixties Scoop purposefully disconnected the dialogue of listening and learning from the values that sustained indigenous life. This disconnection also effected the identities and roles of the indigenous parents between their children, and future generations of the indigenous peoples. It is now necessary for many indigenous families to re-learn, re-listen, and re-engage cultural traditions and expectations of their traditional lifestyles.

Learning from Global Witnesses of Leadership

Hatred and oppressive actions or rules are easy to assign and place upon abstract groups from ideological perspectives, but such stereotypes are much more difficult to sustain when presented in tangible examples and through intimate relationships, where one has to listen and understand. Ian Adams, journalist and author, was one of the first individuals to offer an honest look into the grotesque and horrific experiences of the residential school system. Born in Africa, and raised in boarding schools, Adams felt abounded by his parents who spent their time serving as missionaries in the Congo instead

18. Joseph and Joseph, *Indigenous Relations*, 21–22.
19. Gambrell, "Case for an Indigenous Collectivist Mindset," 29.

of spending time with their son. This isolating experience instilled a desire to advocate for the children in similar situations.

One of the first outspoken advocates to challenge the residential school system and treatment of the indigenous children, Adams used the medium of journalism to advocate the stories to the Anglo community not willing to listen or understand the plight and cultural destruction occurring to the youth of the First Nations. Beginning in 1965, Adams published articles showcasing the treatment of the indigenous in Canada.[20] After hearing about the death of a runaway child, Chanie Wenjack from a residential school in 1966, Adams used his investigative reporting skills to expose the injustices of residential schools through the eyes of the death of a child. This exposé on the death of Wenjack is remembered as one of the catalysts of change to close the school system and hold the Canadian government accountable for their role in the residential school program.

> Charlie Wenjack was an Ojibway Indian attending Cecilia Jeffrey Indian Residential School in Kenora, Ont. He became lonely and ran away. He died trying to walk 400 miles home to his father, who lives and works on an isolated reservation in northern Ontario. It is unlikely that Charlie ever understood why he had to go to school and why it had to be such a long way from home.[21]

Through the article Adams recounted the experience of the children at the residential school, how frequent it was for children to run away, and he also indicated indirectly the frequency of deaths of children at such locations. This article directly challenged the commonly held ascription of the Davin Report, and broadcasted that investigations needed to take place into the inhumane treatment of the indigenous children at residential schools. Adams's article followed the story through to the court and inquisition of the event, where he concluded the article with the following lines of the jury's actions and thoughts:

> The jury found that "the Indian education system causes tremendous emotional and adjustment problems." They suggested that the school be staffed adequately so that the children could develop personal relationships with the staff, and that more effort be given to boarding children in private homes. But the most poignant suggestion was the one that reflected their own

---

20. See Adams, "Indians."
21. Adams, "Lonely Death," 30–31.

bewilderment: "A study be made of the present Indian education and philosophy. Is it right?"[22]

Adams's article was brutally honest and so emotionally jarring that the magazine received hundreds of responses to the article indicating that it was not appropriate as content for the magazine, one of the critiques of Adams's article was written by the CEO of the *Maclean's* publishing company, in which the article was published. Due to the negative response "Mr. Adams quit the magazine to pursue a freelance career. He once said he felt he had wasted his life telling people stuff they didn't want to hear; however, it never stopped him."[23] Adams later pursued writing fiction but continued to infuse his stories with truth-telling narratives as a writing device within the stories.

Just as Adams indicated in his article, Toulouse reminds that "[t]he residential school campaign in Canada left no area of the country untouched. . . . The power of residential schools and the intergenerational damage they inflicted on Inuit and Métis communities are immense."[24] Canadian First Nations populations are still mourning the loss of their children; the children who never returned from the schools or those children who came back and completely unrecognized their culture and traditions. The story of the horrors of the residential schools continues as in the summer of 2021 unmarked mass graves were found on the grounds of two residential schools: one in British Columbia that contained over 200 sets of remains and one in Saskatchewan which had over 750 identified unmarked graves of the remains of children from the schools.[25]

Lessons in Servant Leadership

- **Listening for Understanding:** Servant leaders need to listen to those they serve for understanding. It is essential to know and recognize the unique challenges that they face and how their past experiences have created a lens into aspects of language and the meaning of symbols often taken for granted. By listening with attention to their community,

---

22. Adams, "Lonely Death," 44.
23. Mackay, "Reporter Ian Adams," para. 6.
24. Toulouse, *Truth and Reconciliation*, 11.
25. See Adach, "It Has Never Been a Secret"; and Eneas, "Sask."

servant leaders have the opportunity to grow more in-tune with those they serve and understand their needs.

- **Present the Need of Others Clearly and Deliberately Front and Center:** Servant leaders need to present the needs of others clearly and deliberately in a purposeful way that makes the topic at hand front and center in the view of the conversation, or leadership decision. As demonstrated by Ian Adams's journalistic approach, servant leaders need to exercise clear evidence and transparency to challenge stereotypes that affect the lives of those served. Servant leaders have to become a voice of awareness of community needs to the levels of decision makers not familiar with the issues, as well as present data in a way that attracts the attention of the decisions makers regarding the particular issue at hand for action.

- **Use a Variety of Modes to the Spread the Message:** Servant leaders must not be satisfied that only one method will be enough to advocate the message. They must be willing to use a variety of modes to advocate their message on behalf of those they serve. When one avenue is no longer available servant leaders need to pivot and find other avenues to continue their advocacy for others.

For Further Reflection

- **Listening for Understanding:** Read and reflect on several short stories from Thomas King's *A Short History of Indians in Canada* (2005). How does King use fiction to help the reader understand the social challenges and injustices effecting Indigenous communities? In what ways does King weave humor, grief, and heartache into the stories to keep the reader's attention and focus on the challenging topics of injustice present in the story?

- **Present the Need of Others Clearly and Deliberately Front and Center:** Listen to and reflect on the lyrics of the following songs: Cheryl Bear's "Residential School Song (Indian Boarding School Song)" (2007), Tom Jackson's "Lost Souls" (2021), and The Digging Roots's "Cut My Hair" (2022). How do the lyrics of these songs present the experience and stories of life at a residential school setting in a way to listen for understanding How might the lyrics of these, and similar, songs offer an opportunity to start a dialogue about the horrors and tragedy as well as the grieving process over experiences of the residential schools system? What other artists or musicians have used their talents to promote awareness to acknowledge and understand a social injustice? Explain.

- **Use a Variety of Modes to the Spread the Message:** Ka'ila Farrell-Smith, a contemporary indigenous Klamath Modoc artist offers another mode to express emotion and insight into the experience of the residential schools. Her piece *After Boarding School: In Mourning* (2011) housed at the Portland Art Museum depicts a challenging portrait of a young indigenous girl. Examine the portrait as well as the description at the website for the Portland Art Museum.[26] In what ways does the portrait offer a sense of the gravity and horrific experiences of residential school upon the child? Explain.

---

26. https://portlandartmuseum.org/the-poster-project/after-boarding-school-in-mourning/

6

Racial Stratification

Apartheid

No one is born hating another person because of the colour of his skin, or his background, or his religion. People must learn to hate, and if they can learn to hate, they can be taught to love, for love comes more naturally to the human heart than its opposite.[1]

THIS QUOTATION BY NELSON Mandela offers a conscious reminder that humanity at its core is naturally attuned for a life of deep and intimate relationships through community, not isolation. Similarly, Desmond Tutu consistently reiterated that we, as human beings, receive our initial experiences of self-learning as well as how to act and interact with the world at large through human connectivity by building connections through our family and our first relationships; and when we serve others through our deep-rooted humanity there is a great contentment that is experienced and recognized that by coming together humanity exists not as separate individuals, but as a whole human family.[2]

Apartheid, on the other hand, the sanctioned segregation and separation of black South Africans from white Afrikaans was in existence between 1948 and 1993. Apartheid, meaning apartness, was promoted as a

---

1. Mandela, *Long Walk*, 622.

2. See Shadyac, *I Am*, 32:33–32:52; Tutu, *God Has a Dream*; and Tutu and Tutu, *Book of Forgiving*.

theocratic divine mission perpetuated by the Dutch Reformed Church's influence, and argued that the races needed to be separate by divine command for a future of peace and prosperity. In the early twentieth-century white South African leaders, such as Jan Smuts, established the foundations of apartheid laws and set into motion a half century of galvanized social injustice and oppression against black South Africans.

From the early twentieth-century more and more legal conditions were instituted against black South Africans including where they could live, who they could marry, and where they could work. In 1949, prohibition of mixed marriages legislation was ratified. There was also an addendum to the 1927 Immorality Act, which prohibited white and blacks from having sexual relations. In 1950, additional laws were enacted regarding a population registration act which enforced a mandatory labelling of one's race as: black, colored, white, or Indian. These labels determined where the individual and their family could reside. Between 1960 and 1983, 3.5 million South African residents had to relocate their homes due to their registry status.[3]

To describe this time period, scholar Michael Battle explained that South Africa became predicated upon a new market through the system of Apartheid. Through the legal labelling and separating of races, divisions of worth were created not in terms of commodities, but social capital, identity, and structure.

> In an economic market in which liberty, rights, and freedom were ideals, a new material product could be acquired. This new market was the acquisition of a lower grade of peoples. Along with this new economic market came the justification for racism through the mechanism of apartheid—a religious and legal concept. ... This legal separation of the races ensured both a constant supply of cheap, black labor and complete control over land rights by whites.[4]

These legalistic changes did not occur without retaliation, as the black South Africans came together to defend their dignity and try to regain their autonomy. These groups began as oppositional advocacy groups trying to negotiate in the government spheres but that avenue for response become more and more limited, as black South Africans were soon barred from participating in governmental representation. The resistance movements

3. See Storey, *Protest at Midnight*.
4. Battle, *Reconciliation*, 23.

of black South Africans evolved in into nonviolent protests, where physical actions and demonstrations tried to become a witness to the injustices and need to change. As these demonstrations were ineffective, and further laws were passed that made demonstrations illegal, many South Africans became militant and ultimately espoused violent retaliation. Many black South African leaders believed that violence was a language of best recourse to attack and have the government suffer in some form of retaliation, often through physical and terroristic means. This escalation to violence led to the mass incarceration of many of the black militant leadership, including Nelson Mandela.

Through this forced incarceration Mandela had no choice but to withdraw, be it forced, from his direct advocacy for the cause and reorient his vision of leadership throughout his twenty-seven years of incarceration in prison. Desmond Tutu reflected on this time period and reorientation of Mandela's vision of leadership, while in discussion about the incarnation and transformation that occurred to him as an advocate of violence before his trial and sentence until after his release from prison in 1990: "Nelson Mandela and his fellow political prisoners had used their time to develop their mind and their character so that they would someday be ready to rule the country."[5] Mandela also reflected and studied the work of other global black leaders and educators such as W. E. B. Dubois, Marcus Garvey, and Martin Luther King Jr. as well as athletics such as Joe Louis, who not only defeated his opponents in the sport but also combated racism outside of the athletic ring.[6] Through his withdraw, Mandela used time to deepen and broaden his knowledge and exposure to various perspectives to combat injustices apart from violence.

Servant-Leadership Lens—Withdraw and Reorient

There are moments when failure is evident and there seems to be no recourse than to take time to withdraw and reorient. Within leadership these moments can often be interpreted as times of failure or weakness, but that is far from the case. In the lens of servant leadership such times to withdraw and reorient can be some of the most crucial opportunities to reassess how to best serve for the future. In Scripture, one of the most poignant examples

---

5. Dalai Lama XIV et al., *Book of Joy*, 244.
6. Mandela, *Long Walk*, 583.

of a servant leader who took time to withdraw and reorient within the context of his ministry was the prophet Elijah.

Elijah: A Servant-Leader Who Withdrew and Reoriented His Mission and Vision

Elijah was an Israelite prophet called to challenge, through actions and witness, the royal family of the northern Kingdom of Israel who turned away from the law of the Lord. When Queen Jezebel married King Ahab she was brought into the royal linage of Israel from Sidon. In Sidon she grew up as a devoted worshiper of the god Ba'al, and continued to remain faithful to her religious practice even after moving to the region of Israel. It was against the law of the Israelites to worship other gods; and the Israelites had once before followed the ritual worship of the god Ba'al in their land before the time of King David (Judg 1:11–23). Jezebel not only promoted her beliefs in Israel, but also imported priests of Ba'al to lead worship of her god (1 Kgs 18:19). While she promoted her religion she also called for the death of the prophets of the religion of Israel (1 Kgs 18:13).

Elijah, one of the remaining prophets of YHWH, knew that Jezebel's decree would lead to his execution and did not know how to proceed due to the circumstances. Knowing that he could be killed, and in fear of the royal decree Elijah withdrew from the region of Israel to Mount Horeb, the Mountain of the Lord (1 Kgs 19:3–5). Through the misery and suffering endured from his service Elijah was ultimately ready to give up. But at the mountain, Elijah was able to withdraw and reorient his prophetic mission and service. When he arrived, he hid himself in a cave waiting for a voice of the Lord. While he was waiting in the cave there was a great wind, an earthquake, and a consuming fire, but the presence of the Lord was not in any of the grand events, but only present after a tiny whispering sound that followed (1 Kgs 19:11–13).

Withdrawing and reorienting does not indicate surrender, rather it allows for the opportunity to reassess and realign a vision for a new, creative approach toward the goal or desired outcome. Sometimes when a servant leader's plans do not work the way they initially hoped or anticipated there needs to be a revision and reexamination for the next steps. In the case of Elijah, he was unable to assess how to continue in the midst of certain death, but after withdrawing and reorienting he was renewed with a spirit and vision for another approach to the circumstances.

The importance of servant minded leadership during a time of withdrawal and reorienting is that the leader can gather needed information, otherwise unavailable in a time of continuous action, to listen and better understand the needs of those they serve. Like Elijah, it can be necessary to go away from a familiar location to another setting, or on a pilgrimage to the place of initial inspiration, to reconnect with the sacred presence that served as a catalyst, especially in times of conflict.[7] Desmond Tutu further explained that a time of withdraw and reorienting is not weakness but should be interpreted as a time of refinement. Through such an experience of refinement and reorientation a new perspective can challenge previous ideas or views of others.

> When you have been refined, you want to find out what it is that impelled this other one to do what he did. And so you put yourself in the shoes of the other. So it is almost an axiom that generosity of spirit seems to require that one will have had setbacks to remove the dross. . . . And it seems almost without fail that that generosity of spirit requires that we will have experienced if not suffering, then at least frustrations, things that seem to want to stop us from moving in the particular direction that we have chosen.[8]

The Challenge

Through the 1960s, extreme forms of sanctioned police violence led to countless deaths of black South African demonstrators. This exponential rise of violence and the extreme restrictive legal oppression to black South Africans continued to rise and attracted global awareness. This prompted action, boycotts, and international sanctions against the South Africa throughout the globe. African scholar Matthew Graham illustrated this global effort through the example of the massacre in the township of Sharpeville:

> In March 1960, the brutality of the apartheid state vividly caught the attention of the international community following the police massacre of 69 protesters at Sharpeville. Even the United Nations Security Council, not usually known for its condemnation of South Africa, moved quickly to censure the government.[9]

---

7. See Drodzdzewski et al., "Geographies."
8. Dalai Lama XIV et al., *Book of Joy*, 154.
9. Graham, "Campaigning against Apartheid," 1150.

Racial Stratification

In 1961, South Africa became a republic and officially left the commonwealth. This newfound governmental independence from an outside European overseer altered the course and the trajectory of any tempered view regarding segregation from the perspective of the white minority government and its overreach. With the firm leadership now autonomous in South Africa, the white Afrikaans were able to strengthen Apartheid laws without restriction.[10] African scholar David Chanaiwa stated: "Following ... [the] withdrawal from the Commonwealth, the Nationalist Party moved swiftly to consolidate the *apartheid* system and to turn South Africa into a fully-fledged police state, by passing additional repressive and racialist laws."[11] By 1963, the General Law Amendment Act gave the authority for police officers to detain an individual without communication for 90 days. Two years later, the Criminal Procedure Amendment Act doubled the legal ability of the state to detain a prisoner without communication for 180 days. The Prohibition of Political Interference Act, of 1968, made it illegal for any political party to include inter-racial membership. With this intense stronghold of governmental control and power the struggle for liberation also only continued to intensify, through a growing intense reactionary violence.

As violence often begets violence, the cyclic actions of resistance continued and manifested at greater and greater frenzy throughout the country of South Africa. Even native South Africans who left and returned to their homeland, even within a short period of absence, did not recognize the country that was caught up within the continuous and escalating violence. Anti-Apartheid activist, Molapatene Collins Ramusi, stated:

> When I arrived in South Africa on the third day of July, 1984, I found our youth making South Africa ungovernable. "*Siya yinyova!*" the youths shouted everywhere, meaning "We shall destroy!" The Department of Bantu Education is unable to run its black schools. Rents are uncollectible in municipal areas. The prisons are full, and yet youths are not intimidated. Urban councilors are resigning their offices everywhere, and those who refuse to resign end up with flaming tires around their necks.[12]

During the increased violence of South Africa, leading to the fall of Apartheid, forms of community justice were often dealt out by the hands of the violent resisters, mobs, and rioters. One form of pseudo-justice popular

10. See Chanaiwa, "Southern Africa"; and Graham, "Campaigning against Apartheid."
11. Chanaiwa, "Southern Africa," 275.
12. Ramusi, *Soweto, My Love*, 244.

at the time was called necklacing, which was a time of lynching through which the victim would be bound around the neck or body within a rubber tire, drenched in gasoline, and lit on fire to burn alive. This form of torture was not used on white Afrikaans leaders of the Apartheid regime, but rather reserved for black South Africans who were considered traitors to the cause, or informants who worked with the white government.

A Call for Change

In South Africa, with many of the black militant leaders incarcerated it was left to those remaining outside of the jails to keep the forward momentum going for liberty against the tyranny of the Afrikaans legal segregation. Growing up in the Apartheid culture deep-seeded anger and resentment manifested among black South Africans, from their youth, against the white government and the circumstances of injustice defining life in South Africa. In her memoir, *Part of My Soul Went With Him*, Winnie Mandela, spouse of Nelson Mandela from 1958–1996, reminisced on the feelings of anger she had growing up as a youth in the Apartheid system:

> I became aware at an early age that whites felt superior to us. ... Every tribal child felt that way. ... There is an anger that wakes up in you when you are a child and it builds up and determines the political consciousness of the black man.[13]

Winnie Mandela recalled that the concept of resistance developed from a young age as well. Growing up as a student in her father's classes, she listened to, was taught, and memorized songs of resistance. These traditional South Africa songs dealt with historical events, and were written from traditional tribal composers. The songs became an intimate part of her life as they were also sung consistently in and around her home. Such songs told stories that fueled a fire for change from lyrics that examined black loss at the hands of white bosses and rulers, songs of grief that express the mourning of children for their fathers who worked and died in the mines, and songs that offered hope for a better future away from the injustices of the Apartheid rule. She remembered that such songs elicited a collective emotion that the isolation of the Afrikaans' laws could not put limitations on. The memory of the lyrics and melodies were etched in her consciousness not only as a reminder of the fight against a common foe,

---

13. Mandela, *Part of My Soul*, 48.

but also a rally cry of liberation. "I still know the words today. The white makes a mistake, thinking the tribal black is docile and subservient."[14] As she remembered the songs, she embodied their passionate message and resistance as she grew into adulthood.

Even in the most challenging experiences, Winnie Mandela recounted the comfort that such songs of resistance had for her; they created a withdraw from the pain of reality and allowed her to reorient based on the teachings of her upbringing. In her memoir, she also recounted a family visit with Nelson while he was in prison:

> One day, when Zindzi and I were going to visit him [Nelson] on Robben Island, they had cancelled all the ferries because the sea was too rough. But Nelson insisted on our coming. He wanted to see us. They phoned from the island . . . and we went. Our boat was the only one that day. We were singing all the way and didn't feel the rough seas.[15]

Songs of resistance became an embodiment of the symbol they stood for. The power of song has the ability to define identity, reorient perspectives, and offer healing and witness, especially in times of struggle. Beverley Diamond, Professor of Music and Ethnomusicologist, indicated that there is great psychological and emotional healing power through song: "[t]he longer memories that song elicits demonstrate that health is an ongoing struggle for balance and social well-being and that the sonic continues to be integral to Indigenous healing."[16] A brief or momentary withdraw from events at hand to reflect on memory space and music may create needed solace and reorientation in the moments of leadership.

At the Crossroads

The African historian, J. D. Fage stated that as the increased laws that defined Apartheid in South Africa progressed toward the end of the twentieth-century the system as a whole started to fall apart at its seams. The system which was originally argued to be divinely destined as a prosperous way of life for the peoples of South Africa began to not fulfill the expectations in

---

14. Mandela, *Part of My Soul*, 49.
15. Mandela, *Part of My Soul*, 143.
16. Diamond, "Resisting Containment," 241.

the eyes of the white Afrikaans government. The country was falling deeper and deeper into Civil War and violence consumed the region.

> The policy of *apartheid*—separate development of the races—had been justified by believing that it was a good way for the peoples of South Africa to achieve peace and prosperity. Nationalist thinkers, followed by most of the rest of the party and, indeed, a majority of all of the people of European descent who held the virtual monopoly political power in South Africa, now realized from experience that this belief was wrong, not because the policy was an unjust one (though it was) . . . but essentially because it did *not* bring peace and prosperity.[17]

The unrest of the country's identity at the governmental level was also exacerbated by the continual sanctions placed on it as the injustices from the Apartheid legislation continued to the reach the ears of neighboring countries and the United Nations. This global outreach and influence effected the entire continent as Valentine Iheanacho indicated:

> The African identity crisis arises from the historical context of different competing realities, including traditional culture and religion, Western civilization, Christianity, and Islam. . . . This fact became more manifest since 1989, after the fall of the Soviet Block, when Africa progressively became relegated to the margin in the remaking of a new "world order."[18]

As the conclusion of the twentieth century was dawning upon South Africa a time rose for needed change through a renewed and reoriented goal. British historian Richard Wilson, stated that at this time of crossroads black South Africans began to see a glimmer of light in the darkness through the consistent advocacy of unity preached by an inter-religious coalition of leaders working in solitary for a common goal to end the state-run injustices, such as the advocacy of George Daniel, Peter Storey, and Desmond Tutu, and countless others.

> Out of the ashes of ruined Afrikaner nationalism, a new human rights commission led by a figure of unquestioned moral authority, former Archbishop Desmond Tutu, was explicitly dedicated to building a culture of human rights and an inclusive "rainbow nation."[19]

17. Fage, *History of Africa*, 537.
18. Iheanacho, *Historical Trajectories*, 129.
19. Wilson, *Politics of Truth and Reconciliation*, 223.

This change did not come easily or without issue. Although the Afrikaner nationalism policies were failing, there was hesitation in trusting another path. So much of the twentieth-century South African structure and law was rooted in the stronghold of whites over the black South African peoples that there was fear in what could occur if the tide changed. It was a time of needed reorientation, which was also precipitated through the intervention of global initiatives upon the leadership. Professor and South African international governance scholar Jo-Ansie van Wyk explained the complexities of the transition of power demonstrated in the South African government structure at the conclusion of the Apartheid period.

> For states undergoing democratic transition, change and transformation is complicated by, among other factors, distrust; divergent ideologies and expectations; the integration of the old and new guard, the latter often with no or little experience; insecurities; racial tensions; and leaders' foreign policy ambitions. In South Africa's case, the apartheid government's diplomatic isolation compared with the ANC's extensive international links, and the international expectations and perceptions of the "South African miracle," were additional complicating factors to consider.[20]

Learning from Global Witnesses of Leadership

The international recognition of the need to address the growing racial tension effecting nations across the globe was not a topic that just emerged from the Second World War and its consequential greater attention to human rights and focus on global humanism. There had been a germination and dialogue to address rising racial and human injustice concerns prior. In the Catholic Church there was research and development to craft a papal response of the global racial injustices in the 1930s, as news arrived during the rise of Hitler in Germany.

In 1938, Pope Pius XI commissioned a draft for the development of an encyclical to address the growing racial injustices against black and indigenous peoples as well as the growing anti-sematic movement in Europe at the time. One of the co-authors commissioned to be involved with the writing of the draft was John LaFarge Jr., an American Jesuit. LaFarge was an advocate for racial change in America, using his skills in journalism to raise awareness of the cyclic injustices of America's past. He served in an

---

20. van Wyk, "From Apartheid to Ubuntu," 415.

editorial capacity with *America* magazine during the 1920s, and later wrote a challenging text for the Catholic Church to lead the charge for change of racial injustices in America through his manuscript: *Interracial Justice: A Study of the Catholic Doctrine of Race Relations*, which was published in 1937. He argued vehemently against segregation and the prejudice that any inferiority existed because of racial differences. Cyprian Davis, Black Catholic historian and scholar, stated that the importance of LaFarge's writings in America in the 1920s and 1930s should not be undervalued or underestimated.

> [LaFarge] began to ponder the problem of change in the area of racial injustice. He realized that both blacks and whites had to be educated. Blacks needed education to equip them for a better social condition; whites needed education in the rudiments of justice based on Christian principles.[21]

The co-written draft that Lafarge was involved with for the Pontiff was completed at the conclusion of 1938, and presented to Pius XI. Unfortunately, due to the death of Pius XI in February 1939, the document never developed beyond its draft form.[22] It was stated by scholars that the topic was Pius XI's next major focus and reform in the Church, and that the draft was found on the Pontiff's desk at the time of his death.[23]

Now, known as the hidden encyclical, the draft work of John Farge Jr. offers an insight into the historical context of a recognition of the brewing racial issues that plagued the remainder of the global nations and legislation throughout the twentieth-century. Pius XII would offer his own encyclical to address a need for unity in the world, "Humani Generis," in 1950, but that encyclical focused on human reason through the abstract, and did not follow in the direct language to address ideological global issues of racism and anti-Semitism that would have been plainly addressed in Pius XI's commissioned working draft. As mentioned in the encyclical draft co-authored by LaFarge, racism is often masked through religious justifications:

> Zeal against the sin readily becomes zeal against the sinner; but zeal against the sinner soon throws off its mask and shows itself for what it really is, an assault, under the pretense of protecting

21. Davis, *History of Black Catholics*, 226.
22. See Passelecq and Suchecky, *Hidden Encyclical*.
23. Coppa, "Pope Pius XI's," 775.

society from a single social group, upon the very basis of society, an evocation of limitless hatred, a license for every form of violence, rapacity, and disorder, and an engine against religion itself.[24]

Lessons in Servant Leadership

- **Withdraw and Reorient to Achieve a Goal:** Servant leaders recognize that roadblocks are frequently experience with service and social change. It is essential to effectively utilize time to withdraw and reorient for a clear reassessment and reexamination for a plan forward. This time of reflection can help analyze data and to better appreciate and understand the experience of others, and other perspectives for future action.

- **Passing on the Importance of Memory Space and Song:** Servant leaders also recognize the deep connectivity of memory, space, and song. It is important to remember that the human senses can be a powerful conduit for advocacy and emotion. Servant leaders can help guide others to recall and renew hope through withdrawing to a space or recalling a song for further inspiration.

- **Seeking Growth through Moments of Refinement and Purification:** Servant leaders know that growth is a constant, and that challenges offer experiences to learn from. For servant leaders it is important to approach life experiences, even the most challenging, as a continual learner. Viewing life through this perspective a leader can continue to develop in new perspectives and ways to serve others.

For Further Reflection

- **Withdraw and Reorient to Achieve a Goal:** It is can be detrimental to a goal to just react to a situation. It can be more beneficial in the long term to respond to the situation, instead of just reacting. Compare and contrast the actions and outcomes of two leaders from history; where one reacted to a situation, and the other withdrew and reoriented to ultimately respond to the situation in a more purposeful way. An

---

24. Desbuquois et al., "Draft Encyclical," para. 147.

Truth and Reconciliation

example might be the responses to the brewing American Civil War by both, President James Buchanan and President Abraham Lincoln.

- **Passing on the Importance of Memory Space and Song:** Read the lyrics and compare and contrast the perspectives offered in the following songs: Bruce Cockburn's "If I Had a Rocket Launcher" (1984), Hugh Masekela's "Bring Him Home" (1987), Brenda Fassie "Black President" (1990), and/or Blackie and the Rodeo King/Keb' Mo's "Long Walk to Freedom" (2016). How do the lyrics of these songs incorporate a memory image for the listener? How does the instrumentation and rhythm offer an emotional appeal to the listener of the topic? How might the lyrics of these, and similar, songs offer a springboard for a dialogue regarding injustices of the past?

- **Seeking Growth through Moments of Refinement and Purification:** Read and reflect on the lives of individuals who have endured a forced incarceration for principles of social justice advocacy, such as Mandela's *The Prison Letters of Nelson Mandela* or Martin Luther King Jr.'s "Letter from Birmingham Jail." How do the authors convey this time of refinement and purification in their lives? Compare and contrast this with other civil right or servant leaders who had similar experiences. How did they describe such moments of refinement and purification during their advocacy movements?

7

The Roots of Truth and Reconciliation
Leadership and the Dignity of the Human Person

Basically our first duty today is to human truth in its existential reality, and this sooner or later brings us to confrontation with system and power which seeks to overwhelm truth for the sake of particular interests, perhaps rationalized as ideals. Sooner or later this human duty presents itself in a form of crisis that cannot be evaded.[1]

IN THE SHORT COMMENTARY about the twentieth-century above Thomas Merton, spiritual author and Civil Rights advocate, acknowledged that the escalating racial and ideological tensions of American culture will ultimately come to a head and need to be addressed, likely through crisis, if not addressed before. Throughout the century several movements brought to light needed change of previous deep-rooted ideologies that emerged from the political structures of the nationally defining concept of Manifest Destiny. The twentieth-century brought a time of protest, engagement, and change to systems and power that had been rationalized and sustained since the Industrial Revolution and its affect upon the American consciousness, where the development and finances of industry often took precedent over the rights of human dignity. It was clearly a time of crisis—a crisis created from the division between systematic power structures and the call for

1. Merton, *Courage of Truth*, 159.

equality of sexual and racial identities; but through this struggle the search for existential human truth emerged into a new lens of recognition for the dignity of the human person. This crisis, and the subsequent social and civil rights movements, laid a foundation for an authentic call to the need to assess, with all transparency, the wrongs of America's past and progress to an opportunity for future reconciliation; a step for progress so needed but not yet fully explored.

Servant-Leadership Lens: Being Present on the Now

An important aspect of servant leadership is being present on the now. In the Greek language, the term *kairos* was designated as the time of decision, a sacred time of discernment; a moment of dedicated focus on the weight of the present. An example of recognizing the importance of the moment and living with wisdom of determination was Jesus of Nazareth. In the Gospel of Luke, it is recorded that at the beginning of his ministry he challenged the Jewish population of his home town that it was the time to announce his ministry was to fulfill the prophecy of Isaiah (Luke 4:14–30). There is no time like the present. In the 1960s Thomas Merton posed the question to a racially divided America during the Civil Rights movement:

> The idea of *kairos*—the time of urgent and providential decision— is something characteristic of Christianity, a religion of decisions in time and in history. Can Christians recognize their *kairos*? Is it possible that when the majority of Christians become aware that "the time has come" for a decisive and urgent commitment, the time has, in fact, already run out?[2]

By announcing his ministry Jesus was actively present in the moment to offer an authenticity into the providence of the Lord. To be present in the moment, a servant leader needs to offer courageous transparency. There is no guarantee how the message will be received, but the honesty to the time and the place is unparalleled.

The Challenge

At the conclusion of the Second World War there was a horrific revelation of purposeful and incalculable genocide of human life that had been

---

2. Merton, "Religion and Race," 218.

perpetrated during wartime expansion and malevolence across the globe. Such events continue to remain in the forefront of the scholarship of ethicists and theologians in their analysis of the renewal and re-focus of the dignity of human life which emerged from the events of the twentieth-century. This re-awakening of an ethical call of the worth and dignity of the human person evolved into various movements to ensure that such atrocities would never occur again. Through the dedicated assessment and call for justice of war crimes at the Nuremberg Trials (1946) and through the testimony of the witness at the trial of Adolf Eichmann (1961), as well as the creation of the United Nations Declaration of Human Rights (1948), global oversight recognized the providential moment to clearly define and attempted to protect the rights and dignity of human life throughout the world.

This global leadership perspective, on the rights of the human person, laid a foundation between nations to shift the trajectory of a world governance focused on expansion, control of natural resources, and destruction to one of establishing collaboration, mutuality, and solidarity through a unity of heart, mind, and action. This milestone in the acknowledgement of human rights and societal leadership served as a catalyst that cannot be dismissed, as its influence diffused to local and regional levels throughout the world, especially in an evolving American cultural identity from an Industrial mindset through the Suffrage Movement, Civil Rights Movement, social revolution, and a more contemporary vision of further national and global interconnectedness.

From all sectors of the American consciousness a call for truth was germinated, and is still coming to fruition, through various social movements. While some of the early twentieth-century social leaders and rights advocates evolved beyond their religious-based ideals of their youth to a radical social gospel of action, such as from Baptist, Catholic, Episcopalian, Lutheran, and Quaker roots others remained firmly connected to their religious identities but pushed against traditional barriers and norms within their respected belief systems.

Academics such as African-American sociologists W. E. B. Dubois and Patricia Hill Collins, First Nations leaders Black Elk and Chief G. Anne Richardson, Civil Rights leaders Alice Paul and Martin Luther King Jr., social justice advocates Dorothy Day and Thomas Merton, and global human rights leaders like Eleanor Roosevelt and Eunice Kennedy Shriver championed the call for the rights of the human person throughout the American twentieth-century. Through their examples the American landscape was challenged to address and re-assess with honest transparency the history of the nation with an intensity and a desired progress forward. As illustrated through the racial protests of the summer of 2020, the cyclic focus and dismissal of the dignity of the human person through national policy and leadership still remains to be resolved.

The following examples of scholars, activists, philosophers, and spiritual leaders brought an unabashed witness of servant leadership, through their persistent attitude of being present on the now—as the time and place for change—and commentary of the cultural racism, sexism, stereotypes, and stigmas deep rooted from previous political structures. This chapter will explore some of the relevant events, people, and defining movements that brought the worth of the human person to the forefront of the American culture throughout the twentieth-century—such examples should serve as a call for the foundations for an honest and transparent truth needed to begin dialogue for a national reconciliation to heal ancient wounds and create greater unity for future progress.

Beyond the Veil, Signaling a Change: Challenging Presuppositions of Race and Gender

In his seminal work on the sociological assessment of the African-American experience in America: *The Souls of Black Folk*, W. E. B. Dubois coined an analogy that powerfully demonstrated the inherent separation between the existence and identities of Blacks and Whites at the beginning of the American twentieth-century. Dubois expressed that there existed a veil separating the cultural experiences of African-Americans in the White-dominated culture.

> Leaving, then, the world of the white man, I have stepped within the Veil, raising it that you may view faintly its deeper recesses— the meaning of its religion, the passion of its human sorrow, and the struggle of its greater souls.[3]

Dubois' analogy of the Veil, the Color Line, serves as a dramatic and visual reminder of the stark separation and divided consciousness of the national American identity. He argued that through this atmosphere and environment that not only are African-Americans treated like second-class citizens, but they also possess a "double-consciousness," a schizophrenic life

---

3. Dubois, *Souls of Black Folk*, 3.

of judgment, in thought and action compared to their white counterparts. It was essential to address the truth of the condition of such citizens beyond the physical racial regulations placed on travel, service, and occupation, but also the generational psychological harm and trauma created by the lack of the recognition of the dignity of the human person which eventually erodes the self-perception and personal dignity from living such a divided life.

Dubois argued that equality and justice for African-Americans could only be found from the right to good education and the right to vote, which was still not offered or guaranteed for many throughout the nation. He continued to struggle for his perspective into the mid-twentieth century and well into his twilight years.

> Slowly but surely the working people of the South, white and black, must come to remember that their emancipation depends upon their mutual cooperation; upon their acquaintanceship with each other; upon their friendship; upon their social intermingling.[4]

Authentic human truth of the American experience for both Blacks and Whites, he claimed, was bound in the ability to collaborate, cooperate, and live in social equality.

Mary Church Terrell, an African-American educator and suffragette, similarly demonstrated the challenges of the deep-rooted prejudices especially present in the nation's capital at the beginning of the twentieth-century. Terrell's experience recounted the lack of ability to stay at a hotel, few and minimal occupations, lack of treatment in the local retail locations, and ultimately substandard and poor educational experiences for students and teachers of color. She concluded her famous 1906 speech "What it Means to be Colored in the Capital of the United States" for the Women's Club of Washington, DC, with the following honest condemnation:

> And surely nowhere in the world do oppression and persecution based solely on the color of the skin appear more hateful and hideous than in the capital of the United States, because the chasm between the principles upon which this Government was founded, in which it still professes to believe, and those which are daily practiced under the protection of the flag, yawn so wide and deep.[5]

Similar to the experience of African-Americans, Leaders of First Nations also petitioned for change, for the acknowledgment of the Rights of

---

4. Dubois, "Behold the Land," 201.
5. Terrell, "What it Means," 37.

Native Americans. One such prominent leader was Wassaja, whose name means "Signaling" or "Beckoning." An Apache Native American, he was kidnapped as a child, renamed Carlos Montezuma, and sold as a slave in the Anglo world. Throughout his youth Wassaja acted and travelled with Buffalo Bill's theater troupe before he was settled by his White family for his formal education, while in the care of a Baptist minister near Chicago, Illinois. He came to be the second Native American to earn a medical degree in America and used his education to beckon a new age for the Rights of the Indigenous peoples. He ultimately became an outspoken opponent of the Bureau of Indian Affairs, once stating: "Colonization, segregation and reservation are the most damnable creations of men. They are the home, the very hothouse of personal slavery—and are no place for the free and the 'home of the brave.'"[6] Wassaja later founded the Society of American Indians that sought Civil Rights, a right to good education, and full acknowledge of citizenship for Indigenous.

Through the struggle for change by individuals like Dubois, Terrell, and Wassaja a witness for greater recognition of the dignity of the human person and equal rights under the law was illustrated. The actions of such exemplars could be understood as American advocacy pre-reformers who became catalysts for later movements, especially the Civil Rights movement that defined the American mid-twentieth century; a time of tension and crisis that still remains unresolved because of the lack of an honest acknowledgment of truth and desire for national racial reconciliation.

At the Crossroads

The call of these forerunning advocates for greater dignity to respect unity between the racial and ethnic divide within American culture became a beacon of hope and a voice of the outcast, separated, and disregarded. But with this call a new reformation emerged in the American landscape as well; a schism between advocacy within and without religion proper. This split in the social and civil advocacy movement evolved into two overarching perspectives: a) a secular social gospel, a good news of change for those who had been previously maligned and removed from the freedom of the American Dream, separated and devoid of formal religious affiliation, as well as b) a renewal of an ancient philosophical ethic defined as Christian Humanism which, founded on Christian principles, renewed a call for

---

6. Montezuma, "Light on the Indian Situation," 54.

social advocacy rooted in Scripture. Both of these movements championed the inherent dignity of the human person and argued that authenticity of human existence was rooted in freedom. These movements diverged, though, upon the perspective of why human life has inherent worth and dignity. As will be discussed, for truth and reconciliation to progress it will be essential to establish an ecumenical mindset focused on dignity of the human person to strengthen and continue a complete movement for progress forward.

The Era of the Social Gospel: A Secular View of Dignity

The socio-political landscape of the twentieth-century could be best described as a hyper-progressive evolution. There was a clear call, and need for change, regarding the rights of under-represented groups from within the culture. It was interpreted that traditional moral bodies such as political and religious institutions were not following their beliefs, and not coming to the aid of the vulnerable, in the minds of many civil and social rights advocates. For some, though Christianity laid a foundation of social justice advocacy, there was little move or drive of the leaders of the time to challenge the status quo defining the political atmosphere. The social gospel grew out of the frustration, disappointment, or lack of regard for forward movement from trusted institutions in the lives of many feeling a call for change.

In the suffrage movement, for example, highly regarded feminists and leaders like Susan B. Anthony and Alice Paul separated from their Quaker roots and upbringing for a secular version of social justice advocacy. After being dismissed and censured Alice Paul left the Quakers to fulfill a call to social justice free from the bounds and limited view of the leadership of organized religion. In the struggle for Native American rights, Christian Churches often became associated with the oppressive system of cultural genocide, as many of the schools of Christian education or residential schools attempted to assimilate and Anglicize their Indian students forcibly removing them from their homes, culture, and lifestyle. In the experience of Wassaja, it is recorded that one of his many Anglo caretakers was a Baptist minister associated with the American Baptist Home Mission Society, whose mission was to minster the unchurched and destitute.

Secular social justice was also becoming prominent from the growing popular philosophical and political theorist, Karl Marx. The socialist movement came to be seen as a secular response to the power and governance of religious communities and corrupt Capitalist politicians, and brought a new ethical avenue of social equality apart from the history of religious doctrine. Educator and Civil Rights advocate W. E. B. Dubois, while never specifically espousing a political identity, was known for his strong socialist convictions within his response to the inequalities facing African-Americans, especially regarding his critique of wealth distribution in the American structure. In his novel, *Quest of the Silver Fleece*, Dubois brought the plight of African-Americans front-and-center, as well as the social oppression they face with a clear socialist narrative response to the unjust cultural climate.

With little option within traditional avenues in the mindset of such progressives a new era of secular social movements started to shift the American culture. This Progressive Era focused on the need for modernization in political recognition and governance, including the Suffrage Movement, equality in education, and removal of corruption from traditional institutions that defined, perpetuated, or seemed to enable systems of racial and social injustices.

A Renewal of Christian Humanism: An Incarnational Dignity

Christian Humanism, another ethical perspective that gained prominence in the Progressive Era, was firmly grounded within the history of Christianity from the time of the Early Church. Christian Humanism can trace its theological and philosophical prominence to the era of the Pre-Reformers, most notably Erasmus of Rotterdam. This perspective argued that human life had inherent worth, value, and dignity because of the Incarnation itself. With God becoming human, the dignity of humanity thus arose in its sacredness. Thus, all human life should be respected and treated with a sacred respect.

Within the perspective of Christian Humanism, many social and racial justice advocates pushed the traditional boundaries and expectations of the Christian Churches, often labeled as liberals, radicals, or imprudent within their respected denominations. As chronicled in the his "Letter from Birmingham Jail," Martin Luther King Jr. challenged the lack of action and complacency of a coalition of eight Southern White multi-denominational Christian leaders:

> We have waited for more than three hundred and forty years for our constitutional and God-given rights. The nations of Asia and Africa are moving with jet-like speed toward the goal of political

independence, and we still creep at horse and buggy pace toward the gaining of a cup of coffee at a lunch counter.[7]

From the Catholic perspective, individuals such as Dorothy Day and Thomas Merton frustrated ossified Christian leadership, and struggled against opposing opinions with their work for social justice and non-violent advocacy against war and poverty through a Christian Humanist lens. To the dismay of many conservative-minded Christians at the time, and even today, at certain parts of their lives both of them considered themselves Catholic anarchists, a label of change and progress both Day and Merton were proud to be associated with.

> The theology of love must seek to deal realistically with the evil and injustice in the world, and not merely to compromise with them. Such a theology will have to take note of the ambiguous realities of politics, without embracing the specious myth of a "realism" that merely justifies force in the service of established power. Theology does not exist merely to appease the already too untroubled conscience of the powerful and established. A theology of love may also conceivably turn out to be a theology of revolution. In any case, it is a theology of *resistance*.[8]

This movement of resistance was also illustrated through union strikes throughout the nation, such as the Delano Grape Worker Strike and boycotts in California, through the work of advocates like as Cesar Chavez and Dolores Huerta. From the Christian foundations of non-violence and purposeful fasting, Chavez brought the attention to the struggle of the migrant workers plight to the eyes of the nation, even bringing awareness and attention to democratic Senator and future Presidential nominee Robert Kennedy. Chavez embodied the prophet of Isaiah throughout his purposeful and strategic hunger strikes for the awareness of the injustices against the migrant workers:

> Is not this the fast that I choose: to loose the bonds of injustice, to undo the straps of the yoke, to let the oppressed go free, and to break every yoke? Is it not to share your bread with the hungry and bring the homeless poor into your house; when you see the naked, to cover them and not to hide yourself from your own kin? Then your light shall break forth like the dawn. (Isa 58:6–8)

---

7. Carson, *Autobiography*, 192.
8. Merton, *Faith and Violence*, 9.

The revival of the Christian Humanist movement became a needed voice for the progress of social justice advocacy within Christianity. In the face of a complacent and often Pharisaic style of leadership, but grounded within religious doctrine and virtue ethics, Christian Humanism brought to prominence again the essential nature of the values of the Beatitudes as well as the corporal and spiritual works of mercy. This view reignited a radical imitation of the care for the poor as exemplified in the life of Jesus of Nazareth, through the acknowledgment of the dignity of the those on the fringe of society and a preferential option for the poor and vulnerable that continues to still remain a prominent movement today.[9]

Examples of Collaboration: Predicating a Society on Human Truth and the Dignity of the Human Person

The example of both secular progressives and Christian Humanists of the twentieth-century illustrated that a time for change had come in the political climate of America. Although some political concessions had been made throughout the first decades of the century, the change of law alone did not convert hearts, nor did it penetrate into the deep mindset of the cultural reality. Martin Luther King Jr. blatantly confronted and challenged this perspective of the deep cultural mindset.

Martin Luther King Jr. was no stranger to the theoretical and real challenges involved with changing a culture that valued material objects more than human beings. In light of his faith and a deep thirst of righteousness his call for unity within American culture became a beacon of hope. He had marched, protested, was jailed, and mourned over the callous treatment of Americans separated and segregated by the pigmentation of their skin. Months after his call to arms at the March on Washington, his dream was once again attacked through the death of four innocent children murdered by a terrorist bombing at the oldest Baptist Church in Alabama. King returned to Birmingham, Alabama, to offer the eulogy at the combined funeral of three of the children martyred in the 16th Street Baptist Church bombing. This egregious act shook the nation and for the first time opened many eyes of the passive bystanders to the need and horrors of the struggle for Civil Rights.

---

9. Francis, "Evangelii Gaudium," paras. 186–216.

The Roots of Truth and Reconciliation

> So in spite of the darkness of this hour we must not despair. We must not become bitter, nor must we harbor the desire to retaliate with violence. No, we must not lose faith in our white brothers. Somehow we must believe that the most misguided among them can learn to respect the dignity and the worth of all human personality.[10]

In the midst of such pain, anger, and grief, how can an individual show such magnanimity in the face of vile hate and destruction?

In the midst of the prejudice and disregard for human life, King still believed in hope; hope for redemption in the human heart. He did not commit to a separation between the moral right of the actions of Blacks and Whites but saw racism as a disease that needed to be healed within the heart of all human beings, Black and White. His call for a non-violent alternative did not strive for a victory of one group over another, but was sustained by the belief that equality must be a mutuality leading to recognize unity of the races. King's focus continues to resonate with challenges that still plague the American consciousness: how can the dignity and worth of all human personality be respected, and how can that recognition be perpetuated and sustained at a deep cultural level? Has that time of urgent decision already passed, though? The crisis anticipated by Merton, brought to light by Dorothy Day, Rosa Parks, Martin Luther King, and Cesar Chavez has not yet concluded. The time has not yet passed, but with each passing decade reconciliation within the nation seems more and more difficult.

Collaboration toward Community: Acknowledging That We Are Already One

The witness of the Social and Civil Rights Movements of the twentieth-century converged on the concept of a deeper reality of existence; namely, that humanity at its core is much more connected than different. Beyond the written law, and words on a page, the desire of the human heart is the same through a longing to be included, loved, and to exercise freedom of the rights inherent to all humanity. Similar to King, his Civil Rights contemporary, Thomas Merton, the Catholic hermit and celebrated spiritual author, also firmly stated that beyond the façade humanity, at its core, is bound in a deeper unity than what is seen at face value alone; beyond the skin and bone: we are already one.

10. Carson, *Autobiography*, 232.

Truth and Reconciliation

> [T]he deepest level of communication is not communication, but communion. It is wordless. It is beyond words, and it is beyond speech, and it is beyond concept. Not that we discover a new unity. We discover an older unity. My dear brothers and sisters, we are already one. But we imagine that we are not. And what we have to recover is our original unity. What we have to be is what we are.[11]

This should not be approached as a platitude of hope or an unsubstantiated trite spiritual utopian vision, it is a tangible reality in the physical and metaphysical reality of humanity at its core. Merton stated that dignity and worth defined the foundation of being human. Much like King's perspective of curing the disease of racism, Merton called for the acknowledgement that racism, prejudice, and stigmatization will only begin to change in culture when individuals begin to change their hearts. Hatred and oppression are easy to place upon abstract groups and ideologies, but such stereotypes are much more difficult to sustain with individual and close, intimate relationships.

This is a call, by Merton, for an honest assessment of one's actions in the process of encounter and engagement with others is essential to move forward for a reconciliation built upon transparency and authenticity. Merton does not assume that this is an easy process, but it is a necessary aspect of the process. Without the ability to accurately recognize one's own accountability within the cultural environment the truest form of unity will not be possible.

Learning from Global Witnesses of Leadership

The American twentieth-century political sphere emerged to be much more inclusive than when it first dawned. The work of the Progressive Era, although not yet concluded, continues to challenge and affect the political landscape with every election cycle and agenda through words; but is that always conveyed in action? King's assessment from the year leading up to his assassination could ring true even today: "As the administration has manifested a faltering and fluctuating interest in civil rights during the past year, a flood of words rather than deeds has inundated the dry desert of expectations."[12] Such disappointment at lofty words and lack of action continues to fuel a deep desire for authentic change which unfortunately

---

11. Merton, *Asian Journal*, 308.
12. King, *Where Do We Go*, 228.

has led some contemporary advocacy groups to believe equality can only be achieved or manifested through violence, and that the previous non-violent movements from the twentieth-century had failed.

A Community-Oriented, Focused Leadership

> Our modern world cannot attain to peace, and to fully equitable social order, merely by application of laws which act upon man, so to speak, from outside himself. The transformation of society begins within the person. It begins with the maturing and opening out of personal freedom in relation to other freedoms.... This means a capacity to be open to others as persons, to desire for others all that we know to be needful for ourselves, all that is required for the full growth and even the temporal happiness of a fully personal existence.[13]

The 1960s brought a rupture to the traditional political mindset of administrative oversight about race and social rights. Sit-ins, marches, and nonviolent protests became consistent headline news bringing the raw struggle for rights into the realm of a tangible reality and fully exposed to view. Although laws of segregation were the norm within certain geographical regions, telecommunications broadcasted and illustrated the inhumane treatment of individuals based on racial or ethical differences across the nation. In the 1968, the Memphis Sanitation Workers strike used the phrase "I AM A MAN" to address needed changes for better working conditions and financial equity. These simple words dramatically indicated how disrespected the union workers felt by the policies of leadership of the time; having them feel less than human.

The 1960s also saw that American governmental institutional bodies began to shift from a dedicated philosophy of assimilation, termination, and cultural genocidal approach to Native Americans to more cultural autonomy for tribal self-determination. As President Lyndon Johnson stated also in 1968: "We must affirm the rights of the first Americans to remain Indians while exercising their rights as Americans. We must affirm their rights to freedom of choice and self-determination."[14]

With such momentum, though, 1968 also marked one of the most tragic years in American history with the assassinations of both Martin

---

13. Merton, "Christian Humanism in the Nuclear Era," 154–55.
14. Pevar, *Rights of Indians*, 12.

Luther King Jr. and Robert Kennedy. The nation was in crisis and the voice of change seemed to be stomped out. Human truth when once brought to light cannot be crushed or neglected, nor can hope be lost through the horrific witness of martyrdom. It is said that it is always darkest before the dawn. May we learn from the life and witness of the advocates from the social and civil rights movements of the twentieth-century, and through their work continue an authentic assessment of human truth to help create an avenue for the fruits of future reconciliation and union for leadership and recognition of the dignity of the human person in America, as demonstrated by our brother and sisters in neighboring countries.

Lessons in Servant Leadership

- **Being *Kairos* Minded—Being Present to the Now:** Servant leaders need to stay vigilant for moments of decision throughout their work. Being present to the now allows servant leaders to react when the time warrants without hesitation in a time of needed action. This tenet of servant leadership is directly connected with another servant leadership characteristic, foresight. As foresight focuses on vision, being present in the now takes that vision and puts it into action.

- **The Noble Seeker:** Servant leaders need to depend on access to quality data and continual education. Learning must be understood as a life-long endeavor. To engage with the present and be prepared for an unknowable future, one must learn from the past.

- **A Witness of Courage and Risk:** Servant leaders need to develop a sense of courage and fortitude as their actions may not be accepted or respected at the time. Serving others demands risk, an intimacy that is shared with another that can results in trust building or rejection. It is in the servant leader's lens, of being service-oriented, to initiate relationship, as needed, to encourage others to participate in dialogue.

For Further Reflection

- **Being *Kairos* Minded—Being Present to the Now:** The arts and music are mediums that can cross social barriers and controversial topics to illuminate and challenge stereotypes. Listen and reflect on the following songs: Billie Holiday's "Strange Fruit" (1939), Bob Dylan's "A Hard Rains A-Gonna Fall" (1962), and Marvin Gaye's "What's Going On" (1971). How did the lyrics from the songs present a reality as well as a call for future change? What images or phrases came to focus throughout? How did the instrumentation develop an emotional environment for the topic of the song? What other musicians that you know use topics of racial injustice as the subject matter for their songs? How did they incorporate those topics in the lyrics and musical instrumental to help elicit an emotion from the listener?

- **The Noble Seeker:** In his book, *The Education of Black People*, W. E. B. Dubois offers ten critiques about the American educational system of the twentieth-century. After reading Dubois's critiques reflect on the following questions: Has the contemporary educational system resolved issues regarding race disparities? What role does the advent of technology within educational environments play in bringing greater equality or inequality in the educational experience?

- **A Witness of Courage and Risk:** Listen to/read Dr. Martin Luther King Jr.'s speech at the Memphis Sanitation Worker's strike, "I've Been to the Mountain Top." How does Dr. King acknowledge, through his speech, that his call as a Civil Rights leader influenced his presence to advocate for the Sanitation Workers? What parts of the speech recognize the dangers associated with being a leader in the Civil Rights Movement? Why do you think he would include that in the speech?

8

The Tenants of Truth and Reconciliation
South Africa

We recall our terrible past so that we can deal with it, to forgive where forgiveness is necessary, without forgetting; to ensure that never again will such inhumanity tear us apart; and to move ourselves to eradicate a legacy that lurks dangerously as a threat to our democracy.[1]

NYASHA GURAMATUNHUCOOPER, LEADERSHIP AUTHOR and scholar, pointedly challenged that leadership theory aimed at twenty-first century change needs to expand beyond the usual examples of American leaders alone; that there is much to learn from examples of leaders throughout the world. "There is no shortage of leadership in Africa. It is a matter of those interested in leadership to be intentional in learning about experiences beyond their own social and intellectual spaces."[2] Through the example of the examples of servant leadership demonstrated throughout South Africa's Truth and Reconciliation Commission as well as the movement to seek unity beyond the past racial injustices Guramatunhucooper is absolutely correct, it is past time that America begin to learn from the lessons and witness of the challenges and successes of our global neighbors.

---

1. Mandela, "Special Debate," para. 44.
2. Guramatunhucooper, "Theory Leadership from Africa," 16.

The Tenants of Truth and Reconciliation: South Africa

The concept of Truth and Reconciliation, or Truth and Justice, Commissions have been a global phenomenon since its unconventional and seemingly successful approach of the transformation of the South African government, from its apartheid past into a new era of democracy. Although South Africa was not the first country to utilize the process of truth-telling and investigation through the form of a Truth and Reconciliation Commission (TRC), it became the one of the most publicized and scrutinized. "All of these elements—truth-telling, healing, nation-building, history writing—were integrated by the South African TRC into a potent mixture. This process is not wholly unique, as national politicians have redefined human rights . . . in many other countries."[3]

This process, which included aspects of mediation, adjudication, reconciliation, arbitration and negotiation, was also a natural fit as a model for restorative justice in South Africa in their desire to seek unity and forward movement as a nation, because a similar process was used in traditional pre-contact South African tribal cultures to resolve differences in the past.[4] In the wake of the relative smooth change of political and governmental control, leaders that pursued this form of justice gained global recognition and were welcomed globally with revered status, such as Nelson Mandela and Desmond Tutu. Tutu indicated that the process is methodical, based on taking one step at a time to rebuild trust among the deep divisions in the country.

> In South Africa we are learning to heal through telling stories . . . for it is only through telling that we heal; it is only through revealing the heart's darkest crevices that we can begin to understand, to forgive, and to move forward. . . . After years of mistrust we are beginning to open our hearts and minds to one another; we are learning to see the humanity that lives in each of us.[5]

Although there has already been considerable scholarship written on the process and procedures about Truth and Reconciliation Commissions, much of the previous scholarship has focused on analysis, examination, and exploration of the ethics and morality, law and precedent, as well as political theory of the process. This chapter will examine the crucial dialogue that exists within the fragile balance of mutual listening and storytelling as a methodical process that resonates within a servant leadership model.

3. Wilson, *Politics of Truth and Reconciliation*, 15.
4. See Ajayi and Buhari, "Methods of Conflict Resolution."
5. Tutu, Foreword to *No More Strangers Now*, xi.

Truth and Reconciliation

To understand the goal of the methical process, it is also important to discuss the cultural role that the African perspective and concept, *ubuntu*, served throughout the Commission and process of reconciliation. "Ubuntu can be defined as humanness, a pervasive spirit of caring and community, harmony and hospitality, respect and responsiveness that individuals and groups display for one another."[6] This deep traditional and cultural belief acknowledges that there is an inherent connectivity that defines each human being, not as merely an individual as in a Western perspective, but that the individual is a vital aspect of the relationship with the community as a whole. Namely, to explore and understand leadership through an African lens it is important to remember that the meaning of leadership is not based on an individual outside of the context of the community, as in South African culture a person derives meaning from their connectivity in the community.[7]

Servant-Leadership Lens—Being Methodical: One Action at a Time

Being methodical and approaching leadership systemically allows a servant leader to established a complete vision for the future goal and share the steps of action needed for followers to understand the logic of each of the steps to attain that goal. As servant leadership authors Sipe and Frick stated: "[Servant leaders] guide and empower others to explore positive possibilities for a renewed organization culture, backed by sound strategy and achievable performance."[8]

An individual who exemplified and illustrated strategic leadership in Scripture, Peter, one of the early disciples of Jesus of Nazareth. Although Peter is often remembered for his missteps throughout the Gospels, his decisions were made through steps of action that were purposeful and strategic during his ministry. His strategic decisions of faith included spreading the message of Jesus's teaching beyond groups of Messianic Jews in the Holy Land to include gentile, non-Jewish, communities to fulfill the goal of his ministry.

---

6. Nzimakwe, "Practising *Ubuntu*," 31.
7. Avolio and Locke, "Should Leaders Be," 124.
8. Sipe and Frick, *Seven Pillars*, 149.

Peter: A Methodical Servant Leader Who Learned One Step at a Time

Peter, one of the initial followers of Jesus of Nazareth, became a disciple through a step-by-step process, and later was a leader among the Apostles through the same step-by-step methodical process of reasoning. Unlike his counterpart, the missionary to the Gentiles, Paul of Tarsus who had an intense conversion on the road to Damascus, Peter's conversion was a methodical learning experience full of successes and failures. Throughout the Gospel narratives, Peter is portrayed as an eager disciple who just as easily verbally proclaimed a deep faith as well as fell into just as grave blunders. He is the only one of the Apostles to venture out of the comfort of their boat on the Sea of Galilee and walk toward Jesus on water, while moments later taking his eyes off Jesus, he begins to sink into the depths of the same lake (Matt 14:22–33). Peter is acknowledged as the first to have the awareness and recognize Jesus as the Messiah, the Son of the living God, through his great faith (Matt 16:16), while just a few moments later is rebuked by his master for trying to stop Jesus's destined death in Jerusalem (Matt 16:23).

Although a man of great faith, he had monumental challenges that pressed the limits of his faithfulness, especially at the trial of his rabbi where he denied even knowing his teacher, likely out of the desire of self-preservation in the midst of the angry mob (Luke 22:54–62). Scripture also indicates that Peter was challenged again in his faithfulness, by Jesus himself, after his resurrection, on the shore of the lake of Galilee as a type of three-fold reconciliation (John 21:15–19). But it seems after Pentecost and the reception of the Holy Spirit, Peter finally conquered his fear from any mob attack, and courageously stood his ground to proclaim his faith. This example offers a reminder that a servant-leader grows in their call step-by-step, their engagement is a methodical series of actions focusing on the other.

Peter also served in the defining leadership capacity among the disciples through the strategic decision of the inclusion of gentiles into Christianity, without their needing to be bound to the Jewish law first (Acts 15:1–19). He later methodically moved from Jerusalem, to Antioch, and ultimately to Rome, throughout ministry by expanding the message of Christianity throughout the Roman Empire.

In the first letter attributed to Peter, there is a reminder that a servant leader is one that is methodical, taking one step at a time: "[Jesus] is your example, and you must follow in his steps" (1 Pet 2:21). Peter's letter reminds us that following in the example of a servant-leader one must follow methodical steps that a mentor previously illustrated, through a purposeful series of actions that culminate into the whole.

Peter's leadership included moments of failure through trials and suffering that lay the foundation of conscious decision making for steps toward the future end goal. Leadership is often developed through initial failure and a series of setbacks that create a methodical and purposeful assessment for future engagement. Rabbi Jonathan Sacks reminded that historical leaders that are often remembered as successes experienced continuous challenges, like Peter:

> Lincoln and Churchill faced countless setbacks and were at times exceedingly unpopular. Gandhi failed in his dream of uniting Muslims and Hindus together in a single nation. Nelson Mandela spent twenty-seven years in prison, accused of treason and regarded as a violent agitator. Only in retrospect do heroes seem heroic; only in hindsight do the many setbacks they faced reveal themselves as stepping stones on the road to victory.[9]

Jim Collins, American business consultant and author, also echoed that it is the importance of perspective which creates the difference of failure and weakness through mistakes. Failure is not the moment of setback or struggle but the methodical steps taken to learn from the moment for future determination and growth.

> The signature of the truly great versus the merely successful is not the absence of difficulty, but the ability to come back from setbacks, even cataclysmic catastrophes, stronger than before. . . . Failure is not so much a physical state as a state of mind; success is falling down, and getting up one more time, without end.[10]

The Challenge

The growing pains of the South African government during transition from the Apartheid control to a democratic representation of whole population, both white and black South Africans, lacked a completely cohesive and clear vision. With the continual intense violence in the black townships, more sanctions from the United Nations and neighboring countries, as well as the fear of likely retribution from blacks as apartheid laws became

---

9. Sacks, *Lessons in Leadership*, 68.
10. Collins, *How the Mighty Fall*, 123.

The Tenants of Truth and Reconciliation: South Africa

more lax in the minds of the white Afrikaans leaders, bartering and concessions came slowly. The date, February 11, 1990, became a symbolic time of change and hope for the black South Africans as the political prison, Nelson Mandela, was released from prison after twenty-seven years of incarceration. The release of Mandela became a catalyst and sign of the times of change for black South Africans.

Through the cooperation and desire for a peaceful transition of power in a post-apartheid government a forum for negotiation was set up at the South African World Trade Center called Convention for a Democratic South Africa (CODESA). In 1991, the CODESA 1 drew up a plan of intent for a new constitution for the country of South Africa. These tenets guided the conversation to establish a foundation to ensure: an undivided country among all citizens, to purposefully focus on healing the injustices of the past and recognize the dignity of all human personality, make dedicated efforts to improve economic opportunities, a purposeful desire to quell violence and discord throughout the country, and create a government based on structure that included checks and balances of the power of the offices.[11] Mahmood Mamdani, Professor of Anthropology, Political Science, and African Studies stated that CODESA had a unique and methodical purpose and vision in comparison to previous global peace and justice efforts.

> Whereas Nuremberg was backward-looking, preoccupied with justice as punishment, CODESA sought a balance between the past and the future, between redress for the past and reconciliation for the future. The paradigm shifted from one of victims' justice to that of survivors' justice—where the meaning of survivors changed to include all those who had survived apartheid: yesterday's victims, yesterday's perpetrators and yesterday's beneficiaries [presumed to be bystanders], all were treated as "survivors."[12]

With the initial intent of CODESA, South Africa progressed toward its first free democratic election in 1994; momentum for a Truth and Reconciliation Commission grew as well. This anticipation and tension created an atmosphere of anxiety, betrayal and self-preservation within the white Afrikaans community, especially those who held positions of power that enforced the apartheid laws against the black South Africans.

> During the pre-election period, fear about the coming TRC created a climate in which police officials started "spilling the beans"

---

11. See "Convention for a Democratic South Africa."
12. Mamdani, *Beyond Nuremberg*, 11.

on each other; resulting in a handful of high-profile prosecutions of former security force personnel for apartheid-era abuses. The fear of more prosecutions of police officials was fuelled [sic] by the State's success in prosecuting former South African Police (SAP) hit-squad commander Eugene De Kock. His experience also instilled another fear—that loyal apartheid police officers would be "hung out to dry," unsupported by their former masters.[13]

The decades of anger and political injustices perpetrated against black South Africans still consumed many throughout the country, and violence against whites still persistent leading up to the Truth and Reconciliation Commission. One instance of horrific violence that challenged a hope of reconciliation between the races, and brought the intense violence plaguing the time of democratic transition of South Africa to the forefront of international attention was the murder of American Fulbright scholar, Amy Biehl in August 1993.

Amy Biehl was an anti-apartheid advocate who was in the process of driving three friends from the University home to the Gugulethu township, which resides outside of Cape Town. A mob of black youth stopped the car, attacked the white driver by stoning and tabbing her to death in the street. The exact details surrounding the criminal murder and perpetrators of her death remain unclear, but from within the riotous mob four black South African rights' advocates were singled out and charged for her brutal murder.[14]

In 1997, the four individuals pleaded for amnesty during the Truth and Reconciliation Commission due the argument of the political frenzy that led to the context of the killing. A description of the course of events of her murder were recorded in Peiter Meiring's summary of the Commission:

> It was the slogan "One settler, one bullet" that had inspired them, Manqina said. They were members of Paso, the PAC youth organization, and had been emboldened to the point of mindlessness by the political talk in the township at the time. They wanted, at any price, to make the country ungovernable.... The four young men apologized to the Biehl family but added that they believed that their action at the time was one of the reasons why South Africa today had a black government. To the question as to how the death of a defenceless [sic] and innocent girl—who had come to South Africa precisely to serve black South Africans—could possibly contribute to black people getting their country back, especially

---

13. Rauch, "South African Police," 210–11.
14. See Scheper-Hughes, *We Are Not*; and van der Leun, *We Are Not*.

The Tenants of Truth and Reconciliation: South Africa

in a time when constitutional changes were full steam under way, Mongezi Manqina replied, "We would murder Whites until the government gave in. With the exception of journalists and ambulance drives no Whites were welcome or safe in black townships."[15]

A Call for Change

With the amount of violence and the desire to find dialogue to move forward as a united country, it was imperative for the Truth and Reconciliation to be methodical in response to the chaos of violence and street justice that was occurring in the townships. Steps were taken to ensure that the Truth and Commission process was grounded in strategic principles and specific conditions.

> The task of the [Truth and Reconciliation Commission] was laid down by the Promotion of the National Unity and Reconciliation Act, and included the granting of amnesty, the quest for truth about gross violations of human rights committed during the period of 1960 to 1994, and the drawing up of recommendations to the government concerning reparations and rehabilitation for the victims of such violations.... The Act also provided a definition of what was to be considered as a "gross violation of human rights": a) Killing, abduction, torture or severe ill treatment; b) Any attempt, conspiracy, incitement, instigation, command or procurement to commit an act referred to in paragraph (a), which emanated from conflicts of the past and which was committed (during the mandate period) by any person acting with a political motive.[16]

Claire Moon, author and scholar of political science and sociology of human rights, stated that there were over 21,000 petitions throughout the South African Truth and Reconciliation Commission, with over 7000 people requesting amnesty for their crimes. Out of those petitions, only about ten percent of those requests had their testimonies held within a public venue.[17]

To create an environment of authentic testimony, in the hope of allowing truth-telling evolve into dialogue for purposeful steps toward

---

15. Meiring, *Chronicle of the Truth Commission*, 167–68.
16. Burton, *Truth and Reconciliation Commission*, 27–28.
17. Moon, *Narrating Political Reconciliation*, 42.

reconciliation the environment for the restorative justice process was constructed for healing through understanding and possible forgiveness.

> [The backers of the South African TRC] insisted, a well-run commission could accomplish things no trial could provide. It could focus on the overall pattern of violations, rather than zeroing in on just those cases that happened to be brought to trial. It could keep the focus on testimony and discussion on the victims rather than the perpetrators, and allow victims to testify in a supportive setting more conducive to healing than the sometimes brutal cross-examination of a criminal or civil trial.[18]

Throughout the testimonies at the Truth and Reconciliation Commission grief and trauma was brought to bear and the African perspective of *ubuntu* underlined the proceedings to offer an opportunity for victims to express their loss and the perpetrators to offer explanation of their actions to pave a road of reconciliation. It was not a perfect system, but it attempted to offer more of an opportunity for a confession and interest in reconciliation than criminal procedures alone. Mamdani stated:

> I was part of the audience one grey morning in Cape Town when the TRC questioned F W de Klerk. De Klerk had read out a statement enumerating the wrongs of apartheid and concluded by taking responsibility for apartheid. But the TRC was not interested. Its interest was narrowly focused: on specific human rights violations such as murder, torture, kidnapping: did de Klerk know of these? Had he authorized any of these? It struck me how different this was from what I had read of Nuremberg. At Nuremberg, the greatest responsibility lay with those in positions of power, those who had planned and strategized, not those with boots on the ground. At the TRC, the responsibility lay with the one who pulled the trigger. The greatest responsibility seemed to lie with the one closest to the scene of the crime.[19]

At the Crossroads

Through what ways was the methodical search for an opportunity to grow beyond the injustices of the past demonstrated in a desire for future unity? How was this present as Mandela became President of the new

18. Roht-Arriaza, "New Landscape," 4.
19. Mamdani, *Beyond Nuremberg*, 4.

The Tenants of Truth and Reconciliation: South Africa

democratically led South Africa? South Africa scholar and professor, Sabelo Ndlovu-Gatsheni stated that Mandela strategically balanced the needs of the black South Africans and the charity needed during change for the participation of white Afrikaans to begin a new country founded on a relationship built on trust between the races, which was not an easy task.

> During his presidency, Mandela demonstrated a rare ability and awareness of the motivations of his audiences and tried frantically to appeal to their interests as well as the interests of the new nation that he was creating. He proved to be a very shrewd political calculator and a competent manipulator if not persuader of his enemies into his side. The challenge he faced was that he had to be careful to balance appealing both to the fears of whites and the frustrations of blacks.[20]

Peter Storey recalled an experience of this strategy as he discussed his first visit with Mandela in the Presidential offices after the election in 1994, as Storey was campaigning to end violence through a gun-free South Africa initiative.

> It was the first time I had visited Madiba Mandela in his new offices and was surprised to find the portraits of former prime minsters and presidents lining the anteroom where we waited. The new justice minister was present, and I asked him, "What are these guys still doing here?" he looked at the pictures and said, "Well Peter, they are our history," and then added with a smile, "and believe me, they *are* history!"[21]

Nelson Mandela recognized that by not addressing the past, instead of destroying or removing it, would jeopardize the ability to include a truly united South Africa, from both blacks and whites, for the future. His perspective was for the division to cease, not because of forced laws, procedures, and protocols as was the precedent until the apartheid rule, but rather show a magnanimity through leadership that included both black and white South Africans to guide their future together beyond a desire for retribution from isolation and alienation.

> Ordinary Afrikaners have a deep respect for authority, including governmental and educational authority. Leaders are deeply respected, and their word is taken seriously. . . . It was also the

---

20. Ndlovu-Gatsheni, *Decolonial Mandela*, 117.
21. Storey, *Protest at Midnight*, 216–17.

principled leadership and authority of Nelson Mandela that drew white South Africans and even conservative Afrikaners to this son of royalty. The same people who put him in prison for three decades would embrace him without question. The smallest gesture of friendship or expression of decency among leaders is applauded.[22]

One concrete example of Mandela's principled leadership and strategic magnanimity toward white South Africans can be illustrated through the recognition of the power of sport to bring unity to a country. Mandela recognized that the love for rugby could be harnessed as an avenue of unitive celebration instead of division for the South African people. Instead of removing the symbol of the Springbok, which had become a sign of the white ruling power, Mandela argued for it to be kept so that a new unitive meaning could be applied to it.[23] Mandela also advocated for support of the team throughout its 1995 World Cup run, and eventual victory, in the townships and by wearing a team hat and jersey as sign of support. This was not welcomed by all South Africans, but over the season it became a rally cry of "one team, one country." But Mandela's persistence showed that some activities and symbols are more powerful avenues for change than violence.

> Sport has the power to change the world. It has the power to inspire, it has the power to unite people in a way that little else does. It speaks to youth in a language they understand. Sport can create hope, where once there was only despair. It is more powerful than governments in breaking down racial barriers. It laughs in the face of all types of discrimination.[24]

Throughout the twentieth-century the recognition of the power of sport as an avenue of leadership for inter-cultural development, unity, and ending national racial injustices has been well demonstrated from the courage of athletes, administrators, and analogies utilized by global leaders.[25]

---

22. Jansen, *Knowledge in the Blood*, 238.
23. See Bestall, "16th Man"; and Eastwood, *Invictus*."
24. Mandela, "Speech," para. 3.
25. See John Paul II, "Jubilee of Sports People"; Kahn, *Rickey & Robinson*; Kerr, *Legacy*; and Rembert, "Merton on Sports."

The Tenants of Truth and Reconciliation: South Africa

Learning from Global Witnesses of Leadership

While addressing the challenges of creating a dialogue of forgiveness in situation of genocide and years of racial conflict, Rev. Ubald Rugirangoga explained that story-telling and truth-telling is a strategic method that bring victims and perpetrators into an intimate relational space that removes from one grounded on abstract ideologies but on human encounter. Using his own experiences with his congregation, survivors of the Rwandan genocide Rugirangoga recounted that:

> Some of the victims of the genocide, including family members of those who had been killed, came with me to the prisons to meet their offenders in jail so they could give voice to their decision to forgive. I had taught them that very often it is the victim who must first speak forgiveness in order to give the offender an opportunity to beg pardon.[26]

This type of connection opens to the grace of recognition of humanity, person to person, instead of merely labels victim and perpetrator. This methodical process of one purposeful action establishes a step-by-step deliberation to create new definitions and new relationships through personal encounter instead of distant objectivity. Definition of the relationship is no longer bound to a relationship of negative experience but emerges to new life through the creation of freedom.

Desmond Tutu also echoed this perspective as he stated: "We create a new relationship out of the suffering, one that is stronger for what we have experienced together."[27] Ann Garrido, professor and author of Christian leadership practices in ministry, stated that the course that the South African Truth and Reconciliation Commission created was not about restoring past relationships, but it was a forward seeking movement eager and interested in forging a renewed sense of connectivity and relationship for the future.[28] Ultimately, the methodical process of the Truth and Reconciliation Commission as well as the preceding transition from the apartheid regime to free and democratic elections also noticed globally as Pope John Paul II remarked that: "This great country [South Africa] . . . provides an example to many other nations in Africa and elsewhere, by causing the spirit of

---

26. Rugirangoga, *Forgiveness Makes You Free*, 63.
27. Tutu and Tutu, *Book of Forgiving*, 155.
28. See Garrido, *Redeeming Conflict*, 161.

reconciliation and of compromise to prevail over the tensions which are an inevitable element of transition."[29]

Lessons in Servant Leadership

- **Being Methodical: One Action at a Time:** Servant leaders must be attentive to a method, focusing on action at a time. Are those actions leading to the desired outcome? Does there need to be reassessment? It is the job of a leader dedicated to service of others to ensure that those they service are represented throughout a methodical plan.

- **Developing a Logical and Systematic Approach for a Future Goal:** Servant leaders need to be systematic thinkers, creating a methodical strategy that is goal-oriented. Even though such steps may not always find success, a leader focused on the needs of the community and re-assess each action for the sake of the goal for the community.

- **Redefine Old Symbols through New, Unitive Meanings:** Servant leaders should possess skills to interpret the power of symbols and re-envision how new meaning of symbols could be used to help their community better relate together. It is important for servant leaders to carefully assess the power of the symbol to know how it has been used and the possibility it might have for the future.

For Further Reflection

- **Being Methodical: One Action at a Time:** Read and reflect on one of the following books authored or co-authored by Desmond Tutu: *No Future Without Forgiveness* (1999), *The Book of Forgiving* (2014), or *The Book of Joy* (2016). How did the writing demonstrate Tutu's methodical approach to forgiveness and reconciliation? Do you agree that his perspective is possible? Why or why not?

- **Developing a Logical and Systematic Approach for a Future Goal:** What is one of your future life goals? Have you developed a logical or systematic approach in trying to achieve that goal? Explain what steps would be needed to start that process in an individual's life. Now, expand that thinking and apply it to a city, state, or national level. How

29. O'Connor, *Papal Diplomacy*, 139.

The Tenants of Truth and Reconciliation: South Africa

much planning would be needed to develop a logical or systematic vision for a future goal in your community? Explain why you would, or would not, be interested in serving as a committee member for your local community.

- **Redefine Old Symbols through New, Unitive Meanings:** Watch and reflect on the following films: ESPN's documentary: "The 16th Man" (2010) or *Invictus* (2009). Reflect on how the film(s) portrayed the character of Mandela and how he used the power and symbols of the South African rugby team to try to unite the divided South African country. Explain the ways in which he attempted to use sport in the strategic plan for national unity. Explore other athletes that have, through their sport, tried to resolve racial injustices or helped to push their nation forward through athletics.

9

The Tenants of Truth and Reconciliation
Canada

At the heart of learning is listening to and telling new stories. In particular, we need to tell a new story about how we arrived at this moment in history in the relationship between Indigenous and non-Indigenous peoples in Canada. This story needs to be reflective and inclusive of all of the experiences that have shaped the Canada of today, and it needs to transform the narrative of exclusion that has been prominent.[1]

As mentioned in the previous chapter truth-telling through the form of stories establishes the groundwork for the Truth and Reconciliation process. The victims have the availability for their story to be heard. Through the use of language and imagination an atmosphere of dialogue is created to breathe life into and renew relationship between human beings. This can become a very powerful avenue for human growth and recognition of the dignity of the other, as many do not know or take the needed time to reflect on their own history with the intention to learn from the past. Terry LeBlanc, Mi'kmaq-Acadian and professor of Indigenous studies, stated:

> It is not simply a lack of knowledge of Canadian history, however, that is the roadblock to a significant effort for all of us to be reconciled, rather it is the absence of any real and intentional

1. Wilson-Raybould, *True Reconciliation*, 179.

The Tenants of Truth and Reconciliation: Canada

personal experience to provide a real context into which to insert one's ideas, values, and opinions about that history.[2]

The heart of the response to the genocide of the residential schools was to re-orient survivors with their lost identity, through the storytelling and listening, not for conversion, but rather for understanding. In his book *Leadership Lessons from the Cherokee Nation*, Chad Smith, principal Chief of the Cherokee nation from 1999–2011, offered an important lesson of how the use of language and imagination continued to serve and animate indigenous peoples throughout the genocide of their community and the forced possession of the sacred land.

> The symbol of building one fire is especially fitting when we come and stand together to build one fire; we get and share more heat, greater light, and more comfort. One hundred years ago, the federal government set out to extinguish our national fire. It failed. The flame of this awesome fire and powerful Cherokee Nation burned low for the first 75 years of the last century as the coals beneath the surface burned intensely.[3]

Servant-Leadership Lens: Language and Imagination

One of the tenets of servant leadership is predicated on the purposeful use of language and imagination to offer creative solutions and new ways of engaging others. Servant leaders are called to challenge the traditional bounds of language and expand the limitations to create new forms of meaning and symbols. It is not an easy task as imagination and the use of language in new contexts may create confusion or frustration when not understood in proper context. The following story from Scripture demonstrates how language and imagination can create a new and unitive experience in service.

The Advocate Spirit: Uniting Language and Imagination to Serve Others

The traditional Jewish ritual celebration of the feast of Weeks, also known as Shavuot, was a time of sacrifice, to offer the first fruits of the harvest in thanksgiving and gratitude for the blessings received from God. This ritual

---

2. LeBlanc, "Spirit and Spirituality," 4.
3. Smith, *Leadership Lessons*, 213.

was renamed Pentecost, in Greek language, to designate and focus on the length of time of its occurrence after the high Jewish feast of Passover. In contemporary celebration the Jewish people celebrate this feast as an anniversary of the first reception of the law given to Moses at Mount Sinai and their covenant of service-oriented relationship with God.

After Jesus of Nazareth's ascension, his disciples remained faithful to their Jewish practices and went to Jerusalem for the feast of Pentecost. This experience marked a change in their lives, as Jesus had promised that an Advocate would be sent to help and guide the Apostles after his departure (John 15:26). On this celebration of offering the first fruits of their labors, the promised Advocate descended upon those gathered in the upper room as tongues of fire (Acts 2:1–4). After this encounter with the Spirit, the disciples who were hiding in the upper room, afraid of a similar mob uprising that led to the crucifixion of their teacher a few months earlier, were now gifted with the courage to proclaim the message of Jesus without fear. The fire purified and strengthened their resolve for a ministry and service of evangelization.

This service, through ministry, became a universal message as the story recounts that Peter's speech from the balcony of the upper room was miraculously understood by individuals of various cultures in their various native languages and tongues who were present during the experience (Acts 2:6–11). The sign of the universality of language at that event restored the division present in the world so that a message of unified service could be present and offered as a witness and testimony to all present. This sign and wonder struck the imagination of those present leaving them wondering what this encounter meant (Acts 2:12).

The Challenge

As mentioned previously, memory and space serve an important role to engage in relating language and imagination in a powerful way for the human senses. The Canadian Truth and Reconciliation attempted to create an atmosphere within natural environments for opportunities to allow the witnesses of the indigenous survivors of residential schools to engage their experiences in the openness of the land.

> From the architecture of the spaces used for the TRC events to the spatial orientations of audiences and set-up of places for learning around and within which interaction takes place, the aesthetic

The Tenants of Truth and Reconciliation: Canada

choices implemented by the TRC spatialize connection. In the ease of navigation and informality of outdoor space, new relationships are fostered more easily by chance encounters (as in the Saskatoon TRC's outdoor gathering spaces and at The Forks in Winnipeg). This sits in contrast with the formality of the commissioners' sharing panels, with their raised platform stages, dual large-screen projections, and seating for hundreds of audience members. The aesthetics of space here has an explicit relationship to the kinds of togethering possible.[4]

Just as the space for storytelling was poignant, the atmosphere described of the experiences at the residential schools themselves were designed to quell the ability for dialogue and any form of creative imagination. From the initial moments of the forced abduction of the children from their homes to the buildings and residential areas, the residential schools were barren, sterile, and unwelcoming. As Lena Wandering Spirit, residential school survivor, stated:

> Your number is 34. They called us by number. . . . They used to scrub us and everything: water, lighter fluid. . . . Oh my goodness, bleeding. "Savages" I heard that word lots. . . . We used to get slapped in the mouth if we spoke our language.[5]

Witnesses shared memories that as their indigenous parents fought for their children from being taken, they were labeled as angry, alcoholic, uncivilized, and a danger to the children. When children advocated for their name and cultural identity, administrators and teachers would label them as unruly, disobedient, and stated that the native spirit needed to be exorcized to save the soul. Students tried to run away from the abusive and cultural castrating environment, only to be found, brought back, and punished more severely.[6] The accounts of children dying from exposure while they tried to return home, or children that died on school grounds were kept quiet; and without voices to challenge, the horrors were not questioned for the sake of the progress of education and the identity of the country.

The abuses that the children received in the residential schools were grotesque, violent, and completely unexpected by the children. During the Truth and Reconciliation Commission testimonies, several residential

---

4. Robinson and Martin, "Introduction," 11–12.
5. Villeneuve, *Holy Angels*, 1:47–4:24.
6. See Adams, "Indians"; Truth and Reconciliation Commission of Canada, *Knock on the Door*; and Villeneuve, *Holy Angels*.

school survivors indicated that they had never received any form of physical disciple by their parents before coming to the residential school environment. Many students who tried to run away due to the abuses received: excessive beatings—sometimes by hockey sticks, yardsticks or a whip. They were often caged or locked in rooms for extended periods of time, as well as survival of multiple days only on a "water diet." For those who were caught and forced to return to the resident school in response to their disobedience their hair was completely shaved, while others were forced to stand/sit with inadequate clothing in the snow, and unallowed to change soiled clothing.[7]

Falen Johnson, Mohawk and Tuscarora playwright, indicated that when stating the term school to the residential schools is a disservice, because it completely misses the actual experiences of the life of the children at the institution: "these were re-education and torture camps. I think we have to start naming them for what they were. Too few people know."[8] This sentiment was consistently repeated in the testimony of the survivors of the residential schools who indicated that the actions of the residential school administrators and teachers were focused on trying to civilize the savage.[9] Students were locked away in rooms or cupboards and forgotten until the student broke out of the location for themselves.[10] The discipline policies were aimed at trying to knock the indigenous culture out of the student, indicating that it was bad, evil, and wrong, while European-based were the ideal. Although the skin could not change, residential school staff tried to change everything else to remove any semblance of the indigenous heritage. There was no listening or understanding to the indigenous culture but rather a desire for assimilation and extermination of anything that posed a difference from the definition of civility.

A Call for Change

As international scholar and lawyer Kim Stanton states: "Truth commissions are understood internationally to be mechanisms that assist states with addressing periods of extreme societal rupture. These transitional justice mechanisms enable states to create accurate historical records of such

---

7. Truth and Reconciliation Commission of Canada, *Knock on the Door*, 47–128.
8. Adach, "It has Never Been a Secret that Children Went Missing," para. 8.
9. Truth and Reconciliation Commission of Canada, *Knock on the Door*, 47–128.
10. See Villeneuve, *Holy Angels*.

The Tenants of Truth and Reconciliation: Canada

periods and make recommendations to prevent their recurrence."[11] As with the South African Truth and Reconciliation, the Canadian TRC included very specific mandates for the proceedings as well. The purpose of the Canadian Commission was to unveil the harm perpetrated by the legacy of the church-led and governmental sponsored residential schools, with particular and preferential focus on the strength and resilience of the indigenous victims; and to offer guiding principles toward reconciliation between Anglo and indigenous Canadians for understanding and unity for the future of the country.[12] Like the intentions outlined of the CODESA 1 agreement as South Africa transitioned from apartheid to a democratically governed state, the intentions of the Canadian Truth and Reconciliation were much more challenging to implement and have as an outcome. Mutual respect of indigenous culture must be addressed and incorporated into all sectors that govern the country, throughout education and law, allowing influences of indigenous perspectives define the future direction of Canada.[13]

> At the heart of our success in relationship building across all sectors has been the growing awareness of the harms of colonization [sic], of the value of Indigenous self-determination, and the subsequent partner relationships with communities and equitable engagement by all five health partners—government, health care administration and providers, academia and community.[14]

At the Crossroads

Although there has been progress many indigenous members and indigenous scholars have critiqued the process arguing that too many stories have been dismissed, neglected, removed, or silenced.[15] In this the Canadian TRC has had a difficult challenge to ensure that the tenets of its purpose is fulfilled. It was important that the TRC was founded on language and allowing voice, as the residential school was established on the limitation and silencing of voice. "This official intransigence made the struggle for a truth commission one about voice and respect. Residential school survivors

---

11. Stanton, "Reconciling Reconciliation," 22.
12. See Truth and Reconciliation Commission of Canada, *Honouring the Truth*.
13. See Bell and Friedland, "Introduction."
14. Cook et al., "Structures Last Longer," 3.
15. See Annett, *Murder By Decree*; and Davis et al., "Complicated Pathways."

demanded that Canada open up, listen, learn and start taking responsibility for the damage caused."[16]

This challenge is intensified as there is little knowledge of what healthy advocacy and relationships look like or need to possess to help bridge trust beyond centuries old trauma.

> In reality, many non-Aboriginal people in Canada know little about how Aboriginal and non-Aboriginal relationships have evolved historically, or even the name and provisions of the treaty that makes it possible for them to occupy the community they call "home." Within this context, non-Aboriginal social movement actors are challenged to understand their own social positioning not only as social justice advocates but also as heirs to a history of colonization in relation to Aboriginal peoples. As Aboriginal peoples work to decolonize and heal their communities, non-Aboriginal activists seeking to build relationships are similarly called upon to decolonize their thinking, behaviour, and discourses.[17]

Chief Robert Joseph Kwinkwinxwaligedzi Wakas reminded that the use of deliberate language in apologies is a starting point, and the seeking of forgiveness does matter when desiring to establish reconciliation. Apologies carry a weight that bridges initial rebuilding of trust between words and an offering a concrete action. As he stated:

> It matters because Survivors demand accountability from those responsible for inflicting the harm and trauma imposed on them. . . . It matters to Survivors because apologies can serve as stepping stones to continued healing and reconciliation in their lives . . . so that the world can learn more about the tyranny of colonialization and the spectre of genocide in places like Canada.[18]

In September 2021, the Canadian Bishops of the Catholic Church issued a formal declaration of apology to the First Nations peoples for the injustices of the residential school system and its role in the genocide of indigenous peoples and families by the hands of the school leaders.[19] In July 2022, Pope Francis visited Canada for the specific purpose of apologizing to the First Nations on behalf of the Catholic Church for the history of the residential schools and the injustices perpetrated against the First Nations peoples.

16. James, "Carnival of Truth?," 3.
17. Davis et al., "Aboriginal-Social Justice Alliances," 97.
18. Wakas, *Namwayut*, 229–30.
19. See Canadian Conference of Catholic Bishops, "Statement of Apology."

The Tenants of Truth and Reconciliation: Canada

It is necessary to remember how the policies of assimilation and enfranchisement, which also included the residential school system, were devastating for the people of these lands. When the European colonists first arrived here, there was a great opportunity to bring about a fruitful encounter between cultures, traditions and forms of spirituality. Yet for the most part that did not happen. Again, I think back on the stories you told: how the policies of assimilation ended up systematically marginalizing the indigenous peoples; how also through the system of residential schools your languages and cultures were denigrated and suppressed; how children suffered physical, verbal, psychological and spiritual abuse; how they were taken away from their homes at a young age, and how that indelibly affected relationships between parents and children, grandparents and grandchildren.[20]

Learning from Global Witnesses of Leadership

Trauma affects the inner-most part of our being often without realizing how powerful its effects are within one's identity and actions. It is essential, after the recent traumas of the pandemic isolation as well as the renewal of issues of race relations in the American consciousness, that curriculums realign to a more humanist lens to promote dignity and to try to reconcile a wholeness in humanity through their faculty and student body. Decades ago, Elliot Eisner, Art and Education professor at Stanford University, called for a renewal of arts-based education in the curriculum: "[H]umans experience and give expression to their most deeply held values, beliefs, and through the arts, there can be no adequate form of general education that does not include them."[21] It is through the arts that human beings are able to express emotions and powerful feelings that words alone may not convey.[22] Through the power of the art of imaginative and purposeful storytelling, scholar Eugene Arva, also argued that examining traumatic imagination through literature one can find an avenue of catharsis through the expression of creative and emotional content.[23]

A servant leader that used language and imagination to bring awareness of the social injustices against indigenous children in the residential

20. Francis, "Meeting with Indigenous Peoples," para. 6.
21. Eisner, "Educating the Whole Person," 38–39.
22. See Cioci, "Mural Project," 2020.
23. See Arva, *Traumatic Imagination*.

schools to the forefront of the national consciousness was Canadian musician and poet, Gord Downie. After reading Ian Adams's article on the death of Chanie Wenjack, Downie was inspired to use his gift of language and imagination to bring awareness of the experiences of indigenous children through a new medium, through a graphic novel including lyrics and music. Downie stated that since learning about Chanie through the lens of Adams's article:

> Chanie haunts me. His story is Canada's story. This is about Canada. We are not the country we thought we were. History will be re-written. . . . The next hundred years are going to be painful as we come to know Chanie Wenjack and thousands like him—as we find out about ourselves, about all of us—but only when we do can we truly call ourselves, "Canada"[24]

Gord Downie and Jeff Lamire used the emotional combination of art and poetry as a frame to address the national genocide of First Nations trauma within the Canadian residential school system.[25] After seeking appropriate approval from Chanie's sisters to tell their brother's story he creatively used Adams's 1967 article of the plague of residential schools as inspiration for his album and graphic novel. The musical story of this horrific experience conveys feelings of isolation and desperation that resonate with anyone who has ever been treated as an outcast or has become isolated because of an imposed stigma. Since its release, the Juno Award winning album and graphic novel has been used in classroom curriculums across Canada to educate and give voice to the national tragedy of the residential school history.[26] "Graphic novels . . . reflect a full range of 21st century approaches to communication and arts—integrated storytelling . . . encouraging all students to engage with heavy topics that can generate empathy through multimedia storytelling across humanity courses."[27]

The spirit of Downie and Lamire's storytelling stands as a witness for the dignity of the human person, especially those maligned and isolated by a deep-seeded national prejudice. Through the development of the Downie/Wenjack Fund, and its Legacy Schools Program, *Secret Path* has illustrated that the arts can and should be used as a bridge to seek reconciliation from

---

24. Barclay, *Never-Ending Present*, 369.
25. See Downie and Lamire, *Secret Path*.
26. See Ontario Institute for Studies in Education, "Resources for Teachers"; and Simmons, "Storytelling Resources."
27. Attwood and Gerber, "Comic Books and Graphic Novels," 182.

The Tenants of Truth and Reconciliation: Canada

past national tragedies and injustice, but more so to serve as a bridge for the future of inclusion and diversity especially for populations who have suffered trauma and have no option for a voice in dominant culture.

Although not in the context of arts and music, there have been other advocates in the entertainment industry, such as athletics that have used their voice to raise awareness of the lasting presence of residential schools on the indigenous peoples. Former National Hockey League professional for the Vancouver Canuck, Gino Odjick, who was raised on the Algonquin reserve in Quebec, chose to play throughout his career with the number 29 on his jersey in remembrance of his father's residential school identification number. Odjick also took upon himself the responsibility to represent his indigenous community. He once stated:

> It also means the world to me that my hockey career gave me a chance to open doors for kids in [the] Aboriginal community. I was just a little old Indian boy from the rez. If I could do it, so could they.[28]

The use of language and imagination offer opportunities to create binding memories so that we stay vigilant that future injustices do not occur similarly in the future. It takes one purposeful step at a time to lay the groundwork to build trust for more unity instead of division, in a national identity. It is important to take the time to listen attentive to the language used in stories and listen deeply to the silence present in the missing voices from the past injustices. As Pope Francis included during his apology to the First Nations of Canada:

> On this first step of my journey, I have wanted to make space for memory. Here, today, I am with you to recall the past, to grieve with you, to bow our heads together in silence and to pray before the graves. Let us allow these moments of silence to help us interiorize our pain. Silence.[29]

Lessons in Servant Leadership

- **Creatively Use Language and Imagination:** Servant leaders demonstrate a creative expansion beyond previous ideologies or solutions. This can cause advocates to break-away from the complacent

28. Pawson, "Gino Odjick," para. 14.
29. Francis, "Meeting with Indigenous Peoples," para. 12.

perspectives and seek new and creative avenues for dialogue. It is essential for servant leaders to be adapt to new and emerging problems and to address them with imaginative and diverse solutions.

- **Deliberately Get to Know the Meaning of Traditional Language and Symbols:** Servant leaders need to deliberately recognize and understand the importance of traditional symbols within culture; how those symbols are interpreted and what they mean outside of the culture. It is important for a leader to learn and appreciate the deeper cultural language and symbols of those they serve. Like learning a new language, servant leaders should be open to being corrected and revised with humility when misinterpreting meaning in traditional language or symbols.

- **Use Storytelling Methods to Establish Dialogue:** Servant leaders should be open to the method of storytelling to establish dialogue. Instead of interpreting stories as merely one individual's opinion or perspective of events, it is important to remember that the power of storytelling is that it is a method to appreciate and understand the experience of the other.

For Further Reflection

- **Creatively Use Language and Imagination:** Read, listen, and reflect upon Gord Downie and Jeff Lamire's graphic novel and album, *Secret Path* (2016). How did Downie's lyrics and music create a sonic space to understand the isolation and suffering of the residential school system. How does the coloring of the graphic novel contrast the experience of connection and emptiness throughout the story? In what way do you find a connection with Chanie as you read/listened to the story? Explain.

- **Deliberately Get to Know the Meaning of Traditional Language and Symbols:** Take time to research a culture you are unfamiliar with. What similarities exist between your experiences and the experiences of the culture you chose? What are some of the differences that traditionally define the culture you chose and your own culture? What did you learn from your investigation into that culture that might offer new insights into your own cultural experiences? Explain.

The Tenants of Truth and Reconciliation: Canada

- **Use Storytelling Methods to Establish Dialogue:** Read and reflect on a selection of short stories from Leanna Simpson's *The Gift is in the Making: Anishinaabeg Stories* (2013) or Charles Larson's *Under African Skies* (1997). How did the author establish a dialogue with the reader through the chosen stories? What did you learn about the culture surrounding the topic presented through the short stories? How might reading the literature from another culture help you better appreciate the collective vision of that culture's hopes and dreams for the future? Explain.

10

Racism

A Call for Truth in America

What we need in the United States is not division; what we need in the United States is not hatred; what we need in the United States is not violence or lawlessness; but love and wisdom, and compassion toward one another, and a feeling of justice toward those who still suffer within our country, whether they be white or they be black.[1]

THIS QUOTATION WAS OFFERED by Senator Robert Kennedy during remarks at a stop in Indianapolis, Indiana, on April 4, 1968, while he was in the process of campaigning for the nominee seat as the Democratic candidate for the United States presidential election. Before arriving in Indianapolis, Kennedy received the tragic news that Civil Rights leader Martin Luther King Jr. had been assassinated, and was pronounced dead earlier that day. Although Kennedy had received this news, the primarily African-American audience waiting for him to stop in Indianapolis had not yet been informed or heard about King's death. With the foresight of a servant leader, Kennedy was calm and transparent delivering the tragic news to the awaiting crowd. Remembering the work and hopes of Dr. King, Kennedy laid a message for a nonviolent response to the violence of the murder. Also, in one of the few acknowledgments of his own brother's assassination, Kennedy became

---

1. Kennedy, "On the Assassination," para. 7.

deeply personal and offered an intimate reminder of this connection with the feeling in his audience:

> For those of you who are black and are tempted to be filled with hatred and distrust at the injustice of such an act, against all white people, I can only say that I feel in my own heart the same kind of feeling. I had a member of my family killed, but he was killed by a white man.[2]

The roughly five-minute speech perfectly encapsulated his platform without intending to or ever referring to his campaign—it was a raw moment of grief shared with the audience, and the country. In those few moments, Kennedy embodied the message of a leader who was willing to mourning and serve the needs of the American people, and placing his own needs on hold.

Leadership aimed at systematic change does not occur in one moment alone. There are a connection of moments that set the stage for systematic change. American history has been wrought with stories of the violations of human dignity, as well as moments where individuals stood up to racial injustices as a catalyst for social change. Although the twentieth-century included significant change in race relations through the resistance and suffering of the Civil Rights movement, there remains many more stories to be shared to examine ways in which the current divide and ideologies in the America consciousness can aim toward more unitive future, rather than toward one of further division.

The purpose of this chapter is not to rehash the past, and open old wounds by recalling the horrific injustice and ill treatment of American citizens, but rather to examine the exemplary moments of foresight of mentors and leaders that may have been overlooked in the progression of striving for racial unity and the recognition of human dignity of all. The examples of leadership examined and included in this chapter did not occur in a vacuum, they had back stories that created the circumstances and desire for change. Although I do not have the opportunity to trace the influences of all of these decisions, I hope that you may have the opportunity to further investigate these examples, and similar ones, to mine the wisdom present from those who engaged the challenges of their time. I would also like to remind the reader that these advocates were not often received well or universally accepted at the time of the event. Hopefully, with the passing of time there is

---

2. Kennedy, "On the Assassination," para. 5.

more of an opportunity to reflect and assess the importance of story-telling from multiple perspectives instead of one primary historical lens.

Servant-Leadership Lens: Possessing Foresight

Another tenet included in Greenleaf's model of servant leadership is the quality of possessing foresight;[3] to have an inclination or intuition of the needs of the future from the wisdom of past experiences. Making decisions based on foresight can be a challenge as it is not guaranteed that the intuition of proposed action for the future is going to have the best results in the moment. The trait of foresight is often only appreciated when seen through the reflection on the past. Decisions based on foresight can cause alarm or dissonance as the common perception of the time may not appreciate the decision or direction of the leader who may challenge the expectations or perceptions of the majority. Conversely, it can be easy to demonize leaders of the past who did not possess foresight after the lack of response to significant historical events, or when further knowledge about an event is acquired over time. The old adage states that hindsight is 20/20; foresight on the other hand is not as clear. The failure, or refusal, of a leader of the past to respond with foresight to challenges, issues, or societal injustices of their day may later be held under great scrutiny through the lens of future generations and as a failure to respond ethically in the moment, due to holding the past accountable to the mindset of contemporary ethical perspectives.[4]

Philip: A Servant-Leader Possessing Foresight in His Ministry

One example of foresight illustrated in Scripture is a brief passage in Acts of the Apostles, an account of the development of early Christian ministry and proclamation. As the Apostles start spreading the message of their rabbi, and Messiah, the leaders of the new movement are imprisoned, and then later put to death, by the Jewish authorities of the time (Acts 5:17—8:3)

Philip, one of seven disciples chosen to serve the community in the role of deacon (Acts 6:1–15), a dedicated ministry to the poor, was on the road from Jerusalem to Gaza when he encountered an Ethiopian eunuch, a court official of Candace the Queen of the Ethiopians (Acts 8:28–39).

---

3. See Northouse, *Leadership*, 230.
4. See Barling, *Science of Leadership*, 127–29; and Greenleaf, *Servant Leadership*, 39.

Racism

Philip found that although the eunuch was reading the prophet Isaiah he struggled to discern its meaning. Although eunuchs and foreigners were seen as outcasts, during the culture of that time, Philip approached and started to explained the text to him when he asked. Throughout their exegetical journey of the text, the eunuch saw a body of water on the side of the road and immediately sought baptism, and was he baptized by Philip.

This brief passage of Scripture offers an important reflection on the work of the servant leader Philip. Not only was Philip called to interpret and open the depths of the narrative story of the prophecy of Isaiah, much like the Scripture was opened in the heart of the disciples on the road to Emmaus (Luke 24:13–35), but Philip also had the foresight to baptize the Ethiopian upon his request. This action served as part of the momentum and shift away from merely a message conveyed to a Jewish audience to one that the included individuals outside of the Jewish law. It also set the course of the later evolution from the movement being recognized as sect within Judaism to a distinct way of worshipping God.

Although Scripture scholars continue to debate if the Ethiopian eunuch was an Essene, Gentile, or Jewish, this account does offer a concrete example of an outcast of the time being purposefully incorporated into the Christian community through baptism; and likely the first black individual included into the Christian faith.[5] The foresight of Philip within that moment offers an example of a servant leader who made a deliberate and decisive act of inclusion instead of the traditional Jewish stance of exclusion of an eunuch or outsider who is included in the rituals of the community (Deut 23:1).

The Challenge

The contribution and inclusion of the black American voice in policy and change began to slowly evolve in the twentieth-century. Although there were laws and limitations still firmly in place, in specific regions of the country as well as unwritten customs and policies, more and more advocates recognized and supported the dignity of humanity as a whole, instead of the racial divide that existed throughout the nation. To distance from the harmful stereotypes perpetuated in previous generations civil rights activists continued to push remaining racial barriers placed in the fields of business, education,

---

5. Davis, *History of Black Catholics*, 4.

sciences, and the arts, as the examples of Booker T. Washington, W. E. B. Dubois, and Frederick Douglass had previously accomplished.

> The "race men and women" of the late nineteenth and early twentieth century sought to advance a "politics of responsibility," whereby the personal identities and behaviors of individual African Americans were subsumed under a collective identity of strength. Respectability demanded that every individual in the black community assume responsibility for behavioral self-regulation and self-improvement along moral, educational, and economic lines. The goal was to distance oneself as far as possible from images perpetuated by racist stereotypes."[6]

The following sections offer just a few examples of relationships that displayed foresight in their respective fields to create dialogue and cross racial lines that continued to isolate and segregate inclusion in certain professions and government representation in the 1930s and early 1940s.

Alfred Blalock and Vivien Thomas

Vivien Thomas was a pioneer researcher and cardiac surgeon who broke the color line in the field of American science and research. In 1930, Thomas began a career as a surgical research assistant to Alfred Blalock, at Vanderbilt University. Although Thomas's classification and pay rank, defined by the University, was labelled as a janitor, Blalock had the foresight to appreciate Thomas's work and allow the young assistant be involved in more than menial aspects of surgeries and to even set up surgeries on his own. The data collected from Thomas's work with Blalock on the causes of hemorrhagic shock was used throughout the Second World War, contributing to life saving medical care of countless soldiers.

In 1940, with the recognized success of Blalock's work throughout the medical community, Blalock was invited to the position of Chief of Surgery at John Hopkins. Blalock requested that Thomas be allowed to come with him to the new position at John Hopkins.[7] In 1945, Blalock, Thomas, along with colleague Helen Taussig, successfully created and demonstrated a shunt procedure to increase blood flow to the lungs of a baby to resolve the condition of blue baby syndrome. This procedure has been recognized as the Blalock-Taussig shunt. There has been recent movements to advocate for the

---

6. Walker-Barnes, *Too Heavy a Yoke*, 95.
7. See Thomas, *Pioneering Research*.

inclusion of Thomas's name included in the procedure by scholars.[8] Thomas continued his career at John Hopkins serving a supervisor of the surgery laboratories for over thirty years, and held in reverence by the University.

Eleanor Roosevelt, Mary McLeod Bethune, and the NAACP

With the Second World War, the 1940s brought a dynamic shift to the forefront of the American consciousness as much of the traditional workforce left the country to serve in the effort of global resistance in the conflict that engulfed Europe. The role of citizens who were commonly marginalized up to that point in history was reexamined, not out of a moral conviction, but out of necessity so that the infrastructure of the American life would remain intact as much as possible.

Although the Presidential family were consumed with the war abroad, the Roosevelts were also becoming more and more aware of the racial issues plaguing America, here at home. "Eleanor Roosevelt was awakened to the brutalities of American racism through Mary McLeod Bethune—the educator. . . . The First Lady herself credited the charismatic Bethune with forcing her to confront the depths of her own prejudice."[9] Mary McLeod Bethune was an activist, humanitarian, and philanthropist. She served as an adviser for the Roosevelts on the Black Cabinet, and became the only African American woman to serve on the US delegation for the charter of the United Nations. Through her association with Eleanor Roosevelt, Bethune opened the door for countless African-Americans after her.

Not only was the ear of the President tuned to the work of Bethune, but federal policies throughout the country effecting racial discrimination were starting to shift through the influence of NAACP leaders. A. Philip Randolph and Walter White fought to lobby to ban racial discrimination in the work place throughout the nation. Through threats to march on the nation's capital and through additional pressure from the Eleanor Roosevelt on "June 25, 1941, the president issued the ban in the form of an executive order, the Negro newspapers likened it to the Emancipation Proclamation, freeing the blacks from economic slavery as Lincoln had freed us from physical slavery."[10]

---

8. See Blake, "Change the Name."
9. Watts, *Black Cabinet*, 186.
10. Roundtree, *Mighty Justice*, 43.

A Call for Change

By the end of the 1940s representation and racial changes occurred in more highly visible industries, such as athletics and film. Breaking the racial lines in these fields, prejudices and stereotypes surrounding the weaknesses or the inabilities of black Americans compared to white Americans were shown to be myths.

Branch Rickey and Jackie Robinson

Since 1903, Branch Rickey, major league baseball player and manager, desired to better the experience and opportunities for black baseball players in America. Rickey remained aware of the racial disparities between his players through an incident with one of his players that made him become an advocate for black athletes' access to major league baseball. During his first college coaching experience Rickey traveled with his team to play at Notre Dame University in South Bend, Indiana. When Rickey registered his team with the Oliver Hotel, the clerk would not allow the one black player, Charles Thomas, to register in the hotel. Rickey convinced the clerk to allow Thomas the use a cot and sleep in the room with the coaches. While Rickey was completing the documentation, Thomas went to the room. As the coaches arrived to the room Rickey recounted that they saw:

> Thomas broken down sobbing, scratching at his skin as if he wanted to forcibly remove the stain of its color. "I never felt so helpless in my life," Rickey remembered to Arthur Mann. Though not yet well read on the subject of racial discrimination, Rickey instinctively empathized with Thomas's pain of rejection."[11]

Rickey was known to repeat the story of Thomas often, especially when challenging the hard-pressed racial line of Major League Baseball. Being a devoted Christian, he also connected the experience as a direct analogy to the Biblical story of the first Christmas in Bethlehem, where there was no room in the inn.[12]

In the 1940s, when Rickey became the General Manager of the Brooklyn Dodgers, he was the only general manager willing to have the foresight to break the unwritten color line in Major League Baseball. Rickey was

---

11. Lowenfish, *Branch Rickey*, 23.
12. Kahn, *Rickey & Robinson*, 48.

interested in that prospect with Jackie Robinson, and invited him to Brooklyn. Robinson was also excited about the prospects of playing the in major league. Through the barrage of questions and challenges from Branch Rickey, Robinson stood his ground to Rickey's scenarios. It is recorded that during the interview Rickey stated:

> "I know you're a good ballplayer. . . . What I don't know is whether you have the guts." When physically challenged Robinson always was quick to defend his manhood. He told Rickey that he wasn't afraid of anybody of anything on a playing field. Rickey interrupted. "I'm looking for a ball player with guts enough not to fight back."[13]

Breaking the color line came at great cost for Robinson and the Dodgers, as several players refused to play on a team with Robinson, and were traded. The Captain of the Dodgers, Pee Wee Reese, recalled that as a player on Robinson's team in those years that:

> You'd hear a lot of insults from the opposing benches during the games, guys called him thing like "n*****" and "watermelon eater," trying to rile him up. But that was when Jackie Robinson started to turn the tables. You saw how he stood there at the plate and dared them to hit him with the ball, and you began to put yourself in his shoes. You'd think of yourself trying to break into the black leagues, maybe, and what it would be like—and I know that I couldn't have done it. In a word, he was winning respect.[14]

Even after their profession careers had concluded in the major leagues, both Rickey and Robinson continued to remain advocates for equal access and equal rights. In 1956, Rickey challenged and warned the American society, not just about the lack of including athletes of color, but society in general for its lack of progress in equal rights no matter what the race someone may be:

> [O]nce the Negroes organize effectively in certain areas in this country, we must be prepared to see political control pass locally to colored citizens. If that day comes, it would be too much to expect all Negroes to forgive and to forget the record of the past one hundred years. I am afraid the white man will justly reap as he has sown. How long will the white citizens of this country go on ignoring the agony of the Negro? How long will he be tempted

---

13. Lowenfish, *Branch Rickey*, 375.
14. Monteleone, *Branch Rickey's Little Blue Book*, 87.

to look elsewhere for equal rights—not only civil, political, and educational rights—but just simple human rights?[15]

Robinson also continued to tirelessly advocate for the black voices to be present at the administrative and decision-making level of professional baseball, and in the community. Most notably he supported Curt Flood, when Flood fought and compared the reserve clause in baseball as a human commodity and modern form of slavery.[16] At the 1972 World Series, on the twenty-fifth anniversary of his first year in baseball, Robinson concluded his remarks that with all of the progress of players in baseball, he would be "tremendous more pleased, and more proud, when I look at that third baseball coaching line one day and see a black face managing in baseball."[17]

Walt Disney and James Baskett

Another example of foresight that occurred in the 1940s involved one of the most contentious and controversial Disney movies ever made, *Song of the South* (1946), a live-action/animated film. As with many Walt Disney films, he was interested in taking stories of the American folklore and offering them new life through movie adaptations. Disney was interested in acquiring the rights for the Uncle Remus stories, written by Joel Chandler Harris, as early as the 1930s. By 1939 Disney was able to negotiate with the Harris family and ultimately acquired the rights to create a film. Filming began in 1944 and it was ready for release by 1946.

The title character of Uncle Remis, as well as the voices of Brer Fox and Brer Rabbit, were played by actor, James Baskett (1904–1948). Baskett was a musician who previously worked with in the dance and jazz scene with musicians like Bill Robinson (Mr. Bojangles) and Louis Armstrong. He also had previous acting experience with in the animated Disney film *Dumbo* and feature films like the *African Queen*. Baskett masterfully recorded the classic song "Zip-a-Dee-Doo-Dah" from the film, *Song of the South*, which won the Academy Award for best original song.[18]

---

15. Monteleone, *Branch Rickey's Little Blue Book*, 90.
16. See Ward and Burns, "Inning 6."
17. See Robinson, "Jackie Robinson," 7:56–8:04.
18. That was only the second time that a Disney song received that distinction. The first Disney song to win the Academy Award for best original song was "When you Wish Upon A Star" in 1940.

Racism

Baskett's role in Disney's *Song of the South* also opened wide the doors for black actors ever-after. It was the first dramatic role where the lead actor was a black actor; up to that time when a black actor was a lead actor in a film it was only in a comedic context. When the film was released in 1946, though, Baskett was unable to attend its premier in Atlanta due do the segregation laws still preset at the time in the South. But in March 1948, through the petition of Walt Disney, Baskett received a special "honorary" Academy award for his portrayal of Uncle Remis.[19] This was the first time in the history of the Academy of Motion Pictures that an Academy Award had been given to a black male performer.

The controversial history and the portrayal of the characters in the film have led to the cancellation of distribution or showing of the film since the 1980s. Even Disney entertainment rides associated with the film have been removed and closed. Splash Mountain, a favorite ride in Disneyland, was closed in January 2023, along with the removal of the song 'Zip-a-Dee-Doo-Dah' from the Disney playlist due to its connections with negative racial stereotypes of the film. With the removal of the film and song, the question remains if history will remember the role Disney and Baskett served in opening the doors of acknowledgement for male Black actors in Hollywood in the 1940s?

At the Crossroads

The escalation and violence of American racism was brought to the national forefront as terroristic attacks involved the graphic and racial motivated victimization and death of children. In 1955, a fourteen-year-old boy from Chicago, Emmitt Till was visiting relatives in Mississippi when an altercation at a convenience store with the daughter of the white owner escalated to a racial motivated murder. The exact specifics of the situation still remain unclear, but what is clear is that Till was abducted in the early morning of August 28, 1955, and lynched because of the altercation in the store. Although there was a call for justice for the murder, the perpetrators were never held accountable, as the jury had ruled in favor of not guilty. Later the murders of Till, knowing that they could not be trial again for the same crime, sold their confession of the complete account of the murder to *LOOK* Magazine.[20]

19. See Mitchell, "Indianapolis Actor."
20. See Huie, "Shocking Story."

Truth and Reconciliation

Little Rock Integration and Louis Armstrong

In 1957, during the integration of schools in Little Rock, Arkansas, the struggle of nine black youth for racial integration came to the center stage of the nation, as the National Guard were brought to the state to block children from entering school. The situation caught the attention of musician, Louis Armstrong, and changed his consistent neutral stance on advocating for civil rights through his role as a musician and entertainer.

Armstrong often declared that he was a non-political musician, which was taken with hostility by other black musicians in the 1940s and 1950s, who were overtly political using the arts for their mode for advocacy. While preparing for a concert in Grand Fork, North Dakota during September 1957, Armstrong was watching the national coverage of the blockade by Governor Orval Faubus of Arkansas, of the nine students from attending Central high school. As the students were attempting to enter the school, crowds of whites jeered and spit in the face of the black teenagers.

This act of vileness effected Armstrong, and led him to contact a local reporter and offer a heated interview to the young reporter where he released a litany of harsh and direct criticisms of the cowardness of President Eisenhower, Governor Faubus, and the entire governmental structure that allowed such a situation to occur; an action unprecedented from America's musical ambassador. Not only did the newspaper editor call Armstrong to confirm the quote, but he also double checked to ensure that Armstrong was clear in his meaning by asking him to sign a document to verify the quotation. While signing the document, and confirming the quotation, Armstrong stated: "That's just fine. Don't take nothin' out of that story. That's just what I said and still say."[21] The effect of the direct challenge from an entertainer who had been so closely identified with the nation as America's jazz ambassador to the world, was enormous in public opinion against the officials, as "the consensus of gossip is that Eisenhower never forgive [Armstrong]."[22] As the story broke and captured the attention of the media, Armstrong stated: "You don't pose, never, that's the last thing you do . . . because the minute you pose you're through as a jazzman. Jazz is only what you are."[23]

---

21. Jones and Chilton, *Louis*, 178.
22. Jones and Chilton, *Louis*, 178.
23. Jones and Chilton, *Louis*, 179.

Racism

Birmingham Bombing and Martin Luther King Jr.

As the leader of the Southern Christian Leadership Conference (SCLC) in 1963, Martin Luther King Jr. felt the responsibility to witness through a leadership of service, in his thought and action. His words galvanized the movement of Civil Rights through his powerful skill of oratory. Throughout April and May of 1963, the dedication and sacrifice of the SCLC led by Dr. King held demonstrations, marches, sit-ins, as well as experienced personal injury and incarcerations campaigning for the acknowledgment of racial equality in the city of Birmingham, Alabama, which stood as a witness to the country at a crux between nonviolence resistance and tangible violent racial terrorism.

It was not only the adults who campaigned, but the children of Birmingham also became witnesses. Clayborne Carson's edited autobiography of Dr. King states that on the second of May King recalled: "more than a thousand young people demonstrated and went to jail."[24] Two days later, Commissioner Bull Connor came down in a full force of violence upon the nonviolent resistors with clubs, firehoses, and police dogs. King recalled "this was the time of our greatest stress, and the courage and conviction of these students and adults made it our finest hour. We did not fight back, but we did not turn back."[25] Although a negotiation was finally reached to desegregate and remove signs of separation throughout the city, change did not affect all hearts. Violence continued to ensue through the form of terroristic bombing in white racist retaliation.

Through the trials and tribulations of racial tension, Dr. King culminated an address to the country through an oration of his dream on August 16, 1963, during the march on Washington, DC. There he elicits in memory the struggle earlier in the year in Alabama.

> I have a dream that one day down in Alabama with its vicious racists, with its governor having his lips dripping with the words of interposition and nullification, one day right down in Alabama little Black boys and Black girls will be able to join hands with little white boys and white girls as sisters and brothers. I have a dream today![26]

Roughly a month after the march on Washington, four children became victims of a racist and terrorist bomb attack at the 16th Street Baptist

---

24. Carson, *Autobiography*, 208.
25. Carson, *Autobiography*, 209.
26. Carson, *Autobiography*, 226.

Church on September 15, 1963: Addie Mae Collins, Cynthia Wesley, Carole Robertson, and Carol Denise McNair.[27] King returned to Birmingham, Alabama, and offered the eulogy at the combined funeral of three of the children. This egregious act shook the nation and opened many eyes of the passive bystanders to the horrors experienced for the struggle of Civil Rights.

In the midst of the prejudice and disregard of human life, King still believed and passionately called for hope; hope for redemption in the human heart. He did not commit to a separation between the moral right of the actions of blacks and whites, but saw racism as a disease that needed to be healed within the heart of all human beings, black and white. King's eulogy begins:

> These children—unoffending, innocent, and beautiful—were the victims of one of the most vicious, heinous crimes ever perpetrated against humanity.[28]

In the midst of such violence, King stilled called for a non-violent alternative that was sustained by the belief that equality must be a mutuality of leadership that recognized a unity of the races.

Dovey Johnson Roundtree, American civil rights activist and attorney, admitted throughout the 1960s that it was a continual challenge to trust, that not only would be living conditions improve for racial minorities in America, but also that those who advocated to help with such change in the social structure of America were actually interested in working to resolve the social and racial issues in the country.

> Those of us who thought we'd seen southern hatred and violence peak with the Freedom Riders in the summer of 1961, and then again in the summer of 1963 during Dr. King's Birmingham Campaign, wondered in the spring of 1965 where it would all end, what price would finally have to be paid before the demon spent itself and we could claim what was rightfully ours, in peace. Such times breed a particular kind of distrust and suspicion even among well-meaning people."[29]

---

27. See Huie, "Death of an Innocent."
28. Carson, *Autobiography*, 231.
29. Roundtree, *Mighty Justice*, 202.

Racism

Learning from Global Witnesses of Leadership

As the twentieth-century continued, and the challenge of racial injustices in American culture continued after the death of Martin Luther King Jr. and Malcolm X, other individuals became the voice of racial change. One of the most animated was the boxing legend and religious convert to Islam, Muhammad Ali. Ali used his bravado and celebrity to bring awareness to the injustices perpetrated by the social structure throughout the nation. Growing up as a resident of Louisville, Kentucky, Ali was familiar with the unjust racial treatment found in urban life still present in the Southern states of the nation.

In his memoir, *The Greatest*, he recalled that even after he won a gold medal on behalf of his country, his return was empty as the racial issues remained the same. After being denied service at a restaurant in his hometown, because of the color of his skin, Ali decided that the symbol of his accomplishments that was so tied to the racial divide of his country, and remained a consistent reminder of his lack of equality, needed to have no more of a hold over his life. "The Olympic medal had been the most precious thing that had ever come to me. I worshiped it. It was proof of performance, status, a symbol of belonging, of being a part of a team, a country, a world."[30] But earning it still did not change the treatment he received in restaurant or by the local police officers. Ali wrote:

> So what I remember most about the summer of 1960 is not the hero welcome, the celebrations, the Police Chief, the Mayor, the Governor, or even the ten Louisville millionaires, but that night when I stood on the Jefferson County Bridge and threw my Olympic Gold Medal down to the bottom of the Ohio River."[31]

Through his words and actions Ali continued to challenge injustice with foresight, not allowing others to control him. When he was drafted for the Vietnam War, he refused on religious grounds and was convicted of dodging the draft. He was also stripped of his heavyweight title. Ali remained true and steadfast to his conscience in the midst of the challenges of losing the honors bestowed on him in the media and his sport. In 1971, the Supreme Court overturned Ali's conviction. He continued to promote

---

30. Ali and Durham, *Greatest*, 77.
31. Ali and Durham, *Greatest*, 59.

nonviolence and Civil Rights throughout the remained of his life.[32] During his funeral, comedian and friend, Billy Crystal stated:

> He [Ali] was a tremendous bolt of lightning, created by Mother Nature out of thin air; a fantastic combination of power and beauty.... Muhammad Ali struck us in the middle of America's darkest night in the heart of its most threatening gathering storm. His power toppled the mightiest of foes and his intense light shined on America, and we were able to see clearly injustice, inequality, poverty, pride, self-realization, courage, laughter, love, joy, and religious freedom for all. Ali forced us to take a look at ourselves.[33]

Similar to other theologians and Civil Rights activists, like John Paul II and Mandela[34], Thomas Merton also recognized and appreciated the analogy of the discipline involved with athletics and spirituality: "Souls are like athletes, that need opportunity worthy of them, if they are to be tried and extended and pushed to their full use of their powers, and rewarded according to their capacity."[35]

Lessons in Servant Leadership

- **Be Keenly Aware and Develop Foresight:** Servant leaders remain keenly aware and develop foresight from the wisdom of the past to assist in decision making for the future. They follow their intuition to make decisions that may not be appreciated or completely understood at the time. Leaders who serve others focus on how future outcomes will affect those they serve.

- **Keep a Tenacious Focus for Change:** In the midst of challenge and opposition, servant leaders must remain focused on the needs of the community. This may result in the leader having to stay tenacious for change to better the live experiences of those they serve.

- **Remain Strong and Courageous when Opposed:** Servant leaders will develop a disciplined sense of courage in the face of opposition. Many decisions to serve others will result in a witness for greater change and will demand a sense of courage and conviction to be able to persevere.

---

32. See Gorsevski and Butterworth, "Muhammad Ali's Fighting Words."
33. ABC News, "Muhammad Ali Funeral," 11:59–12:50.
34. See Bestall, "16th Man"; and John Paul II, "Homily."
35. Merton, *Seven Storey Mountain*, 92.

For Further Reflection

- **Be Keenly Aware and Develop Foresight:** Listen and read the lyrics of the following songs: Bob Dylan's "The Times They are A-Changing" (1964), Grandmaster Flash and the Furious Five's "The Message" (1982), Peter Mulvey's "Smell the Future" (1995), and/or Lennie Gallant's "Lifeline" (1997). In what ways did the composer illustrate foresight through the lyrics throughout the topic of the song? How might the lyrics of these, and similar, songs offer an opportunity to dialogue about societal changes in the past, for the future?

- **Keep a Tenacious Focus for Change:** Many advocates and servant leaders from the twentieth-century created new groups or avenues for communication to unite their movements, through the use of periodicals or magazines to address issues not previously discussed in traditional literature or professional associations. How has the growth of the internet and social media allowed new communications for advocacy groups to emerge and develop? What role can technology play within servant led advocacy leadership in the twenty-first century?

- **Remain Strong and Courageous when Opposed:** Explore and examine moments of servant leadership that offered an example of courage in the face of global issues of injustice (i.e. the Greensboro sit-in, Cesar Chavez's hunger strike, the lone protester in front of the tank at Tiananmen Square . . .) Through what ways did their action and courage bear witness to an injustice? Explain.

11

Genocide

A Call for Reconciliation in America

Reconciliation is an ancient imperative. We can sustain the environment, the resources, the cultures, the rituals, and the ceremonies of us all. This is a well of rich history—of practice and tradition, values and ethics. And all we've got to do is open the door to all of those sources of knowledge, recognizing our value in all the different ways that we live.[1]

IN HER BOOK LEADING *with Cultural Humility,* Lyna Nyamwaya, registered nurse and Diversity, Equity, Inclusion, and Belonging expert offered: "*humility* is not *humiliation.* Humility is not discrediting. Pausing to listen to your followers, acknowledging that you do not know everything, and then asking to learn is essential in building trust in leadership."[2] This trust building process requires acceptance and empathy, especially when entering the intimate presence of the stories and testimonies from individuals of trauma. South African professor, T. I. Nzimakwe, explained that the communal concept of *ubuntu* offers an inherent model of acceptance and empathy which laid the cultural foundation of the South African Truth and Reconciliation Commission truth-telling sessions:

---

1. Wakas, *Namwayut,* 96.
2. Nyamwaya, *Leading with Cultural Humility,* 127–28.

> It seems that thinkers take the African family as a model for a wider kinship system. This interpersonal character of Ubuntu is, according to scholars, the source for many of the distinctive virtues such as patience, hospitality, loyalty, respect, sociability, liveliness, health, endurance, sympathy and magnificence.[3]

The Truth and Reconciliation Commission process is predicated not just on the opportunity to offer witness of truth through a story-telling experience, but also the initial steps toward reconciliation that is found through the listening with empathy of the truth being shared and spoken aloud. Through the monologic culture common place in social media environments there is often little room for dedicated listening and opportunity to create a dialogue built on trust and rooted in relationship. Nyamwaya's quotation and manuscript is a reminder of the need for servant leaders to approach others with humility and a vigilant reminder of the fragility present in the sharing and truth-telling process, which is at the heart of Truth and Reconciliation proceedings. It also serves as a warning about how tenuous the bond can be in restorative justice environments if there is a lack of acceptance and empathy between the participants involved.

To learn from the stories of others, it is essential then to listen with a posture of acceptance and empathy and to encounter the other through the dialogic narrative. When reflecting on the hopeful future for his congregation and nation, through the reconciliation process from genocide in his country of Rwanda, Rev. Ubald Rugirangoga offered the insight that "The past is never entirely forgotten, but there is a new sense of purpose and unity."[4] It should also be remembered, that Gord Downie similarly challenged that through the recognition of the horrors of the residential schools, Canada too will need to face its own marred past. Although it will take time, decades or centuries, of purposeful awareness to accept, learn, and offer empathy for the injustices perpetuated in the past, that will never be forgotten, but hopefully the desire for a more united future will over shadow the darkness of the past.

Rugirangoga offers a cautionary reminder of the power and reach of America's international influence throughout the globe: "When darkness comes from America, it spreads all over the world—I like to think that if

---

3. Nzimakwe, "Practising *Ubuntu*," 33.
4. Rugirangoga, *Forgiveness Makes You Free*, 122.

light comes from America, that too will spread all over the world. . . . Light is coming from America, and that is good."[5]

Servant-Leadership Lens—Acceptance and Empathy

Servant leadership is exemplified through the tenets of acceptance and empathy. Leadership scholar, Peter Northouse explained the importance of empathy within servant leadership by indicating, "[e]mpathic servant leaders demonstrate that they truly understand what followers are thinking and feeling. When a servant leader shows empathy, it is confirming and validating for the follower. It makes the follower feel unique."[6]

These two aspects of servant leadership are extremely difficult perspectives to cultivate, as they both take much dedication, effort, and sacrifice to execute well. Acceptance is established in a holistic reception of the other. Beyond merely tolerating the other, acceptance extends a generosity and willingness to be open to the sacred presence and dignity of the other. Empathy also involves a dedicated openness to emotional connectivity to the joys, struggles, and needs of the other. Both acceptance and empathy can help create a trust in a relationship, but may also place the leader in a situation of vulnerability the others in a service-oriented relationship.

Abraham: A Servant of Empathic Sacrifice and Acceptance

The father of the Jewish faith, Abraham, demonstrated empathy and acceptance as a servant leader throughout the Scriptural text. There are several stories that can be used to illustrate these aspects of his character.

The first example of his empathy involved the relationship with his nephew, Lot. When Abraham traveled to a new land, led by the voice of God, he was accompanied by his family which included his nephew. Abraham and Lot eventually separated ways, while Abraham remained a nomad within the land while Lot decided to take his family to live in the near city of Sodom (Gen 13:5–13). When Abraham receives news that Lot has been captured during a sack of the city of Sodom, he was empathic to the situation of suffering of his nephew and led a successful rescue campaign (Gen 14:12–16). Abraham remained empathic to his nephew's plight when

---

5. Rugirangoga, *Forgiveness Makes You Free*, 122.
6. Northouse, *Leadership*, 229.

Genocide

he learns that the cities of Sodom and Gomorrah were to be destroyed. Abraham pleads with the three angelic visitors to spare the inhabitants of Sodom, if there were any faithful citizens that still remained in the city (Gen 18:16–33).

Abraham also demonstrated acceptance and faith in the will and narrative of God, even when he did completely not understand it during the moment. Abraham following the tradition of offering one's most prized possession to God, planning to sacrifice his promised son back to the Lord (Gen 22:1–19). Before Abraham completed the holocaust offering, a divine messenger intervened to stop the sacrifice. Through this unnerving story, Abraham came to the acceptance of a new perspective, namely that his son cannot be valued as just one of many of his possessions. Abraham needed to let go of his previous cultural perspectives that believed that children were objects, or pieces of property within the family, to evolve in his recognition that human dignity exists beyond material or objective value.

Benedictine monk and theologian, David Steindl-Rast offered an African proverb that may offer further insight of this process:

> The Ibo in Nigeria have a proverb that says, "It is the heart that gives, the fingers just let go." Giving is something only the heart can do. And this is true not only for gift-giving, but of all forms of giving. . . . The heart knows that all belongs to all.[7]

Steindl-Rast's proverb creates a new perspective on the power of encountering narrative and storytelling. The type of acceptance demanded in listening for understanding, similar to what Steindl-Rast indicates, is the process that allows the heart to listen to the heart of the other. This interconnectivity, which emanates from within a process of active listening in storytelling, creates a binding encounter between the listener and storyteller; and encourages the listener to metaphorically open their fingers to let go of their pre-conceived expectations or prejudices about the story and storyteller. This type of acceptance demands an uncomfortable sacrifice of one's ego to recognize that the story is not one of the listener's list of possessions, but that the listener is an engaged participant in the intimate gift-giving of the other. Only through such an intimate connection can a listener truly accept and become empathic to context of the narrative, and become in tune with the story teller to reach understanding.

---

7. Steindl-Rast, *Gratefulness*, 200.

The Challenge

Through American history the pushing and movement of the indigenous peoples from their land and onto reservations has created a cataclysmic effect still harming generations afterward. Between 1830 and 1850, the forced migration and displacement of roughly sixty thousand indigenous created a genocide to five tribes of indigenous: Cherokee, Creek, Seminole, Chickasaw, and Choctaw nations. This Trail of Tears, was instigated by the passage of the Indian Removal Act of 1830, a law that took possession of all indigenous land to the Mississippi and forced removal of indigenous peoples to the lands West of the Mississippi river. As the indigenous nations had not acclimated to the new climates, nor did they understand the land for proper harvesting exposure, and starvation occurred during and after the expulsion. There was also a high concentration of contracted diseases in the process that led to additional deaths in the process. A similar displacement and ethnic cleansing took place in the 1860s when the Navajo were forcibly removed and took the three-hundred-mile-long walk to a new reservation.

Although time and history has begun to acknowledge these, and similar, broken treaties, forced relocations, and genocidal events, the stories told of this time period for radio and television entertainment throughout the mid-twentieth century were completely different. The American stories continued to romanticize and perpetuate the glories of the West throughout radio dramas like *The Lone Ranger* and *Frontier Town*, where one Indian may serve as a bumbling but faithful side-kick to the hero. Although fictional, stories like the *The Lone Ranger* included episodes depicted historical indigenous as wild and dangerous, like Geronimo; lacking any contextual insight into the plight and fight for survival of the indigenous, but rather a focus on the villainous foe who attacked and murdered settlers and US soldiers.

A Call for Change

Randy Woodley, indigenous theologian and wisdom keeper, has argued that one of the greatest challenges in American society is that adults have lost the art of authentic storytelling and the growth that comes from the narrative relationship between listener and storyteller.

> Something terrible has happened in modern American society. In our effort to survive modernity and replace actual place with

> America *the* place, we have failed to develop real stories.... Story (or narrative) takes people to a different realm and a more relaxed frame of mind. Modern Americans seldom make time for story in our lives. We usually relegate story to children, even though science is now discovering that listening to stories has a healing effect on adults.[8]

Through the influence of the Enlightenment, contemporary American truth is based on some definable measurable evidence. These stories based on science need to be historically verifiable and resolve through one outcome. But real stories, as Woodley, indicate are not strictly verifiable by the physical senses, or based on a defined historical timeline, or have clear conclusions. Real stories are not reflections of just the past historical actions or events of one's life, but rather they bind the past, present, and future within its context. With these types of real stories, a historical timeline and verifiable contradictions to the narrative actions are not as significance, but rather the lesson and the relationship formed by the moment that binds the storyteller and listener are of the utmost importance. Richard Twiss summarized this concept best when he stated:

> Stories are people, people are their stories, and stories are alive. Traditionally, Native American stories are never fully explained. The power and influence of the story does not lie in the exact correctness of its telling, but in the life of the "teller" and in the "telling."[9]

With a better understanding of the importance and power of storytelling within First Nations culture, it must be acknowledged that the genocide perpetrated against the indigenous throughout North America included the loss of life, conquest of land, and also the elimination and silencing of their voice for the sharing and telling of stories; the mode through which the indigenous peoples communally shared their life with others. This elimination of indigenous culture began with the call to change the traditional structures of the indigenous tribal leadership and governance.

> [Pre-contact] governance structures weren't granted by any other government. At Confederation, Canada began its assimilation policy, consolidated the *Indian Act*, and moved to replace hereditary or traditional forms of governance with elected chiefs and councils. This action of replacing traditional leadership represents a direct imposition on self-governing communities that requires

---

8. Woodley, *Shalom*, 137.
9. Twiss, *Rescuing the Gospel*, 191.

them to elect a chief and council and forgo their traditional systems of governance.[10]

Chad "Corstassel" Smith, principal Chief of the Cherokee Nation from 1999–2011, offered additional insights that traditional forms of leadership selection within some indigenous communities were structured in a way where:

> Leaders are identified not by title but by example, through the attributes they exhibit. . . . By studying those who lead by example, we can learn to improve our own leadership, know what traits are desirable in recruiting staff, and understand the leadership development needs of an organization.[11]

At the Crossroads

One of the challenges of story-telling is where to begin. Indigenous theologian, Terry LeBlanc indicated that it is essential to go back to the very beginning and start the narrative from the perspective of creation stories, as it is from creation stories that our foundations are originally laid.

> Two myths concerning Native peoples have continued to play out over the centuries—one, the fairy tale of Eden; the other, the polar opposite lie of the godless heathen in the godless heathen land. Perhaps the most grievous in Western mission, the latter falsehood not only affronts the clear teaching of Scripture—that God exists in all times and in all places—but it makes a rude mockery of the Son's creative activity.[12]

From revisiting the stories of creation and examining them from a different perspective it can be illuminating to see how distortions have crept into the re-telling of the story over the millennia. Through exploring the stories of creation, a listener can open their attention to the focus of the goodness of creation, instead of focusing the on the divisions and labels that have defined and perpetuated that the only one group has the correct perspective of the story.

---

10. Joseph and Joseph, *Indigenous Relations*, 21–22.
11. Smith, *Leadership Lessons*, 36–37.
12. LeBlanc and LeBlanc, "NAIITS," 93.

> Truth telling from multiple perspectives not only reveals those situations where respect for human rights and dignity has been violated but creates space for dialogue about what concrete steps must be undertaken to rectify current policies and practices that may perpetuate similar harms into the future.[13]

Without the opportunities of multiple perspectives in storytelling the narrative can easily be modified and adapted to create another cycle of injustice, under a different name for future generations. As Joel Edward Goza similarly indicated:

> The foundation for keeping the illusion of racial progress in the colorblind age was the perpetuation of segregation. Though the color line proved every bit as entrenched as the days of segregation, the lack of explicitly racial laws formed the illusion of racial inclusivity.[14]

LeBlanc also offered this challenge and insight that without the time to develop empathy or acceptance of new perspectives cyclic ideologies can easily come back in new forms.

> [W]e find that the same ideas that gave rise to the original wrongs and injustices still exist today, albeit in modified form. Often, in the day-to-day behaviours of these very same people we continue to find wilful [sic] ignorance, apathy, judgment and stereotyping; we find expectations of cultural assimilation, and support for policies whose ultimate aim is extinguishment of pre-existing Indigenous rights.[15]

The heart of a Truth and Reconciliation Commission is the process of storytelling, listening, and allowing story to the reality shaping any forward movement. The power of story offers a realty where storyteller and listener create a reality bound to a new experience. Without the ability to create this lived experience there is an inability to recognize the need of the other. One individual sharing his experience through ministry is Rev. Maurice Henry Sands, executive director of the Black and Indian Mission for the United States Catholic Church. Sands is a member of the Ojibway, Ottawa and Potawatomi tribes. Similarly echoing Chief Joseph's speech to the federal government in 1879, Sands also reminded that assimilation is

---

13. Regan, *Unsettling the Settler Within*, 64.
14. Goza, *America's Unholy Ghosts*, 17.
15. LeBlanc, "Walking in Reconciled Relationships," 8.

Truth and Reconciliation

not what America needs to do to include indigenous peoples into the nation; it needs to allow them to be in peace without federal definition or cultural colonialization.[16]

> The most important thing for me is to forgive the injustices that have been committed, and to forgive the people who did it.... Genocide, mass murder, annihilation, elimination, termination, removal, relocation, assimilation, integration, and the best one of all, Americanization. We are the first Americans and for some reason the U. S. government thinks we needed to be Americanized.[17]

To begin a conversation for forward movement toward reconciliation, it is important to first understand and accept stories of truth from the past as a groundwork to build upon, and then begin to empathize with the challenges and injustices that have occurred through those historical accounts. As Indigenous scholars Dunbar-Ortiz and Gilio-Whitaker have indicted, it is much easier for the American federal government to silently acknowledge the transgression of the past than it is to be authentically transparent and willing apologize to show ownership of the actions of the past:

> After several unsuccessful attempts to pass legislation issuing a formal apology to Native Americas, in 2009 a bill was passed without fanfare, having been slipped quietly—and ironically—into a defense appropriations bill. The joint resolution acknowledges historical events like the massacres at Wounded Knee and Sand Creek, forced removals of entire nations from their homelands, and the taking of children from their families for education in distant boarding schools. It acknowledges "years of official depredations, ill-conceived policies, and the breaking of covenants by the Federal Government regarding Indian tribes" and expresses "regret for the ramifications of former wrongs." But nowhere is the word "genocide" used.[18]

It is time for America to learn from the wisdom of global servant leaders to be courageous and start the process for future unity, instead of further division.

---

16. See Chief Joseph, "Indian's View."
17. Pattison, "To End Racism Tomorrow," para. 5–6.
18. Dunbar-Ortiz and Gilio-Whitaker, "*All of the Real Indians*," 59.

Learning from Global Witnesses of Leadership

A witness of acceptance and empathy can be illustrated through the arts, especially music. Each of the countries examined throughout this manuscript has had an example of the power and reach that music has had on bringing awareness to injustices. Some of these examples are controversial, as they were not received well at the time, but challenged the audience with having to engage in conversation regarding the nation's past, and how that could affect its future.

The South African National Anthem

The example from South Africa involved Mandela's request to merge two anthems together: "Sikelel' iAfrika" (Lord, Bless Africa) the African National Congress' official anthem, and "Die Stem van Suid-Afrika" (The Call of South Africa) the anthem of the Afrikaans throughout the rule of apartheid. Staying consistent to his belief that symbols have power, and that their meaning can change, Mandela requested that melodic parts of the two anthems be fused together for the new national anthem of South Africa. The lyrics for the South Africa national anthem also incorporated five of the most spoken dialects into the stanzas to create a musical tapestry of lyrics and melody illustrating the history and composition of the peoples throughout the nation. Recently, there has been a movement to petition the removal of the Afrikaans section of the South African National Anthem, as it is a reminder of the apartheid regime. This debate offers an example of the how symbols and their meaning can very easily change or be misinterpreted by different generations without a complete context of the purpose of their original acceptance or empathy for their development or evolution of their current status and meaning.

The United States

Similarly, America experienced debate over the use of symbolic songs at national sporting events. Since 1917, the hymn "Lift Every Voice and Sing" has been adopted and used by The National Association for the Advancement of Colored People (NAACP) as the Black National Anthem. With the protests after the death of George Floyd in 2020, the anthem "Lift Every Voice and Sing" was incorporated at the beginning of major athletic events throughout that year. During NASCAR 2020 musicians quoted the hymn during the Star-Spangled Banner. The National Football League (NFL) also incorporated the hymn throughout the beginning ceremonies of the 2020 season. Most notably it has gained controversy, as the hymn was played during the pre-game ceremonies at the Superbowl LV, in 2021. This tradition has continued for three years to Superbowl LVII, where the hymn was performed live and in the stadium for the first time. The proximity of the anthem with the traditional pre-game singing of the American National Anthem created controversy as some audience members and pundits cited that playing two anthems broadcasted a divisive identity within America and that there should only be one anthem played for the sporting event, while other viewers saw the gesture as a sign of unity that helped to raise awareness of the injustices still present throughout the country.

Canada

Another example of a recent controversy and adaptation of the symbolic meaning to an anthem was witnessed at the 2023 National Basketball Association (NBA) All-Star game. During the Canadian National Anthem, singer Jully Black adapted one word in the lyrics that created a controversy. Instead of singing "O Canada! Our home and native land!," Black sang "O Canada Our Home on Native Land." When interviewed about the change in the lyrics she simply replied: "I sang the facts."[19]

These three examples illustrate in a small way, an acknowledgment of acceptance and empathy to the power of the symbolic meaning that the anthems had in the past and their role in the present. The question remains as to how debates or controversies will affect the future use of the anthems, or if changes will occur to adapt them for a new purpose. Nevertheless, the parallels within the power of music and identity is an important reminder of the challenges associated with change at a national level. With the controversies involving the use of anthems or adapting lyrics, one can only image the complexities that surround debates and discussions of national reparations or restitution of land as Dunbar-Ortiz discussed:

> Indigenous peoples offer possibilities for life after empire, possibilities that neither erase the crimes of colonialism nor require the disappearance of the original peoples colonized under the guise of including them as individuals. That process rightfully starts by

---

19. See CBC News, "'I sang the facts.'"

Genocide

honoring the treaties the United States made with Indigenous nations, by restoring all sacred sites, starting with the Black Hills and including most federally held parks and land and all stolen items and body parts, and by payment of sufficient reparations for the reconstruction and expansion of Native nations.[20]

Although reflecting on the cyclic war and violence in Europe, Jonathan Sacks's comment offers a psychological parallel and reminder for the generation trauma of injustices in America; that without a method to break or change the cyclic ideologies present from history it is likely that they will only continue to perpetuate from generation to generation:

> Nothing is more dispiriting than the cycle of revenge that haunts conflict zones and traps their populations into a past that never relaxes its grip. . . . Historical grievances are rarely forgotten. They become part of a people's collective memory, the narrative parents tell their children, the story from which a group draws its sense of identity.[21]

Lessons in Servant Leadership

- **Create Opportunities for Acceptance and Empathy:** Servant leaders need to acknowledge that acceptance and empathy are at the heart of service. To be a leader of empathy and acceptance of the other, it is important to let go of any pre-conceived biases or expectations, and allow the encounter of the presence or story within the community to become part of your story.

- **Make Time to Celebrate and Grieve Together:** Servant leaders should routinely celebrate the successes and mourn in grief with those they serve. A leader of service should connect to the emotional spectrum of the community, knowing appropriate and expected ways to revere community rituals and when protocol indicates when the presence of the leader would not be welcomed.

- **Walk with Those You Serve:** Servant leaders should have the opportunity to walk with those they serve. It is important to experience and recognize what live is like from a different point of view. To serve

---

20. Dunbar-Ortiz, *Indigenous Peoples' History*, 236.
21. Sacks, *Dignity of Difference*, 178.

others authentically it is essential to have a tangible working knowledge of some of their common daily experiences.

For Further Reflection

- **Create Opportunities for Acceptance and Empathy:** Read the lyrics and compare and contrast the perspectives offered in the following songs: The Tragically Hip's "Fiddler's Green" (1991), Spirit of the West's "Bulembu" (2011), and Leonard Cohen's "You Want It Darker" (2016). How do the lyrics of these songs incorporate an opportunity to develop empathy in the listener? How does the instrumentation and rhythm offer an emotional appeal to the listener of the topic? How might the lyrics of these, and similar, songs offer opportunities to be readily able to accept the challenges of others?

- **Make Time to Celebrate and Grieve Together:** After the COVID-19 pandemic, what rituals did you miss during the lockdown? In what ways can you now remember and celebrate or grieve those moments with family or friends? What new rituals could you start to remember important events in your life, and the lives of your family and friends? Investigate how other cultures celebrate birthdays or funerals, what are some of the similarities or difference between your ritual traditions? Explain some of the symbolic meanings of those rituals and yours.

- **Walk with Those You Serve:** Take time to sit and authentically listen to someone else. Let go of pre-conceived ideas or expectations of the encounter. Just be present to the individual and their story. What did you learn about the storyteller through that encounter? How did recognizing that you received a gift, through the form of a story, instill a responsibility to respect that narrative as well as create a little empathy toward the individual who shared that with you? What ways can you be more present and accepting of others in your family, social groups, or work life?

12

Truth and Reconciliation

A Vision for Servant Leadership in National Dialogue

And so we shall have to do more than register and more than vote; we shall have to create leaders who embody virtues we can respect, who have moral and ethical principles we can applaud with an enthusiasm that enables us to rally support for them based on confidence and trust.[1]

MARTIN LUTHER KING JR.'s words continue to echo true today. Current waves of power and ideological influence based on a two-party political system have seen a growth in identity politics in America over the past decades. Since the social revolution throughout the American 1960s, the assassination of governmental representatives and Civil Rights leaders, the disclosure of the horrors of the Vietnam War, and scandals that have left lasting defining legacies on the Presidential office, there has been a growing obsession of defined moral rights and wrongs based on a party line. The enthusiasm and romanticism that once existed with youth during the social change of the American 1960s has changed to a despair and malaise of youth to political change in 2020s.

Throughout the past five decades, the American executive office has become a continually object of scrutiny, for good or for ill. There has been much time and focus devoted to demanding representatives be held

---

1. King, *Where Do We Go*, 217.

Truth and Reconciliation

accountable based political views and based on the party that holds office. There also seems to be a rising feeling of conflict, aggression, and underlined frustration because of a lack of transparency, hypocrisy, and propaganda projected in the media.

> Our global situation today is not unlike the condition of European nations during the great wars of religion of the sixteenth and seventeenth centuries in the wake of the Reformation. Then, as now, there were many societies riven by conflict. The question arose: how can people of violently conflicting beliefs live peaceably together?[2]

As Rabbi Jonathan Sacks reflected in the above quotation, over the past five hundred years, it does not seem like much has changed in human behavior. There are similar parallels in history, as the during the age of expansion and colonialization of Europe of the 1500s. There remain global conflicts include Europe and America, theological debates continue to rise throughout the globe, a post-pandemic reality has affected economic realities, and we are in the midst of a new technological age that is redefining humanity and its relationship with others. All of these factors have the possibility of creating new forms of injustice and divisions throughout the country, and the world. This is a time of transition in human development, where leaders should remain vigilant to a servant-mindedness that could stop cyclic ideologies and offer a nonviolent alterative and narrative for future perspectives of culture and national identity.

This manuscript has used Robert Greenleaf's servant leadership model as a lens to examine the wisdom of the past in the hope of offering insights to start a conversation and assist in addressing a more purposeful posture of national unity. Storytelling and narrative can serve a vital role in the ability to discuss past injustices and to build trust for the future. Throughout this book examples of the following servant leadership traits have already been examined: being service-oriented, possess awareness and openness to a new lens and perspective, being community-oriented, being goal-oriented, listening for understanding, purposefully withdrawing and orienting, remaining present on the now, being methodical, creatively using language and imagination, developing foresight, and creating opportunities of acceptance and empathy.[3] All of these aspects lead to the one culminating trait, namely healing and serving; the putting into action

---

2. Sacks, *Dignity of Difference*, 205
3. Greenleaf, *Servant Leadership*, 21–53.

of the servant leadership model. This chapter will conclude with examples of how this has been demonstrated, and might continue to be accomplished to seek reconciliation of America's past.

Servant-Leadership Lens

As servant leadership scholars Sousa and van Dierendonck indicated that, although one can: "speak about servant leadership as one specific way of leadership, at a deeper level, and as mentioned before, there seem to be two overarching encompassing dimensions: a humble service-oriented side and an action-driven side, both co-existing and complementing each other."[4] Servant leadership is demonstrated through a service-oriented action.

The final tenet of servant leadership to be examined in this book will be the importance of the focus of healing and serving, the culmination of service-oriented action. At the heart of a truth and reconciliation commission is the goal of healing and serving others, through which to find a process for some semblance of catharsis and common ground to progress forward in a more unitive future. All of the previous tenets of servant leadership are essential to offering healing through service. It is essential to engage in attentive listening for understanding to create the foundations for healing of past wrongs by the very act of creating a bond of recognition that had not been present in the past. The component of service offers a second feature that reminds that future actions are called for the betterment of all, instead of only personal gains. To offer one's gifts and strengths for others allows to create a balance against individual weaknesses. As the spiritual author and theologian, Henri Nouwen stated: "Christian leaders are called to live the Incarnation, that is to live in the body, not only their own bodies but also in the corporate body of the community, and to discover there the presence of the Holy Spirit."[5] This incarnate reality of leadership is the living embodiment of the service demonstrated by the Apostle to the Gentiles, Paul of Tarsus.

---

4. Sousa and van Dierendonck, "Servant Leadership," 14.
5. Nouwen, *In the Name of Jesus*, 68.

Paul of Tarsus: A Leader of Service and Healing

Although Paul of Tarsus's ministry includes healings, his own and those he served, one particular example illustrates the complications that can arise from serving and healing others when change is not welcomed (Acts 16:16–34). As Paul and Silas were traveling on a mission, they came upon a girl who could tell fortunes through a demonic possessed. The possessed girl was of great value for her master because she was used by him to increase his fortune. Through his ministry, Paul exorcised the demon from the girl and gave her liberty from the possession and objectification of her master. The slave owner became outraged at Paul because of this healing, because he could no longer make money off of the girl's talent, and accused Paul and Silas of crimes against Rome. Paul and Silas were taken by a mob, beaten and then thrown in jail for their act.

During their incarceration, there was a great earthquake that broke the doors of the jail and would have allowed the escape of Paul and Silas. The guard of the jail, who believed that all of the prisoners had escaped on his watch, lost hope when he thought about what he would have to be held responsible for with the escape of the prisoners to the Roman authorities, and was about to fall on his sword when Paul and Silas indicated that they were still present in the jail. Through this encounter, the guard had a conversion of heart that changed from despair to gratitude.

Servant leadership offers the ability for those who lost hope to find a new way, a fresh start, and a new connection. The servant leadership of Paul and Silas offered a new and liberating way of life for both the servant-girl from possession of a demonic force, objectification at the hand of her master, as well as the healing of the prison guard from the possession of despair and hopelessness. These moments of service create a way of hope through struggle and bondage. Healing offers a liberation from a damage of the past, while service offers a purposeful calling and hope for the future. As Henri Nouwen elaborated:

> [Christian leadership] is not a leadership about power and control, but a leadership of powerlessness and humility in which the suffering servant of God, Jesus Christ, is made manifest. . . . I am speaking of a leadership in which power is constantly abandoned in favor for love.[6]

---

6. Nouwen, *In the Name of Jesus*, 82.

The Challenge

Similar to Nouwen, Thomas Merton also offered the powerful reminder: "He who attempts to act and do things for others or for the world without deepening his own self-understanding, freedom, integrity, and capacity to love, will not have anything to give others."[7]

This does not only hold true for individuals, but for communities as well. Although America may be a nation that is involved with the global realities of many countries it is essential to remember that it is important to take care of the identity and unity of the country as well. In his book, *The Clash of Civilizations and the Remaking of World Order*, Samuel Huntington warned that:

> The West is overwhelming dominant now and will remain number one in terms of power and influence well into the twenty-first century. Gradual, inexorable, and fundamental changes, however, are also occurring in the balances of power among civilizations, and the power of the West relative to that of other civilizations will continue to decline.[8]

So, how can we learn from the examples of our neighbors to start addressing aspects of the country that will allow the nation to continue to progress forward together, instead of become more divided?

First, it must be stated that Truth and Reconciliation hearings have always been convened based on a national wrong still present in living memory. The two Truth and Reconciliation Commission exemplars examined in this text, South Africa and Canada, were founded on the narrative lived experience of individual testimonies experienced in their past. Witnesses in South Africa explained their part, experiences, and survivorship from the plight of Apartheid, while survivors of the Canadian residential schools told of the horrific experiences of their childhood as well as the lingering psychological effects that continue to plague their lives and the nation. For America, both the events of slavery and conquest are rooted in history, and do not have tangible survivors to bear witness.

But, the effects of those egregious aspects of the nation's past still bear their weight today. Although reparations for past injustices have been continued to be discussed in scholarly and civil circles, financial payments will

---

7. Merton, "Contemplation," 375.
8. Huntington, *Clash of Civilizations*, 82.

Truth and Reconciliation

not resolve injustices alone.[9] There are stories than can be shared from survivors of the Birmingham bombing and youth effected by Jim Crow laws. One of the last recorded lynchings at the hands of Ku Klux Klan members of a black American was perpetrated against Michael Donald in 1981, in Alabama. Impoverish living conditions of First Nation members on reservations are still exponentially disproportion to the entire nation. The United Nations Declaration of Human Rights of Indigenous Peoples was recently ratified in 2007. These Rights ought to be discussed, examined, and implemented across the nation.

> Starting with the national or political level, the fact that a government sets up a truth commission may in itself be perceived as an effort to uncover crimes of the past, thus publicly acknowledging that violence has taken place—which is important for those who have suffered repression and violence.[10]

To start the conversation of the viability of a Truth and Reconciliation Commission in the United States it is still foundational to recognize that the history of the country is woven with injustice and wrongs perpetrated against multiple nationalities, religions, and groups. It would be impossible to examine the history of the atrocities against each group throughout one commission. In the modern consciousness the plight of Black America has been the focus of the contemporary media. Dating back to 1619, when the first ship carrying human beings to be sold as property, slaves, arrived there has been an intergenerational trauma and consistent fear in the legacy of the nation's relationship with racial difference. As demonstrated from 1800's through the 1900's and into the protests of 2020, the changes to the law alone have not changed hearts. There continues to be reoccurring cycles that remind the population of the cultural genocide and human disregard that has occurred, and continues to occur.

The addressing of disregard for human dignity in 1619 and the cultural tragedy that followed will not resolve the racial discord present in America if discussed in isolation. There was another group present before the developed of the country that experienced genocide and a cultural extermination in the same land, the First Nations, Native Americans. From the 1565, the relationship of regime expansions and colonialization created a determination to acquire material at the price of human life. The very act

---

9. See Dickerson, "Designing Slavery Reparations."
10. Skaar, "Reconciliation," 74.

of establishment of American colonies that led to a national independence was a sign of rebellion from an authoritarian force in England. Unfortunately, through this action a new type of authoritarian force was placed upon another group of individuals. The atrocities of war, forced migration, indentured servitude, and industrial/residential schooling became a norm for numbers of First Nations that did not have a voice.

At the Crossroads

> Two things are necessary in a revolutionary transition [of Truth and Reconciliation]: acknowledgment of wrongdoing and its seriousness, and a forward-looking effort of reconciliation. A further helpful element suggested by . . . the practice of Mandela is the cultivation of empathy, the ability to see how the world looks from the other party's perspective.[11]

America is not devoid of such examples of magnanimity in the midst of a life time of suffering. Anthony Ray Hinton was arrested in Alabama in 1985, falsely identified as the suspect of two murders, and had inadequate counsel leading to his conviction. He was convicted and spend twenty-eight years on death row before his conviction was overturned by the United States Supreme Court, allowing his release in 2015. In his memoir, *The Sun Does Shine: How I Found Life and Freedom on Death Row*, Hinton stated: "But pain and tragedy and injustice happen—they happen to us all. I'd like to believe it's what you choose to do after such an experience that matters the most—that truly changes your life forever."[12]

Instead of being full of resentment and desire for retaliation, Hinton was clear that bitterness and hate corrupt the soul. Although half of his life was taken, he was clear that his soul would not be taken as well. While the media reports of his release focused on the injustice of the situation, failure of the courts, and lack of willingness of the Alabama Court of Appeals to examine the case, Hinton focused on his future, displaying gratitude for the tireless work of the Equal Justice Initiative for pursuing his case, and treasuring what he has, instead of what he has lost.[13] Hinton exemplifies that retributive justice may not be the most effective process to move forward,

---

11. Nussbaum, *Anger and Forgiveness*, 238.
12. Hinton and Hardin, *Sun Does Shine*, 1.
13. See Hinton, "Sun Does Shine."

Truth and Reconciliation

though it still remains the common position for many people as a response to injustice. His time of reflection while incarcerated allowed him to think deeply about his future.

> Was that day just the culmination of a whole series of fateful moments, poor choices, and bad luck? Or was the course of my life determined by being black and poor and growing up in a South that didn't always care to be civil in the wake of civil rights? ... When you are forced to live out your life in a room the size of a bathroom—a room that's five feet wide by seven feet long—you have plenty of time to replay the moments in your life...[14]

A Call for Change

The history of America does include an attempted at a local version of a Truth and Conciliation Commission. The Greensboro Truth and Reconciliation Commission (2004–2006) offered an initial example of what the process could look like. This community led initiative examined an event of injustice that occurred in the location in 1979. This examination allowed story telling from witnesses from the event.

> Opportunities for victims and others to tell their stories, and for public acknowledgement of wrongs, accurately told—the most common objectives of truth commissions—are usually justified as measures to ease past suffering. Reparations processes, to the extent that they aim to remedy past harms, are also past-focused. In addition, trials of perpetrators, fall within the response to past violations goal.[15]

Greensboro: A Case Study for Further Reflection in the United States

Through the international acclaim of the South African Truth and Reconciliation process, a local community in Greensboro, North Carolina was inspired to explore the form of transitional justice for a racial injustice within their own recent past. On November 3, 1979, an altercation between members of the communist workers party and members of the Ku Klux Klan (KKK) escalated into racial motivated violence. As the protesting

---

14. Hinton and Hardin, *Sun Does Shine*, 1.
15. Lutz, "Transitional Justice," 325.

Truth and Reconciliation

intensified members of the KKK retrieved firearms, and five protesters were killed while ten more were wounded in the melee.[16] The event received the moniker, the Greensboro Massacre. Due to the coinciding Hostage Crisis in Iran (1979–1981) the events in Greensboro became overshadowed by the international events and media coverage.

On the twentieth anniversary of the event, there was discussion of organizing a Truth and Reconciliation Commission to help unify and find a path forward for the citizens of Greensboro. Although there had been three previous juridical proceedings regarding the event, it did not offer the transparency the community was seeking.

> The Greensboro commission was established through a largely private effort of civil society and Church groups, working closely with victims and survivors of the 1979 event. The city council discussed and gave consideration to formally backing the initiative, but a vote on the matter fell short. However, the mayor of Greensboro appointed the chair of the selection panel, upon being invited to do so.[17]

In 1999, this movement was officially known as the Truth and Reconciliation Commission Project. In 2004, five years after the initial discussion, a Truth and Reconciliation Commission was established to investigate the events surrounding November 3, 1979. This became the first example of a Truth and Reconciliation style transitional justice mentioned in the United States. The process was not a blind attempt of implanting that the style of restorative justice, as figures of the South Africa Truth and Reconciliation Commission presented their wisdom in preparation for the Commission, such as Peter Storey and Desmond Tutu.[18] Bongani Finca, a member of the South African Truth and Reconciliation was present and challenged the members of the commission to not shy away from difficult questions but to seek the level of transparency needed to legitimize the project after the first hearing.[19]

The Greensboro Truth and Reconciliation Commission was compiled in a thorough 529-page report that outlined the findings from the Commission and action statements to assist with serving and healing the

---

16. See Jovanovic, *Democracy*, 3–16; and Magarrell and Wesley, *Learning*, 3–38.
17. Hayner, *Unspeakable Truths*, 62.
18. Jovanovic, *Democracy*, 69.
19. Magarrell and Wesley, *Learning*, 199.

community.[20] As evidenced with the South African and Canadian Truth and Reconciliation Commissions, after the Commission findings education efforts increased in the community of Greensboro to help the healing process, some of these community activities included use of the arts, the development of conversation spaces, and vigils.[21]

Learning from Global Witnesses of Leadership

To offer an example of service and healing at the national level, there is no easy example to use for America, as a whole. There still needs to be considerable exploration of the narratives of the nation before a Truth and Reconciliation Commission is possible to address indigenous and racial injustices. Possibly the closest and controversial example in the recent history of America was an attempt to seek reconciliation to a palpable anger throughout the country due to an example of broken trust from the highest office in the nation.

In 1974, Gerald Ford came into office of the President of the United States, never voted in by the people, but by the resignation of Richard Nixon due to the Watergate scandal. Ford had the insurmountable task of re-orienting a country that was devastated by a scandal leading to the resignation of the only sitting President in the history of the United States. With the departure of Richard Nixon from the presidency, and the aftermath of the Watergate investigation and impeachment, Ford had to make a decision for the course of the country as a whole; to proceed with the prosecution against the former President and appease much political anger and frustration, or to pursue actions that he thought would heal and serve the country. On September 8, 1974, Ford made the decision to grant an unconditional pardon to Richard Nixon, through Proclamation 4311.

> Jerry Ford acted in accord with what he sincerely felt were the best interests of the country; that there was no secret quid pro quo with Nixon for a pardon in return for resignation; and that Ford, a compassionate man, was moved by the palpable suffering of a man who had lost so much.[22]

---

20. See Jovanovic, *Democracy*, 91–114; and Magarrell and Wesley, *Learning*, 118–31.
21. See Jovanovic, *Democracy*, 115–39.
22. Ben-Veniste, "Pardon in History's Hindsight," para. 9.

Truth and Reconciliation

Although extremely criticized, and being personally accused of participating in a cover up of the truth surrounding the scandal, Ford courageously persevered in his conviction and felt compelled by the legal structure of the law that a pardon would not only heal the country for the future, but could also limit the fascination and obsession of rehashing Nixon's actions over and over, which could leave a lasting legacy of disgrace on the office of the President of the United States.

> Citing reasons of national reconciliation, the difficulty Nixon would have in obtaining a fair trial by jury, and the suffering that Nixon and his family had already endured, Ford announced that he had pardoned Richard Nixon for all crimes he committed or "may have committed" while president[23]

It is a commonly held belief that one of the major contributing factors of Ford's election loss of 1976 was because of the decision of giving Nixon the pardon. Through the standfast courage of his decision of the pardon, Ford jeopardized and sacrifice his future career in service of the nation for its healing. This example of servant leadership offers an authentic perspective in the struggles of being a servant leader when the majority of the community does not agree with the foresight, goal, and methodical process.

Over time Ford's decision has been reexamined and has been appreciated with much more reverence and acknowledgment of being the right course of action for the nation at the time. In 2001, Ford was recognized for the action of his pardon of Nixon, a quarter of a century afterward, through the John F. Kennedy Profile in Courage Award® presented by Senator Ted Kennedy. Kennedy who originally was furious the decision of the pardon discussed the deliberation of awarding the honor to Ford:

> I think there were people in that room, including the historians that had been critical at the time. But once, we had the benefit of hindsight and once we had a benefit of history, it became much clearer. And I must say, I was both inspired and enlightened, and enormously encouraged, and incredibly proud that at the end of the deliberations.[24]

During his acceptance speech for the award, Ford did not focus on his own achievements, but rather used the time to highlight the achievements

---

23. Ben-Veniste, "Pardon in History's Hindsight," para. 6.
24. See National Public Radio, "Sen. Kennedy."

of others and of their service to change the trajectory of the country and the world.

> In the course of almost 88 years, I have seen more than my share of miracles. I have witnessed the defeat of Nazi tyranny and the destruction of hateful walls that once divided free men from those enslaved. Here at home, thanks to the bravery of men like John Lewis, we are belatedly honoring the promises we made to one another at the founding of the Republic. We have at last begun to recognize women for their talents and revere them for their contributions. . . . None of this just happened. It happened because people of conscience refused to be passive in the face of injustice, or indifferent to the demands of democracy.[25]

In Conclusion

As illustrated throughout this manuscript, servant leadership offers a lens to engage in service and healing in the most challenging divisions of a nation's history. Although America has not yet had the opportunity to start an earnest investigation into the truths of the past to seek the initial steps of reconciliation for the future, this manuscript attempted to offer some brief reflections to open the door for discussion of past injustices as well as snippets of the wisdom of leaders from the past who have acted through service to heal their country's indigenous and racial divisions. The Truth and Reconciliation model is not a perfect process for justice, but it opens the door to an essential aspect of truth-telling to listen, learn, and dialogue.

With the current polemic divisions present in America today, the country may not be ready to focus on the needs of the other enough to authentically listen and encounter past injustices. Without the interest to withdraw and reorient in times of cyclic violence, it can be a challenge for leaders to reflect on past events and try to resolve new approaches for movement for the future. There is always a possibility, though, to follow in the footsteps of our neighboring nations. This type of action may need to take the willingness to put individual needs to the side and approach injustices as a servant leader to offer steps needed to start to heal the country as a whole.

---

25. Ford, "Acceptance Speech," paras. 5–7.

Truth and Reconciliation

Stand therefore, and fasten the belt of truth around your waist, and put on the breastplate of righteousness. As shoes for your feet put on whatever will make you ready to proclaim the gospel of peace. (Eph 6:14–15)

Lessons in Leadership: Trends from Models of Servant Leadership

- **Focus with Humility toward Healing and Serving Others:** Servant leaders should approach their leadership actions through humility. It is important to remember that for a servant leader that the focus is not on the successes of the leader, but on the ability to empower others.
- **Purposefully Be Active in Community Life:** Servant leaders need to be purposely active in the life of their community. This tangible connectivity allows for the opportunity to learn and assess the needs of the community being served.
- **Set Aside Time Dedicated to Building Unity:** Servant leaders also need to set time aside to develop relationships and build unity with those they serve. The further away from direct contact with the community, the less able one is to accurately recognize and understand the dreams and goals of those being served.

For Further Reflection

- **Focus with Humility toward Healing and Serving Others:** Listen and read the lyrics of the following songs: USA for Africa's "We Are the World" (1985), Leonard Cohen's "Anthem" (1992), and/or Dave Matthews Band's "Mercy" (2010). How do the lyrics challenge the listener to think about healing and serving community? What feelings did you experience through the song? Through what ways did these musicians offer insight into encouraging actions and movements of service and healing, locally of globally?
- **Purposefully Be Active in Community Life:** Explore some of the ways you could volunteer in your local community. What ways do you offer your time to serve the community? Take time to experience volunteering in a soup kitchen, homeless shelter, nursing home, or with individuals with special needs. What did you learn from

the experience? How did the experience help you learn more about yourself?

- **Set Aside Time Dedicated to Building Unity:** How do you build unity in your family? Take time to play a board game, call a distant loved one on the telephone/Zoom, and/or visit a friend or family member who is lonely or isolated. Let that friend or family member know through your presence that they are not alone.

Bibliography

Adach, Kate. "'It Has Never Been a Secret That Children Went Missing': Will the Loss of 215 Be a Watershed Moment?" *CBC News*, Jun 11, 2021. https://www.cbc.ca/radio/unreserved/what-happens-when-hidden-histories-become-a-national-conversation-1.6059520/it-has-never-been-a-secret-that-children-went-missing-will-the-loss-of-215-be-a-watershed-moment-1.6059530.

Adams, Ian. "The Indians: An Abandoned and Dispossessed People." *Weekend Magazine*, Jul 31, 1965.

———. "The Lonely Death of Chanie Wenjack." *Maclean's*. Feb 1967. https://www.macleans.ca/society/the-lonely-death-of-chanie-wenjack/.

Ajayi, Adeyinka Theresa, and Lateef Oluwafemi Buhari. "Methods of Conflict Resolution in African Traditional Society." *African Research Review* 8.2 (Apr 2014) 138–57.

Alexander VI. "Inter Caeter: Division of the Undiscovered World between Spain and Portugal." 1493. https://www.papalencyclicals.net/alex06/alex06inter.htm.

Ali, Muhammad, and Richard Durham. *The Greatest: My Own Story*. Los Angeles: Graymalkin Media, 2015.

Annett, Kevin. *Murder by Decree: The Crime of Genocide in Canada*. Toronto, ON: International Tribunal for the Disappeared of Canada, 2016.

Arva, Eugene L. *The Traumatic Imagination: Histories of Violence in Magical Realist Fiction*. Amherst, NY: Cambria Press, 2011.

Attwood, Adam I., and Jill L. Gerber. "Comic Books and Graphic Novels for the Differentiated Humanities Classroom." *Kappa Delta Pi Record* 56 (2020) 176–82.

Avolio, Bruce J., and Edwin E. Locke. "Should Leaders Be Selfish or Altruistic? Letters on Leader Motivation." In *Ethics, the Heart of Leadership*, edited by Joanne B. Ciulla, 105–28. Westport, CT: Praeger, 2004.

Barclay, Michael. *The Never-Ending Present: The Story of Gord Downie and the Tragically Hip*. Toronto, ON: ECW Press, 2019.

Barling, Julian. *The Science of Leadership: Lessons from Research for Organizational Leaders*. Oxford, UK: Oxford University, 2014.

Bartolomé de las Casas. *A Short Account of the Destruction of the Indies*. Urbana, IL: Project Gutenberg, 2007. https://www.gutenberg.org/ebooks/20321.

Battle, Michael. *Desmond Tutu: A Spiritual Biography of South Africa's Confessor*. Louisville, KY: Westminster John Knox Press, 2021.

———. *Reconciliation: The Ubuntu Theology of Desmond Tutu*. Rev. ed. Cleveland, OH: Pilgrim Press, 2009.

Bibliography

Bell, Catherine, and Hadley Friedland. "Introduction: Law, Justice, and Reconciliation in Post-TRC Canada." *Alberta Law Review* 56.3 (2019) 659–67.

Ben-Veniste, Richard. "The Pardon in History's Hindsight." *Washington Post*, Dec 29, 2006. https://www.washingtonpost.com/wp-dyn/content/article/2006/12/28/AR2006122801054.html.

Bestall, Cliff, dir. "The 16th Man." *ESPN 30 for 30*. United States: ESPN, 2010.

Blake, Kathleen. "Change the Name of the Blalock-Taussig Shunt to Blalock-Thomas-Taussig Shunt." *JAMA Surgery* 157.4 (2022) 287–88.

Blight, David W. *Frederick Douglass: Prophet of Freedom*. New York: Simon & Schuster, 2018.

Block, Alan A. *The Classroom: Encounter and Engagement*. New York: Palgrave Macmillan, 2014.

Boahen, A. Adu. *Africa under Colonial Domination 1880–1935: The UNESCO General History of Africa VII*. Berkeley, CA: University of California Press, 1990.

Bowman, Thea. *In My Own Words*. Edited by Maurice Nutt. Liguori, MO: Liguori, 2009.

Brown, Dee. *Bury My Heart at Wounded Knee: An Indian History of the American West*. New York: Holt, 2007.

Brown, Joseph Epes, ed. *The Sacred Pipe: Black Elk's Account of the Seven Rites of the Oglala Sioux*. Norman, OK: University of Oklahoma, 1989.

Burton, Mary Ingouville. *The Truth and Reconciliation Commission*. Athens, OH: Ohio University Press, 2016.

Canadian Conference of Catholic Bishops. "Statement of Apology by the Catholic Bishops of Canada to the Indigenous People of This Land." Sep 24, 2021. https://www.cccb.ca/letter/statement-of-apology-by-the-catholic-bishops-of-canada-to-the-indigenous-peoples-of-this-land/.

Carson, Clayborne, ed. *The Autobiography of Martin Luther King Jr*. New York: Grand Central Publishing, 2001.

Chanaiwa, David. "Southern Africa Since 1945." In *Africa Since 1935: The UNESCO General History of Africa VIII*, edited by Ali A. Mazrui, 249–84. Berkeley, CA: University of California Press, 1999.

Chief Joseph. "An Indian's View of Indian Affairs." *North American Review* 128.269 (Apr 1879) 412–33. https://www.washington.edu/uwired/outreach/cspn/Website/Classroom%20Materials/Reading%20the%20Region/Texts%20by%20and%20about%20Natives/Texts/9.html.

Cioci, Will. "Mural Project Brought Black Voices to a Shuttered State Street." *Wisconsin Watch*, Jun 23 2020. https://www.wisconsinwatch.org/2020/06/mural-project-brought-black-voices-life-to-a-shuttered-state-street/.

Clark, Meredith D. "Drag Them: A Brief Etymology of So-Called "Cancel Culture." *Communication and the Public* 5.3–4 (2020) 88–92.

Collins, Jim. *How the Mighty Fall: And Why Some Companies Never Give In*. New York: HarperCollins, 2009.

"Convention for a Democratic South Africa (CODESA)." *South African History Online: Towards a People's History*. https://www.sahistory.org.za/article/convention-democratic-south-africa-codesa.

Cook, Catherine, et al. "Structures Last Longer than Intentions: Creation of Ongomiizwin—Indigenous Institute of Health and Healing at the University of Manitoba." *International Journal of Circumpolar Health* 78 (2019) 1–4.

Bibliography

Coppa, Frank J. "Pope Pius XI's 'Encyclical' Humani Generis Unitas against Racism and Anti-Semitism and the 'Silence' of Pope Pius XII." *Journal of Church and State* 40.4 (1998) 775–95.

Crenshaw, Kimberlé W., et al. *Say Her Name: Resisting Police Brutality against Black Women*. Columbia Law School Scholarship Archive, 2015. https://scholarship.law.columbia.edu/faculty_scholarship/3226.

Crystal, Billy. "Muhammad Ali Funeral | Billy Crystal Imitated Ali." *ABC News*, Jun 10, 2016. https://www.youtube.com/watch?v=7XB3sD9QJCI.

Csontos, Janet. "Truth and Decolonization: Filling the Educator Achievement Gap Darn It!" *American Review of Canadian Studies* 49.1 (2019) 150–86.

Dalai Lama XIV, et al. *The Book of Joy*. New York: Avery, 2016.

Davis, Cyprian. *The History of Black Catholics in the United States*. New York: Crossroad Publishing, 1990.

Davis, Lynne, et al. "Aboriginal-Social Justice Alliances: Understanding the Landscape of Relationships through the Coalition for a Public Inquiry into Ipperwash." *International Journal of Canadian Studies* 36 (2007) 95–119.

Davis, Lynne, et al. "Complicated Pathways: Settler Canadians Learning to Re/frame Themselves and Their Relationships with Indigenous Peoples." *Settler Colonial Studies* 7.4 (2017) 398–414.

Deloria, Vine, Jr. "The Indians of the American Imagination." In *Merton & Indigenous Wisdom*, edited by Peter Savastano, 1–20. Louisville, KY: Fons Vita, 2019.

Desbuquois, Gustave, et al. "Draft Encyclical: Humani Generis Unitas." *Council of Centers on Jewish-Christian Relations*. https://ccjr.us/dialogika-resources/primary-texts-from-the-history-of-the-relationship/hgu1938.

Diamond, Beverley. "Resisting Containment: The Long Reach of Song at the Truth and Reconciliation Commission on Indian Residential Schools." In *Arts of Engagement: Taking Aesthetic Action in and Beyond the Truth and Reconciliation Commission of Canada*, edited by Dylan Robinson and Keavy Martin, 239–66. Waterloo, ON: Wilfrid Laurier University Press, 2016.

Dickerson, A. Mechele. "Designing Slavery Reparations: Lessons from Complex Litigation." *Texas Law Review* 98 (2020) 1255–82.

Douglass, Frederick. "What, to the Slave, Is the Fourth of July." PBS, Jul 4, 1852. https://www.pbs.org/wgbh/aia/part4/4h2927t.html

Downie, Gord, and Jeff Lemire. *Secret Path*. New York: Simon & Schuster, 2016.

Doyle, Arthur Conan. *The Hound of the Baskervilles*. Urbana, IL: Project Gutenberg, 2001. https://www.gutenberg.org/ebooks/2852.

Drodzdzewski, Danielle, et al. "Geographies of Memory, Place and Identity: Intersections in Remembering War and Conflict." *Geography Compass* 10.11 (2016) 447–56.

Drury, Bob, and Tom Clavin. *The Heart of Everything That Is: The Untold Story of Red Cloud, an American Legend*. New York: Simon & Schuster, 2013.

Dubois, W. E. B. "Behold the Land (October 20, 1946)." In *Great Speeches of the 20th Century*, edited by Bob Blaisdell, 162–72. Mineola, NY: Dover Publications, 2011.

———. *The Souls of Black Folk: With "The Talented Tenth" and "The Souls of White Folk."* New York: Penguin, 2018.

Dunbar-Ortiz, Roxanne. *An Indigenous Peoples' History of the United States*. Boston, MA: Beacon Press, 2014.

Dunbar-Ortiz, Roxanne, and Dina Gilio-Whitaker. *"All of the Real Indians Died Off" and 20 Other Myths about Native Americans*. Boston, MA: Beacon Press, 2016.

Bibliography

Duran, Eduardo, and Bonnie Duran. *Native American Postcolonial Psychology*. Albany, NY: State University of New York Press, 1995.

Duriga, Joyce. *Augustus Tolton: The Church Is the True Liberator*. Collegeville, MN: Liturgical Press, 2018.

Dysinger, Luke, trans. *The Rule of Saint Benedict: Latin and English*. Santa Ana, CA: Source Books, 2003.

Eastwood, Clint, dir. *Invitcus*. United States: Warner Brothers, 2009.

Echo-Hawk, Walter R. *In the Light of Justice: The Rise of Human Rights in Native America and the UN Declaration on the Rights of Indigenous Peoples*. Golden, CO: Fulcrum, 2013.

Eder, Richard. "1492 Ban on Jews Is Voided by Spain." *The New York Times*, Dec 17, 1968. https://timesmachine.nytimes.com/timesmachine/1968/12/17/76918699.html.

Eisner, Elliot W. "Educating the Whole Person: Arts in the Curriculum." *Music Educators Journal* 73.8 (1987) 37–41.

Ekeocha, Obianuju. *Target Africa: Ideological Neocolonialism in the Twenty-First Century*. San Francisco: Ignatius Press, 2018.

Eneas, Bryan. "Sask: First Nation Announces Discovery of 751 Unmarked Graves near Former Residential School." *CBC News*, Jun 24, 2021. https://www.cbc.ca/news/canada/saskatchewan/cowessess-marieval-indian-residential-school-news-1.6078375.

Escher, Constance K. *She Calls Herself Betsey Stockton: The Illustrated Odyssey of a Princeton Slave*. Eugene, OR: Resource, 2022.

Fage, J. D. *A History of Africa*. 3rd ed. New York: Routledge, 1995.

Fast, Elizabeth, and Delphine Collin-Vézina. "Historical Trauma, Race-Based Trauma and Resilience of Indigenous Peoples: A Literature Review." *First Peoples Child & Family Review* 5.1 (2010) 126–36.

Ford, Gerald. "Acceptance Speech for the John F. Kennedy Profile in Courage Award." JFK Library, May 21, 2001. https://www.jfklibrary.org/events-and-awards/profile-in-courage-award/award-recipients/president-gerald-ford-2001.

Francis. "Evangelii Gaudium." *The Holy See*, Nov 24, 2013. http://www.vatican.va/content/francesco/en/apost_exhortations/documents/papa-francesco_esortazione-ap_20131124_evangelii-gaudium.html.

———. "Laudato sí." *The Holy See*, May 24, 2015. https://www.vatican.va/content/francesco/en/encyclicals/documents/papa-francesco_20150524_enciclica-laudato-si.html.

———. "Meeting with Indigenous Peoples: First Nations, Métis and Inuit." *The Holy See*, Jul 25, 2022. https://www.vatican.va/content/francesco/en/speeches/2022/july/documents/20220725-popolazioniindigene-canada.html.

Gambrell, Kem. "The Case for an Indigenous Collectivist Mindset." In *Global and Culturally Diverse Leaders and Leadership: New Dimensions and Challenges for Business, Education and Society*, edited by Jean Lau Chin et al., 21–39. Bingley, UK: Emerald Publishing, 2018.

Garrido, Ann M. *Redeeming Conflict: 12 Habits for Christian Leaders*. Notre Dame, IN: Ave Maria Press, 2016.

Goodwin, Doris Kearns. *Leadership in Turbulent Times*. New York: Simon & Schuster, 2018.

Gorsevski, Ellen W., and Michael L. Butterworth. "Muhammad Ali's Fighting Words: The Paradox of Violence in Nonviolent Rhetoric." *Quarterly Journal of Speech* 97.1 (2011) 50–73.

Goza, Joel Edward. *America's Unholy Ghosts: The Racist Roots of Our Faith and Politics*. Eugene, OR: Cascade, 2019.

Bibliography

Graham, Matthew. "Campaigning against Apartheid: The Rise, Fall and Legacies of the South Africa United Front 1960–1962." *The Journal of Imperial and Commonwealth History* 46.6 (2018) 1148–70.

Greenleaf, Robert K. *Servant Leadership: A Journey into the Nature of Legitimate Power and Greatness*. 25th anniversary ed. New York: Paulist Press, 2002.

Guramatunhucooper, Nyasha M. "Theory Leadership from Africa: Examples of Trait Theory." In *Global and Culturally Diverse Leaders and Leadership: New Dimensions and Challenges for Business, Education and Society*, edited by Jean Lau Chin et al., 3–20. Bingley, UK: Emerald Publishing, 2018.

Hayner, Priscilla B. *Unspeakable Truths: Transitional Justice and the Challenge of Truth Commissions*. 2nd ed. New York: Routledge, 2011.

Heinlein, Michael R., ed. *Black Catholics on the Road to Sainthood*. Huntington, IN: Our Sunday Visitor, 2021.

Hinton, Anthony Ray. "The Sun Does Shine." Talks at Google, Apr 24, 2018. https://www.youtube.com/watch?v=ZfnTdQ28Hbo.

Hinton, Anthony Ray, and Lara Love Hardin. *The Sun Does Shine: How I Found Life and Freedom on Death Row*. New York: St. Martin's, 2018.

House, Robert J., et al. *Strategic Leadership across Cultures: The GLOBE Study of CEO Leadership Behavior and Effectiveness in 24 Countries*. Los Angeles: SAGE, 2014.

Huie, William Bradford. "Death of an Innocent: What Kind of Mind Could Have Planted the Bomb That Killed Four Children in Birmingham?" *LOOK*, Mar 1964. http://sixtiessurvivors.org/ft_innocent.html.

———. "The Shocking Story of Approved Killing in Mississippi." *LOOK*, Jan 1956. http://xroads.virginia.edu/~public/civilrights/0161.html.

Huntington, Samuel P. *The Clash of Civilizations and the Remaking of World Order*. New York: Simon & Schuster, 2011.

Iheanacho, Valentine Ugochukwu. *Historical Trajectories of Catholicism in Africa: From Catholicae Ecclesiae to Ecclesia in Africa*. Eugene, OR: Resource, 2021.

James, Matt. "A Carnival of Truth? Knowledge, Ignorance and the Canadian Truth and Reconciliation Commission." *The International Journal of Transitional Justice* 6.2 (2012) 1–23.

Jansen, Jonathan D. *Knowledge in the Blood: Confronting Race and the Apartheid Past*. Stanford, CA: Stanford University Press, 2009.

John Paul II. "Homily: Jubilee of Sports People." *The Holy See*, Oct 24, 2000. http://www.vatican.va/content/john-paul-ii/en/homilies/2000/documents/hf_jp-ii_hom_20001029_jubilee-sport.html.

Jones, Max, and John Chilton. *Louis: The Louis Armstrong Story*. Boston, MA: Little, Brown and Company, 1971.

Joseph, Bob, and Cynthia F. Joseph. *Indigenous Relations: Insights, Tips & Suggestions to Make Reconciliation a Reality*. Vancouver, BC: Indigenous Relations Press/Page Two Books, 2019.

Jovanovic, Spoma. *Democracy, Dialogue, and Community Action: Truth and Reconciliation in Greensboro*. Fayetteville, AR: University of Arkansas Press, 2012.

Kahn, Roger. *Rickey & Robinson: The True, Untold Story of the Integration of Baseball*. New York: Rodale, 2014.

Kennedy, Robert F. "On the Assassination of Martin Luther King Jr." JFK Library, Apr 4, 1968. https://www.jfklibrary.org/Research/Research-Aids/Ready-Reference/RFK-Speeches/Statement-on-the-Assassination-of-Martin-Luther-King.aspx.

Bibliography

Kerr, James. *Legacy: What the All Blacks Can Teach Us about the Business of Life*. Croydon, UK: Constable, 2013.

Kimmerer, Robin Wall. *Braiding Sweetgrass: Indigenous Wisdom, Scientific Knowledge, and the Teaching of Plants*. Minneapolis, MN: Milkweed, 2013.

King, Martin Luther, Jr. "Beyond Vietnam: A Time to Break Silence" [The Riverside Church Speech]. Apr 4, 1967. https://www.commondreams.org/views04/0115-13.htm.

———. *Where Do We Go From Here? Chaos or Community*. Boston, MA: Beacon Press, 2010.

King, Thomas. *The Inconvenient Indian: A Curious Account of Native People in North America*. Minneapolis, MN: University of Minnesota Press, 2012.

———. *The Truth about Stories: A Native Narrative*. Minneapolis, MN: University of Minnesota Press, 2003.

Kouzes, James M., and Barry Z. Posner. *Learning Leadership: The Five Fundamentals of Becoming an Exemplary Leader*. San Francisco: The Leadership Challenge, 2016.

Kroeber, Theodora. *Ishi in Two Worlds: A Biography of the Last Wild Indian in North America*. 50th anniversary ed. Berkeley, CA: University of California Press, 2002.

Kushner, Harold S. *The Lord Is My Shepherd: Healing Wisdom of the Twenty-Third Psalm*. New York: Anchor Books, 2003.

LeBlanc, Terry. "Spirit and Spirituality: New Old Perspectives." *Journal of NAIITS* 8 (2010) 65–78.

———. "Walking in Reconciled Relationships." *Consensus* 37.1 (2016) 1–13. http://scholars.wlu.ca/consensus/vol37/iss1/4.

LeBlanc, Terry, and Jennifer LeBlanc. "NAIITS: Contextual Mission, Indigenous Context." *Missiology: An International Review* 39.1 (2011) 88–100.

Lowenfish, Lee. *Branch Rickey: Baseball's Ferocious Gentleman*. Lincoln, NE: Bison Books, 2009.

Lutz, Ellen. "Transitional Justice: Lessons Learned and the Road Ahead." In *Transitional Justice in the Twenty-First Century: Beyond Truth versus Justice*, edited by Naomi Roht-Arriaza and Javier Mariezcurrena, 325–41. Cambridge, UK: Cambridge University Press, 2006.

Mackay, Susan Ferrier. "Reporter Ian Adams Told the Story of Chanie Wenjack's 'Lonely Death.'" *The Globe and Mail*, Nov 30, 2021. https://www.theglobeandmail.com/canada/article-reporter-ian-adams-told-the-story-of-chanie-wenjacks-lonely-death/.

Mamdani, Mahmood. "Beyond Nuremberg: The Historical Significance of the Post-Apartheid Transition in South Africa." *Politics & Society*, 43 (1) 61–88. https://doi.org/10.1177/0032329214554387.

Mandela, Nelson. *Conversations with Myself*. London, UK: Picador, 2011.

———. *Long Walk to Freedom*. New York: Back Bay Books, 2013.

———. "Special Debate on Report of Truth and Reconciliation Commission." Feb 25, 1999. http://www.mandela.gov.za/mandela_speeches/1999/990225_trc.htm.

———. "Speech at the Inaugural Laureus Lifetime Achievement Award." Monaco, May 25, 2000. http://db.nelsonmandela.org/speeches/pub_view.asp?pg=item&ItemID=NMS1148&txtstr=Laureus.

Mandela, Winnie. *Part of My Soul Went with Him*. New York: W. W. Norton, 1985.

Magarrell, Lisa, and Joya Wesley. *Learning for Greensboro: Truth and Reconciliation in the United States*. Philadelphia, PA: University of Pennsylvania Press, 2008.

Bibliography

Martin, Michael. "Healing U. S. Divides through Truth and Reconciliation Commissions." *All Things Considered: National Public Radio*, Oct 11, 2020. https://www.npr.org/2020/10/11/922849505/healing-u-s-divides-through-truth-and-reconciliation-commissions.

McGregor, Deborah. "From 'Decolonized' to Reconciliation Research in Canada: Drawing from Indigenous Research Paradigms." *ACME: An International Journal for Critical Geographies* 17.3 (2018) 810–31.

Meiring, Pieter. *Chronicle of the Truth Commission: A Journey through the Past and Present into the Future of South Africa*. Eugene, OR: Wipf & Stock, 1999.

Merton, Thomas. *The Asian Journals of Thomas Merton*. Edited by Naomi Burton et al. New York: New Directions, 1980.

———. "Christian Humanism in the Nuclear Era." In *Love and Living*, edited by Naomi Burton Stone and Patrick Hart, 151–69. San Diego, CA: Harcourt, 1979.

———. "Contemplation in a World of Action." In *Thomas Merton, Spiritual Master*, edited by Lawrence S. Cunningham, 368–87. New York: Paulist, 1992.

———. *The Courage of Truth: Letters to Writers*. Edited by Christine M. Bochen. New York: Farrar, Straus & Giroux, 1993.

———. "A Devout Meditation in Memory of Adolf Eichmann." In *Raids on the Unspeakable*, 45–49. New York: New Directions, 1966.

———. *Faith and Violence: Christian Teaching and Christian Practice*. Notre Dame, IN: University of Notre Dame Press, 2015.

———. *Ishi Means Man: Essays on Native Americans*. New York: Paulist Press, 2015.

———. "Letter to Betsi Baeten, October 2, 1967." In *The Road to Joy: Letters to New and Old Friends*, edited by Robert E. Daggy, 358–59. New York: Farrar, Straus & Giroux, 1989.

———. *The Literary Essays of Thomas Merton*. Edited by Patrick Hart. New York: New Directions, 1985.

———. "Religion and Race in the United States." In *Faith and Violence: Christian Teaching and Christian Practice*, 130–44. Notre Dame, IN: University of Notre Dame Press, 2015.

———. *The Seven Storey Mountain: An Autobiography of Faith*. 50th anniversary ed. New York: Mariner, 1999.

Mitchell, Dawn. "Indianapolis Actor Famous for 'Zip-a-Dee-Doo-Dah' Was Groundbreaking Oscars Recipient." *Indianapolis Star*, Feb 22, 2019. https://www.indystar.com/story/news/history/retroindy/2019/02/22/oscars-james-baskett-indianapolis-actor-groundbreaking-academy-award-recipient-retroindy/2927638002/.

Monteleone, John J., ed. *Branch Rickey's Little Blue Book: Wit and Strategy from Baseball's Last Wise Man*. New York: Macmillan, 1995.

Montezuma. "Light on the Indian Situation (October 5, 1912)." In *Great Speeches of the 20th Century*, edited by Bob Blaisdell, 38–47. Mineola, NY: Dover Publications, 2011.

Moon, Claire. *Narrating Political Reconciliation: South Africa's Truth and Reconciliation Commission*. New York: Lexington Books, 2008.

National Centre for Truth and Reconciliation at the University of Manitoba. "The Davin Report." Mar 14, 1879. https://dev.nctr.ca/wp-content/uploads/2021/01/Davin-Report.pdf.

National Park Service. "Learn & Explore." *National Park Service U.S. Department of the Interior*. https://www.nps.gov/learnandexplore/index.htm.

National Public Radio. "Sen. Kennedy on Ford's Courageous Decision." Dec 27, 2006. https://www.npr.org/2006/12/27/6685819/sen-kennedy-on-fords-courageous-decision.

Bibliography

Ndlovu-Gatsheni, Sabelo J. *The Decolonial Mandela: Peace, Justice and the Politics of Life.* New York: Berghahn Books, 2016.

Norris, Pippa. "Cancel Culture: Myth or Reality?" *Political Studies* 71.1 (2023) 145–74.

Northouse, Peter G. *Leadership: Theory and Practice.* 8th ed. Los Angeles: SAGE, 2019.

Nouwen, Herni. *In the Name of Jesus: Reflections on Christian Leadership.* Chestnut Ridge, PN: Crossroad, 1992.

Nussbaum, Martha C. *Anger and Forgiveness: Resentment, Generosity, Justice.* Oxford: Oxford University Press, 2016.

Nyamwaya, Lyna. *Leading with Cultural Humility: 12 Inclusive Practices to Manage Biases, Promote Equity, and Cultivate Cultures of Belonging.* New Hope, MN: Bold Impact Group, 2022.

Nzimakwe, T. I. "Practising *Ubuntu* and Leadership for Good Governance: The South African and Continental Dialogue." *African Journal of Public Affairs* 7.4 (Dec 2014) 30–41.

O'Connor, Bernard. *Papal Diplomacy: John Paul II and the Culture of Peace.* South Bend, IN: St. Augustine's Press, 2005.

Ochs, Stephen J. *Desegregating the Altar: The Josephites and the Struggle for Black Priests 1871–1960.* Baton Rouge, LA: Louisiana State University, 1990.

Ong, Walter J. *Fighting for Life: Contest, Sexuality, and Consciousness.* Eugene, OR: Wipf & Stock, 2011.

Ontario Institute for Studies in Education. "Resources for Teachers." *University of Toronto.* https://www.oise.utoronto.ca/deepeningknowledge/Teacher_Resources/.

Passelecq, Georges, and Bernard Suchecky. *The Hidden Encyclical of Pius XI.* San Francisco: HarperOne, 1998.

Pattison, Mark. "To End Racism Tomorrow, Confront the Past Today, Panelist Says." *National Catholic Reporter*, Feb 5, 2019. https://www.ncronline.org/news/end-racism-tomorrow-confront-past-today-panelist-says.

Paul III. "Sublimis Deus: On the Enslavement and Evangelization of Indians." 1537. https://www.papalencyclicals.net/paul03/p3subli.htm.

Pawson, Chad. "Gino Odjick, Canucks Fan Favourite, Dead at 52." *CBC News*, Jan 15, 2023. https://www.cbc.ca/news/canada/british-columbia/gino-odjick-vancouver-canucks-obituary-1.6715005.

Pevar, Stephen L. *The Rights of Indians and Tribes.* 4th ed. Oxford: Oxford University Press, 2012.

Prazan, Michaël, dir. *The Adolf Eichmann Trial.* Paris, France: Kuiv Production, 2011.

Ramusi, Molapatene Collins, and Ruth S. Turner. *Soweto, My Love: A Testimony to Black Life in South Africa.* New York: Holt & Co., 1989.

Rassool, Ciraj, and Leslie Witz. "The 1952 Jan van Riebeeck Tercentenary Festival: Constructing and Contesting Public National History in South Africa." *The Journal of African History* 34.3 (1993) 447–68.

Rauch, Janine. "The South African Police and the Truth Commission." *South African Review of Sociology* 36.2 (2005) 208–37.

Regan, Paulette. *Unsettling the Settler Within: Indian Residential Schools, Truth Telling, and Reconciliation in Canada.* Vancouver, BC: University of British Columbia Press, 2010.

Rembert, Ron B. "Merton on Sports and Spirituality." *The Merton Seasonal* 42.1 (2017) 18–25.

Bibliography

Robinson, Dylan, and Keavy Martin. "Introduction: The Body Is a Resonant Chamber," In *Arts of Engagement: Taking Aesthetic Action in and Beyond the Truth and Reconciliation Commission of Canada*, edited by Dylan Robinson and Keavy Martin, 1–20. Waterloo, ON: Wilfrid Laurier University Press, 2016.

Robinson, Jackie. "Jackie Robinson Gives Final Speech at 1972 World Series." Baseball on Fanatics View, Aug 30, 2020. https://www.youtube.com/watch?v=PdgoWApbYjI.

Roht-Arriaza, Naomi. "The New Landscape of Transitional Justice." In *Transitional Justice in the Twenty-First Century: Beyond Truth versus Justice*, edited by Naomi Roht-Arriaza and Javier Mariezcurrena, 1–16. Cambridge: Cambridge University Press, 2006.

Roundtree, Dovey Johnson, and Katie McCabe. *Mighty Justice: My Life in Civil Rights*. New York: Algonquin Books, 2019.

Rugirangoga, Ubald. *Forgiveness Makes You Free*. Notre Dame, IN: Ave Maria Press, 2019.

Sacks, Jonathan. *The Dignity of Difference: How to Avoid the Clash of Civilizations*. Rev. ed. London, UK: Bloomsbury, 2003.

———. *Lessons in Leadership: A Weekly Reading of the Jewish Bible*. New Milford, CT: Maggid Books, 2015.

———. *Morality: Restoring the Common Good in Divided Times*. New York: Basic Books, 2020.

———. *To Heal a Fractured World: The Ethics of Responsibility*. New York: Schocken Books, 2005.

Savastano, Peter. "Introduction." In *Merton & Indigenous Wisdom*, edited by Peter Savastano, xiii–xx. Louisville, KY: Fons Vita, 2019.

Scheper-Hughes, Nancy. "We Are Not Such Things: The Murder of a Young American, a South African Township, and the Search for Truth and Reconciliation [Book Review]." *Anthropology Southern Africa* (2017) 224–40.

Shadyac, Tom, dir. *I Am*. Universal City, CA: Homemande Canvas/Shady Acres Entertainment, 2010.

Shaler, Andrew. "Indigenous Peoples and the California Gold Rush: Labour, Violence and Contention in the Formation of a Settler Colonial State." *Postcolonial Studies* 1 (2020) 79–98.

Simmons, Andrea. "Storytelling Resources for *Secret Path* Week." *Learning Bird Resources*, Oct 2, 2018. https://learningbird.com/resources-for-secret-path-week/.

Sinclair, Raven. "Identity Lost and Found: Lessons from the Sixties Scoop." *First Peoples Child & Family Review* 3.1 (2007) 65–82.

———. "The Indigenous Child Removal System in Canada: An Examination of Legal Decision-Making and Racial Bias." *First Peoples Child & Family Review* 11.2 (2016) 8–18.

Sipe, James W., and Don M. Frick. *Seven Pillars of Servant Leadership: Practicing the Wisdom of Leading by Serving*. Rev. and expanded ed. New York: Paulist Press.

Skaar, Elin. "Reconciliation in a Transitional Justice Perspective." *Transitional Justice Review* 1.1 (2012) 54–103.

Smith, Chad "Corntassel." *Leadership Lessons from the Cherokee Nation: Learn from All I Observe*. New York: McGraw Hill, 2013.

Smith, Linda Tuhiwai. *Decolonizing Methodologies: Research and Indigenous Peoples*. 3rd ed. London: ZED Books, 2021.

Bibliography

Sousa, Milton, and Dirk van Dierendonck. "Servant Leadership and the Effect of the Interaction between Humility, Action, and Hierarchical Power on Follower Engagement." *Journal of Business Ethics* 141 (2017) 13–25.

Stanton, Kim. "Reconciling Reconciliation: Differing Conceptions of the Supreme Court of Canada and the Canadian Truth and Reconciliation Commission." *Journal of Law and Social Policy* 26.2 (2017) 21–42.

Steindl-Rast, David. *Gratefulness, the Heart of Prayer: An Approach to Life in Fullness*. New York: Paulist Press, 1984.

Storey, Peter. *Protest at Midnight: Ministry to a Nation Torn Apart*. Eugene, OR: Cascade, 2022.

Sumanac-Johnson, Deana. "'I Sang the Facts,' Says Jully Black about 1-Word Change to O Canada at NBA All Star Game." *CBC News*, Feb 20, 2023. https://www.cbc.ca/news/entertainment/jully-black-anthem-lyrics-1.6754405?fbclid=IwAR0XCQ1dx-fhHCxD0Ocyy6WVvhcDvt1-2g4uzE0ALLfJowObWaXwz9OMnzk.

Swoyer, Alex. "Alexandria Ocasio-Cortez Calls for a Commission to 'Rein in Our Media.'" *Washington Times*, Jan 14, 2021. https://www.washingtontimes.com/news/2021/jan/14/alexandria-ocasio-cortez-calls-commission-rein-our/.

Terrell, Mary Church. "What It Means to Be Colored in the Capital of the United States (October 10, 1906)." In *Great Speeches of the 20th Century*, edited by Bob Blaisdell, 25–31. Mineola, NY: Dover Publications, 2011.

Thomas, Vivien T. *Pioneering Research in Surgical Shock and Cardiovascular Surgery: Vivien T. Thomas and His Work with Alfred Blalock: An Autobiography*. Philadelphia, PA: University of Pennsylvania Press, 1985.

Toulouse, Pamela Rose. *Truth and Reconciliation in Canadian Schools*. Winnipeg, MB: Portage & Main, 2018.

Truth and Reconciliation Commission of Canada. *Honouring the Truth, Reconciling for the Future: Summary of the Final Report of the Truth and Reconciliation Commission of Canada*. Winnipeg, MB: Truth and Reconciliation Commission, 2015. https://nctr.ca/records/reports/.

———. *A Knock on the Door: The Essential History of Residential Schools from the Truth and Reconciliation Commission of Canada*. Edited and abridged. Winnipeg, MB: University of Manitoba Press, 2016.

Tutu, Desmond. Foreword to *No More Strangers Now: Young Voices from a New South Africa*, by Melanie Kroupa, xi. New York: Dorling Kindersley Publishing, 1998.

———. *God Has a Dream: A Vision of Hope for Our Time*. New York: Random House, 2005.

———. *No Future without Forgiveness*. New York: Random House, 1999.

Tutu, Desmond, and Mpho Andrea Tutu. *The Book of Forgiving: The Fourfold Path for Healing Ourselves and Our World*. New York: HarperOne, 2014.

Twiss, Richard. *Rescuing the Gospel from the Cowboys: A Native American Expression of the Jesus Way*. Downers Grove, IL: IVP, 2015.

van der Leun, Justine. *We Are Not Such Things: The Murder of a Young American, a South African Township, and the Search for Truth and Reconciliation*. New York: Random House, 2016.

van Dierendonck, Dirk, and Kathleen Patterson. "Servant Leadership." In *Servant Leadership: Developments in Theory and Practice*, edited by Dirk van Dierendonck and Kathleen Patterson, 3–10. New York: Palgrave Macmillan, 2010.

Bibliography

van Wyk, Jo-Ansie. "From Apartheid to Ubuntu: Transition, Transaction and Transformation in South Africa's Post-Apartheid Foreign Ministry." *South African Journal of International Affairs* 26.3 (2019) 413–34.

Villeneuve, Jay Cardinal, dir. *Holy Angels*. Montreal, Canada: National Film Board of Canada, 2017. https://www.nfb.ca/film/holy-angels/.

Wakas, Robert Joseph Kwinkwinxwaligedzi. *Namwayut: We Are All One—A Path to Reconciliation*. Vancouver, BC: Page Two, 2022.

Walker-Barnes, Chanequa. *Too Heavy a Yoke: Black Women and the Burden of Strength*. Eugene, OR: Cascade, 2014.

Burns, Ken, and Lynn Novick, dir. "Inning 6 The National Pastime (1940–950)" (Episode 6) [TV Series Episode]. In *Baseball*, Ken Burns. PBS, Sep 25, 1994.

Watts, Jill. *The Black Cabinet: The Untold Story of African Americans and Politics during the Age of Roosevelt*. New York: Grove Press, 2020.

Wente, Jesse. *Unreconciled: Family, Truth, and Indigenous Resistance*. Toronto, ON: Allen Lane, 2021.

Wilkerson, Isabel. *Caste: The Origins of Our Discontents*. New York: Random House, 2020.

Wilson, Richard A. *The Politics of Truth and Reconciliation in South Africa: Legitimizing the Post-Apartheid State*. Cambridge: Cambridge University Press, 2005.

Wilson, Tom. *Beautiful Scars: Steeltown Secrets, Mohawk Skywalkers and the Road Home*. Toronto, ON: Doubleday Canada, 2017.

Wilson-Raybould, Jody. *True Reconciliation: How to Be a Force for Change*. Toronto, ON: McClelland & Stewart, 2022.

Winston, Bruce, and Barry Ryan. "Servant Leadership as a Humane Orientation: Using the GLOBE Study Construct of Humane Orientation to Show That Servant Leadership Is More Global Than Western." *International Journal of Leadership Studies* 3.2 (2008) 212–22.

Woodley, Randy S. *Shalom and the Community of Creation: An Indigenous Vision*. Grand Rapids, MI: Eerdmans, 2012.

Index

Abraham, 144–45
Adach, Kate, 118
Adams, Ian, 67–70, 117, 122
Ajayi, Adeyinka, 40–41, 101
Alexander VI, 9
Ali, Muhammad, 139–40
Amos, 36–37, 42–43, 48
Anthony, Susan B., 91
Armstrong, Louis, 134, 136
Arva, Eugene, 121
Attwood, Adam, 169
Avolio, Bruce, 124

Barclay, Michael, 122
Barling, Julian, 40, 128
Bartolomé de las Cases, 10–12, 15–16
Baskett, James, 134–35
Battle, Michael, xiv, 33, 73
Bear, Cheryl, 70
Benedict of Nursia, 62
Berry, Wendell, 31
Bethune, Mary McLeod, 131
Biehl, Amy, 2, 106–7
Black Elk, 45, 87
Black, Jully, 152
Blackie and the Rodeo Kings, 84
Blalock, Alfred, 130
Blight, David, 54
Block, Alan A., 12
Boahen, Adu, 37–38
Bonaparte, Napoleon, 25
Borja, Rodrigo de. See Alexander VI
Bowman, Thea, 57
Brown, Dee, 45, 52

Brown, Joseph Epes, 50, 53
Buchanan, James, 84
Buffy Sainte—Marie, 16
Buhari, Lateef, 40–41, 101
Burton, Mary Ingouville, 107

Carson, Clayborne, 93, 95, 137–38
Cases, Bartolomé de las. See Bartolomé de las Cases
Chanaiwa, David, 38, 77
Chavez, Cesar, 93, 95, 141
Chilton, John, 136
Clavin, Tom, 50
Cockburn, Bruce, 31, 84
Cohen, Leonard, 154, 167
Collin-Vézina, Delphine, 63
Collins, Jim, 104
Collins, Patricia Hill, 87
Columbus, Christopher, 9, 18, 21, 33
Connor, Bull, 137
Cook, Catherine, 119
Cooke, Sam, 44
Coppa, Frank, 82
Crystal, Billy, 140

Dalai Lama XIV, 74, 76
Daniel, George, 42, 80
Davin, Nicholas, 63
Davis, Cyprian, 10, 55, 56, 82, 129
Davis, Lynne, 119–20
Day, Dorothy, 87, 93, 95
Desbuquois, Gustave, 82–83
Diamond, Beverley, 79
Dierendonck, Dirk van, 49, 157

Index

Digging Roots, The, 70
Disney, Walt, 134–35
Donald, Michael, 160
Douglass, Frederick, 53–54, 58, 130
Downie, Gord, 122, 124, 143
Drexel, Katherine, 55
Drury, Bob, 50
Dubois, W. E. B., 55, 74, 87–90, 92, 99, 130
Dunbar—Ortiz, Roxanne, 18, 25, 150, 152
Duran, Eduardo, 17
Duran, Bonnie, 17
Durham, Richard, 139
Duriga, Joyce, 56–57
Dylan, Bob, 99, 141
Dysinger, Luke, 62

Echo—Hawk, Walter, 23–24
Egawa, Chenoa, 31
Eichmann, Adolf, xii–xiii, 87
Eisenhower, Dwight, 136
Eisner, Elliot, 121
Ekeocha, Obianuju, 32
Elijah, 75–76
Erasmus of Rotterdam, 92
Escher, Constance, 29–30

Fage, J. D., 35, 79–80
Farb, Peter, 26
Farrell—Smith, Ka'ila, 71
Fassie, Brenda, 84
Fast, Elizabeth, 63
Faubus, Orval, 136
Ferdinand II, 8–9
Finca, Bongani, 163
Floyd, George, 151
Ford, Gerald, 164–66
Francis, Pope, 19, 94, 120–21, 123
Frick, Don M., 61, 102

Gallant, Lennie, 141
Gambrell, Kem, 67
Garrido, Ann, 111
Garvey, Marcus, 74
Gaye, Marvin, 99
Gerber, Jill, 122

Geronimo, 146
Giddens, Rhiannon, 58
Gilio—Whitaker, Dina, 25, 150
Goodwin, Doris Kearns, 26–27
Goza, Joel Edward, 46, 149
Graham, Matthew, 76
Grandmaster Flash and the Furious Five, 141
Grant, Ulysses S., 63
Greenleaf, Robert, xv, 35, 61, 128, 156
Guramatunhucooper, Nyasha, xvii, 100
Guster, 58

Heinlein, Michael, 56
Hinton, Anthony Ray, 161–62
Holiday, Billie, 99
Huerta, Dolores, 93
Huntington, Samuel, 23, 159

Iheanacho, Valentine Ugochukwu, 34, 80
Isabella I, 8–9
Isaiah, xi, 86, 93, 129
Israel. *See* Jacob

Jacob, 6–7, 11
Jackson, Andrew, 51
Jackson, Michael, 31
Jackson, Tom, 70
James, Matt, 120
Jansen, Jonathan, 110
Jefferson, Thomas, 139
Jeremiah, 47–49, 52, 54
Jesus of Nazareth, xi, 86, 94, 102–3, 116
Joel, Prophet, 18
John Paul II, 111, 140
Johnson, Falen, 118
Johnson, Lyndon, 97
Jones, Max, 136
Joseph, Bob, 59, 65, 67, 148
Joseph, Chief, 52–53, 149–50
Joseph, Cynthia F., 59, 65, 67, 148
Jovanovic, Spoma, 163–64

Keb' Mo', 84
Kennedy, Robert, 93, 98, 126–27
Kennedy, Ted, 165
Kimmerer, Robin Wall, 21–22

Index

King, Jr., Martin Luther, 12–13, 45, 74, 84, 87, 92–96, 98–99, 126, 137–39, 155
King, Thomas, 17, 51, 70
Klerk, F. W. de, 108
Kock, Eugene de, 106
Kouzes, James, xvi
Kroeber, Theodora, 47, 51–52
Kushner, Harold, 12

Ladysmith Black Mambazo, 44
LaFarge Jr., John, 81–82
Lamire, Jeff, 122, 124
Larson, Charles, 125
LeBlanc, Jennifer, 148
LeBlanc, Terry, 59–60, 114–15, 148–49
Lewis, John, 166
Lincoln, Abraham, 84, 104, 131
Locke, Edwin, 102
Louis, Joe, 74
Lowenfish, Lee, 132–33
Lutz, Ellen, 162

Macdonald, John A., 63
Mackay, Susan Ferrier, 69
Magarrell, Lisa, 163–64
Malcolm X,
Mamdani, Mahmood, 105, 108
Mandela, Nelson, 13–16, 39–40, 42, 72, 74, 78–79, 84, 100–101, 105, 108–10, 113, 140, 151, 161
Mandela, Winnie, 78–79
Martin, Keavy, 117
Marx, Karl, 91
Masekela, Hugh, 84
Matthews, Dave Band, 44, 167
McGregor, Deborah, 28
Meiring, Pieter, 106–7
Merton, Thomas, xiii, 11, 13, 16, 22–23, 60–61, 85–87, 93, 95–97, 140, 159
Monteleone, John, 133–34
Montezuma, Carlos. *See* Wassaja
Moody, James, 58
Moon, Claire, 107
Moses, 20–23, 35–36, 61–62, 116
Mulvey, Peter, 141

Ndlovu—Gatsheni, Sabelo, 109
Nixon, Richard, 164–65
Northouse, Peter, 128, 144
Nouwen, Henri, 157–59
Nussbaum, Martha, 161
Nyamwaya, Lyna, 142–43
Nzimakwe, T. I., 102, 142–43

Ocasio—Cortez, Alexandria, 5
Ochs, Stephen, 56
O'Connor, Bernard, 112
Odjick, Gino, 123
Old Crow Medicine Show, 58
Ong, Walter, 1–2

Parks, Rosa, 95
Paul, Alice, 87, 91
Paul of Tarsus, 103, 157–58
Paul III, 10
Peter, the Apostle, 102–4, 116
Pevar, Stephen, 46, 97
Philip, the Deacon, 128–29
Pius XI, 81–82
Pius XII, 82
Posner, Barry, xvi

Ramusi, Molapatene Collins, 77
Randolph, A. Philip, 131
Rauch, Janine, 106
Red Cloud, 50
Reese, Pee Wee, 133
Regan, Paulette, 149
Richardson, G. Anne, 87
Rickey, Branch, 132–34
Riebeeck, Jan van, 33–34
Robinson, Dylan, 117
Robinson, Jackie, 132–34
Rogers, Nathan, 16
Roht-Arriaza, Naomi, 108
Roosevelt, Eleanor, 87, 131
Roosevelt, Theodore, 26–27
Roundtree, Dovey Johnson, 131, 138
Rudd, Daniel, 57
Rugirangoga, Ubald, 111, 143–44

Sacks, Jonathan, xiii, 3, 20, 104, 153, 156
Samuel, 61–63

Index

Sands, Maurice Henry, 149
Shadyac, Tom, 26, 72
Sheridan, Philip, 52
Shriver, Eunice Kennedy, 87
Simeoni, Giovanni, 56–57
Simon, Paul, 44
Simpson, Leanna, 125
Sinclair, Raven, 66
Sipe, James W., 61, 102
Skaar, Elin, 160
Slattery, John R., 57
Smith, Chad "Corntassel," 115, 148
Smith, Linda Tuhiwai, 8
Smuts, Jan, 73
Sousa, Milton, 49, 157
Spirit of the West, 31
Savastano, Peter, 13
Simpson, Leanna, 125
Stanton, Kim, 118–19
Stegner, Wallace, 27
Steindl—Rast, David, 145
Stockton, Betsey, 29–30
Storey, Peter, 42–43, 73, 80, 109, 163

Terrell, Mary Church, 89–90
They Might Be Giants, 58
Thomas, Charles, 132
Thomas, Vivien, 130, 131
Thoreau, Henry David, 31
Till, Emmitt, 135
Tragically Hip, The, 154
Tolton, Augustus, 55–57

Tosawi, 52
Toulouse, Pamela Rose, 64, 69
Turtle, Alex, 31
Tutu, Desmond, xiv, 33, 42, 72, 74, 76, 80, 101, 111–12, 163
Twiss, Richard, 24, 147

USA for Africa, 167

Villeneuve, Jay Cardinal, 117

Walker-Barnes, Chanequa, 54–55, 130
Wandering Spirit, Lena, 117
Wakas, Robert Joseph Kwinkwinxwaligedzi, 120, 142
Washington, Booker T., 55, 130
Washington, Jesse, 51
Wassaja, 90–91
Watts, Jill, 131
Weis, Michael, 56
Wenjack, Chanie "Charlie," 68, 122
Wente, Jesse, 63–64
Wesley, Joya, 163–64
Wilkerson, Isabel, 49–51
Wilson, Richard, 80, 101
Wilson—Raybould, Jody, 28, 114
White, Walter, 131
Woodley, Randy, 27–28, 146–47
Wovoka, 58
Wyk, Jo—Ansie van, 81

X, Malcolm. *See* Malcolm X

www.ingramcontent.com/pod-product-compliance
Lightning Source LLC
Chambersburg PA
CBHW051741230426
43670CB00012B/2106